THE BOOK OF THE GRADUAL SAYINGS

(ANGUTTARA-NIKĀYA)

OR

MORE-NUMBERED SUTTAS

Pali Text Society

TRANSLATION SERIES, NO. 27

(EXTRA SUBSCRIPTION)

THE BOOK OF THE GRADUAL SAYINGS (ANGUTTARA-NIKĀYA)

OR MORE-NUMBERED SUTTAS

VOL. V

(THE BOOK OF THE TENS AND ELEVENS)

TRANSLATED BY

F. L. WOODWARD, M.A.

TRANSLATOR OF "MANUAL OF A MYSTIC"; "THE BUDDHA'S PATH OF VIRTUE"; "KINDRED SAYINGS, PARTS III, IV, V"; "GRADUAL SAYINGS, PARTS I, II"; "SOME SAYINGS OF THE BUDDHA"; "BUDDHIST STORIES"; "VERSES OF UPLIFT" AND "AS IT WAS SAID" (UDĀNA AND ITIVUTTAKA, S.B.B. SERIES); "BUDDHIST STORIES"; ETC.

WITH AN INTRODUCTION BY

MRS. RHYS DAVIDS, D.Litt., M.A.

'Say on, sayers! sing on, singers!
Delve! mould! pile the words of the earth!
Work on, age after age, nothing is to be lost,
It may have to wait long, but it will certainly come in use
When the materials are all prepared and ready, the architects shall appear!"

WALT WHITMAN.

Published by
THE PALI TEXT SOCIETY, LONDON

Distributed by
ROUTLEDGE & KEGAN PAUL
LONDON, BOSTON, AND HENLEY
1986

First published - - - 1936
Reprinted - - - - - 1955
Reprinted - - - - - 1961
Reprinted - - - - - 1972
Reprinted - - - - - 1986

ISBN 0 86013 018 5

Distributed by Routledge & Kegan Paul plc

14 Leicester Square, London WC2H 7PH, England

9 Park Street, Boston, Mass. 02108, USA and

Broadway House, Newtown Road,
Henley-on-Thames, Oxon, RG9 1EN, England

Printed in Great Britain by
Redwood Burn Ltd, Trowbridge, Wiltshire

INTRODUCTION

WITH this volume an important objective has been attained—the publication, in fifteen volumes, of a complete English translation of the Four Nikāyas, also called Āgamas, of the Pali Canon. Five of the fifteen appeared in the series *Sacred Books of the Buddhists*, a series started by Max Müller after he had stopped his earlier series *Sacred Books of the East*, and of which he only lived long enough on earth to edit, of the fifteen, the first. The second and third volumes (of this, the Dīgha-Nikāya) were published by the generosity of former kings of Siam; the last twelve have been published by the Pali Text Society. A list of the volumes appears on another page.

For not one of these volumes can it be claimed that the workmanship amounts to the meticulous long-drawn-out care and collaboration bestowed on the English Bible, either in the translation of the 17th century or in that of the 19th. The Nikāyas have as yet found but their Wyclifs, their Tyndales. An 'authorized' English edition is not yet upon the horizon. The translators have worked alone, or, at best, as a pair, and with too little co-operation. It could hardly as yet have been otherwise. The English reader has been given some notion of the contents of these four Collections. But he has not seldom borne away misleading ideas.

These, with many oversights and other errors, posterity will in time come to correct. My more present business is to express the Pali Text Society's deep indebtedness to the two Englishmen who, in lands unluckily far distant, have devoted time, energy and labour to the translation of the five volumes of which this is the last, the one in the leisure hours of a business career, the other when resting from agricultural toil, neither looking for any reward save that which good work done brings, both helping this Society by annual subscriptions. Fortunate Society to be so blessed!

More especially is our tribute due to him of the twain who has borne the major burden, translating alone six of the fifteen volumes, giving aid in a seventh, and now crowning our labours with this last volume. To all this must be added his recently issued translation of two minor anthologies in the *Sacred Books of the Buddhists* Series: Udāna and Iti-vuttaka, and his first edition of the Saṃyutta-Commentary, the third and, I believe, final volume of which we shall publish a year hence. Very worthily has he stood in the breach left by the untimely death of such concentrated helpers as Richard Morris and Edmund Hardy. That we can look forward, in a few years, to completing our scheduled programme is largely due to him.

Lest by writing thus I get into trouble with this remote recluse, I pass to his renderings, and what therein they have made so much more accessible to us. His 'home-leaver' for *pabbajito* is new—so I believe—and should 'catch on.' The contexts specify the leaving with reference, not to the world, but to 'the house': "having gone forth from the house to the houseless." Of his 'wayfarer' for *tathāgata*, that gnawn bone of exegesis, I have worded my appreciation in his *Minor Anthologies*, VIII. I am glad also to see he has approved of 'very man' for *sappurisa* (see his note, p. 79); and, I hold, gets nearer to literal accuracy in rendering *vedanā* by 'knowings' rather than by the more usual 'feeling' or 'sensation.' And he has virtually discovered for us the noun *yattako*: 'striver' (p. 67), a word which Childers knew only as an adjective: 'of so much.' This escaped the notice of the promising neophyte, alas! lost to our work, who compiled the Anguttara Index, and eluded my husband and myself when bemargining our Childers, let alone the compiler of the Dictionary, depending too much on our uncertainties. Finally he has, O joy! used, for the first time in this work, the bracketed corresponding page of the text, whereby the work of reference is immensely expedited.

As to the contents of the Tens and Elevens, a comment here on (*a*) persons, (*b*) ideas.

(*a*) Familiar to readers will be the brahman Jāṇussoni, coming to have a matter of ritual spiritualized into a matter of religious conduct, and ever, as usual, made promptly to repeat a patter of lay-adhesion to the Order. Likewise the ever-faithful cousin Ānanda, now saving his great relative's face by an ingenious apologetic parable, now finding himself apologized to as a very distinguished man. Of *Upāli* (pp. 50, 140) we are glad to hear more, yet is there here too the disadvantage that we know not for certain *which* of the three Upālis it is: the Sakyan valet, the learned Jain, or a third. Once more we are at the faithful Vesālī, meeting Mahāli of the Dīgha Suttanta, and seeing the brilliant Licchavi cavaliers ride by. But the outstanding person in the Sakyan following is the mysterious woman-teacher known as the Kajangalan nun, with her lay congregation, her formulas as differing in part from those of the Khuddakapāṭha's ten heads, and the high tribute paid her by the Founder.[1] The 'Etad-agga' list knows her not, nor the Therīgāthā, nor the Apadāna. Who was she? And where was Kajangala?

Finally, in references to the Founder, we note here, and not in the Majjhima only, allusions showing the growth of Buddha-cult, and of a tendency to terms of Bhaktimarga, reminding us of the Bhagavadgītā—"Whoever have come to the goal in me . . . whoever has unwavering faith in me . . ." (p. 81). Compare in the Majjhima: "all who have but faith in me and love for me have *svarga* as their destiny" (No. XXII).

(*b*) *Dhamma-sota* (p. 96 *f.*). Mr. Woodward's note here of contexts with *sota*, meaning now 'hearing,' now 'stream,' is of much interest. I readily agree that, in this context, whereas I must have been led by the association *sotâpatti*: attainment of the stream (as usually rendered), to use 'stream,' the meaning is more probably 'hearing' or 'ear' (the word is the same). It points to the emergence of *dhamma* as *coming to mean*, not so much 'conscience,' the inner divine monition, as an externalized code of 'teaching,' becoming ever more scheduled and formularized.

It is of interest to compare the variant versions of the reply to Migasālā's very pertinent inquiry—treated by the monk-editor with deprecating patronage—as given in Saṃ-

[1] Pages 37 *ff.* See *Minor Anthologies*, VII, pp. lvi *f.*

yutta and here, and to wonder what the single-minded and appreciative Founder would say, did he see the sophisticated misty teaching here fathered upon him! (p. 94).

Attha, anattha (pp. 38, 155 *ff.*, 173). I have elsewhere tried to show all that this term meant for original Buddhism, and how, as becoming ever more in demand for growing literary purposes, and so, ambiguous, it was superseded by *aññā* and by *nibbāna*. It certainly meant, as the translator gives it (p. 38), 'aim': the thing in religion *needed*, the thing *sought*. So the seeking needing man is (p. 155) called *-atthiko*. It was the Buddhist *summum bonum*, as the later-emerging *nibbāna* was at one time *not*. This was but a cathartic discipline made in the quest of the Aim. But with the monk *nibbāna* made famous headway, and editors got busy with it. Emerging in other Indian literatures as the consummation of the Man or soul (*Brahma-nirvāṇaṃ*, Gītā), in Buddhism it prevailed as Man's final wiping out *as man*. *Attha* having meant at one time religious quest—king Bimbisāra is shown pointing to it, with the express qualification of *samparāyika* (belonging to other worlds) as the Bhagavan's teaching (*Vin. Mhv.* v, 1)—I regret to see it often elsewhere rendered by 'use,' 'profit.' The fact that (α) urgent admonition here lays *attha* beside, as equal to, *dhamma*, (β) the solemn mantra of the First Utterance names, as to be avoided, 'what does not belong to *attha*,' and doubtless, as originally spoken, named the Middle Way as 'belonging to *attha*,' calls for an English word of high religious import. This is not easy, as both translators of the Anguttara have admitted. By an accident in the Christian tradition, and so in the English language, we have the urgent importance of the religious quest handed down in a verb, rather than in its noun:

> "*Seek* ye FIRST the kingdom of God and his righteousness. . . ."

We might have had this as: Be your first search. . . . There remain the alternatives: weal, aim, quest. The translator has used the first two. But he is not to be held responsible for the literary uncouthness of "aim and not-aim" (*attho anattho ca*). Here he had faltered and followed the herd, and I have barged in. 'Profit' is in itself excellent, but current use has tied it up tightly with that other kind of *attha*, referred to by Bimbisāra as 'of things seen,' *i.e.* worldly. It is true that, in Indian usage, *dharma* and *artha* were, in the 3rd century B.C., on the verge of becoming used (with *kāma*) as the three absorbing features in a man's worldly life. But no such institutional meaning is revealed here (p. 167); the words *dhamma, attha* were still not so much what a man did as what a man *ought to do and seek.* They were still high words of the religious quest, and I earnestly beg readers to see them here in that light: *dhamma*, the ought to be done (or ought not); *attha*, the ought to be sought after. "One should fare onward according to these two things" (p. 173).

Vuḍḍhi, bhāvanā. No less do I exhort the reader not to overlook, as overlooked it invariably is, the reiteration and deep significance of these two terms (*e.g.*, pp. 84, 94, 110, 151). Not till we see, *first*, the insistence on man's religious progress as, not a 'being,' but a 'becoming,' everywhere stressed in the pre-Buddhist Upanishads, *then*, the gospel of the Son of the Sakyas as a way of growth (inspired by seeing the lilies: "how they grow!"), a growth to which there need be no decay (*parihāni*), shall we ever understand that gospel. And further, even if we note the insistence, we tend to overlook *wherein* should be the growth. We think too much of growth in terms of body, mind, character; we lose sight, in the instruments and the sign (character) of their growth, of growth in that which is supremely worth while, *i.e.* in religion. It is the man, user of the instruments, who has to grow. It is good to see how the verses, hoary it may be with age, keep this in view: it is not just "faith, virtue," and the rest that grow; it is

YO *'dha vaḍḍhati:*

whoso by faith, by virtue ('in' is here not literally correct),
by wisdom, generosity and lore
alike makes growth . . .

Nor, notice, is it enough not to decay, to fall back. Like the gallant Nurse Cavell with her "Patriotism is not enough," we find Sāriputta affirming that to maintain, to hold ground gained is not enough: " I praise not standing still, let alone waning in what is good. I praise growth, not standing still, not waning. . . . Herein is a man a striver !" Can we find anything equal to this save in the Christian Epistles ?

Such a divine growing was called *bhāvanā*, literally a making-become. It doesn't make elegant English, and the translator has preferred 'culture' and 'cultivating.' I regret this, because the reader thereby tends to lose the *historic* significance in the 'making-become.' We get *but one use* of the causative 'make-become' in those early Upanishads[1] with their frequent use of 'become.' Their sky was not yet darkened by the rise of monasticism, nor had they heard of the close intermondial intercourse of the early Sakyans with men who had gone before to a better world. The early Buddhist horizon is full of denizens other than those of earth. Man's right of way in the worlds had become a very present thing to them. Words were wanted for 'lives,' 'worlds' in the plural, and 'becomings' (*bhavā*) was chosen for both. But growing monkdom shrank from the opportunities given for growth by 'lives' and 'worlds,' and hastened (α) to forge a short-cut, or as in the North a cut-short, to consummation by an arahan theory, (β) to pour shame and abhorrence on the word chosen for lives, for worlds: *bhavā*. But, to preserve the old ideal of life as growth or becoming, the causative form of *bhava* was upheld, and so we get *bhava* condemned, but *bhāvanā*, *bhāveti* commended.

I apologize if I repeat myself, but this historical fact is of deep significance, and while it is still not listened to, the one thing left me is to say it over again.

The 'eightfold path' as tenfold. Elsewhere I have pointed to the way in which, in the first volume, the Way as eightfold is being tentatively used, alternatively with other scheduled things, for the Middle Course (i, p. 275).[2] Also to the fact that the Way as eightfold finds no place in the subjects classed as eight in number (iv, p. x). Here we find the Way explicitly classed *under the Tens* (p. 185 *ff.*), as if when the

[1] *Aitareya*. [2] *Manual of Buddhism*, 135.

original draft of that section was compiled, the Way was taught as tenfold.

And, as I pointed out in the preceding volume to this, the passing over the Way as eightfold in the titular subjects of the Eights-Nipāta is but one surprise among many surprises awaiting us, if we, with Buddhists and most writers on Buddhism, see in the present iron-bound formularization of Hīnayāna or Theravāda Buddhism the gospel as originally taught by Gotama called Buddha. I have listed these 'surprises' briefly in the *J.R.A.S.*, for October, 1935, and more fully in *Indian Culture*, Calcutta, I, 4, 1935. Here they are. The following groups are *not among the titular Suttas:*

Among the Threes, the three Refuges (later *Ratana*'s or Jewels), the three Marks (*lakkhaṇa*): *anicca, dukkha, anattā.*

Among the Fours: the Four Truths.

Among the Fives: the *Khandha*'s or Aggregates.

Among the Eights: the eightfold path.

And there are irregularities, so to speak, in the handling of the Four *Satippaṭṭhāna*'s and of the Five *Indriya*'s and of the Six *Abhiññā*'s, as I have also pointed out.

No historical research in the problem of the compilation and arrangement of the Pali Canon can afford to ignore, as all have as yet ignored, these anomalies. Our English issue of this Fourth Nikāya would alone, for the light thrown here, have been worth the expended trouble and cost. But there is much else to be gathered of sidelights on the older teaching. A little of that 'much' I have sketched in these Introductions, but there is more that will reward research. In none of the Four Nikāyas is the '*man*' kept in view and shown as being in a process of becoming, of growth so clearly as he is in this Book of the Gradual Sayings. By what happy accident (?) was it that among the judges, listening to the endless series of parallel varying versions at Patna's great Eisteddfod of Asoka's day, was a man, or men in sympathy, relatively speaking, with the older tradition?

C. A. F. RHYS DAVIDS.

TRANSLATOR'S PREFACE

THE translation of this last volume of *Anguttara-Nikāya*, which completes the Pāli Text Society's (together with the *Sacred Books of the Buddhists* Series) translations of the Four Great Nikāyas, has fallen to my lot, for Mr. E. M. Hare, who translated Vols. III and IV, found it impossible to give the necessary time to the work. I owe him thanks for sending me the draft of a few early suttas, and for the use of his own copy of the text which contained many valuable references, also for transliterating the greater part of the Sinhalese edition of the Commentary on this volume.

There is not much for me to say about the Tens and Elevens, as much of the matter appears in previous volumes; the Elevens contain hardly anything new. So I have left it to Mrs. Rhys Davids, who kindly writes her usual Introduction, to remark upon points of interest.

I may, however, mention that, as in my recent volume, *Verses of Uplift* and *As it was Said* (*Udāna* and *Itivuttakā S.B.B.* Series), I have used 'The Wayfarer' for *tathāgata.* As I have remarked in my notes, in the stock list of *diṭṭhī* (or views) held by non-adherents to the Buddha's teachings the one question always put is, quite naturally: 'Does the man, human being, *satta*, survive death or does he not?' Here the word used is always *tathāgata* (taken generally by the commentator as *satta*, a being). I do not hold the usual view that *tathāgata* here means the Teacher, for I believe this was a much later title for him. In this list it seems to mean 'one who has come-to-be in this world and will fare on in this and other worlds.' The Teacher is the Wayfarer *par excellence.* He is often called *Sugata*, the Well-farer, he who has fared successfully in this world. It is worth while noting that later on his followers, or some of them, were called by this name, the *Sugatas* or *Saugatas*, 'a sect who believe that religion consists only in kindness ' (Hopkins, *Religions of India*, 448), or who held, according to other accounts, that 'something exists but only momentarily.'

Also I have used Lord Chalmers' term 'cankers' for *āsavā*, a word which has been translated by 'drugs,' 'intoxicants' (in Skt. a distilled spirit); but it seems to mean 'a running sore.' *Santaŋ* (*sat*), I have translated as 'the Real' in preference to 'peaceful' in the phrase *idaŋ santaŋ*, *paṇītaŋ*, etc., where the context seems to demand an epithet stronger than 'peaceful.' I have also taken *makkha* (hypocrisy) to mean 'depreciation of others' in accordance with the commentarial explanation as 'one who smears over (*makkheti*) the virtues of others.'

F. L. WOODWARD.

TASMANIA, 1935.

CONTENTS

THE BOOK OF THE TENS AND ELEVENS

PART V

(The Book of the Tens)

(The Book of the Elevens)

Indexes

THE BOOK OF THE GRADUAL SAYINGS

(*AṄGUTTARA-NIKĀYA*)

Honour to that Exalted One, Arahant, the Fully Enlightened One

---

THE BOOK OF THE TENS AND ELEVENS

PART V

THE BOOK OF THE TENS

CHAPTER I.—PROFIT.

§ i (1). *What is the object?*[1]

THUS have I heard: On a certain occasion the Exalted One was staying near Sāvatthī at Jeta Grove, in Anāthapiṇḍika's Park. Then the venerable Ānanda came to see the Exalted One, and on coming to him saluted the Exalted One and sat down at one side. So seated the venerable Ānanda said this to him: 'Pray, sir, what is the object, what is the profit of good conduct?'[2]

'Why, Ānanda, freedom from remorse[3] is the object, freedom from remorse is the profit of good conduct.'

---

[1] *Kim-atthiyaṃ*. It is not easy to translate this, the adjective of *attha* (*cf. G.S.* iv, pp. vii, x, xix). The root-idea is 'thing-sought,' or '-needed,' and so 'aimed at.' This is well shown in the much-used parable of the man *sār-atthiko* (*-ika=iya*), 'seeking (or needing) timber': see below again, p. 201; also five times in the Majjhima and four times in *K.S.* The 'forward view' in the contexts makes such a term as 'of what use' not quite so suitable.

[2] *Sīlāni* (good conduct) is more literally habits, then, moral habits. The English words give too wide and deep a range.

[3] *Avippaṭisāro*; *cf. D.* i, 73; *S.* iv, 351; *A.* iii, 21=*G.S.* iii, 16. In the Elevens the same set is made into eleven by taking revulsion-and-fading as two terms.

'Pray, sir, what is the object, what is the profit of freedom from remorse?'

'Joy, Ānanda, is the object, joy is the profit of freedom from remorse.'

'But, sir, what is the object, what is the profit of joy?'

'Rapture, Ānanda, is the object, rapture is the profit of joy.'

'But pray, sir, what is the object, what is the profit of rapture?'

'Calm, Ānanda, is the object, calm is the profit of rapture.'

'But, sir, what is the object, what is the profit of calm?'

'Happiness, Ānanda, is the object, happiness is the profit of calm.'

[2] 'Pray, sir, what is the object, what is the profit of happiness?'

'Concentration,[1] Ānanda, is the object, concentration is the profit of happiness.'

'But pray, sir, what is the object, what is the profit of concentration?'

'Knowing and seeing things as they really are, Ānanda, is the object and profit of concentration.'

'What is the object, sir, what the profit of knowing and seeing things as they really are?'

'Revulsion and fading of interest, Ānanda, is the object of it.'

'Pray, sir, what is the object and profit of revulsion and fading of interest?'

'Release by knowing and seeing, Ānanda, is the object and profit of these. So you see, Ānanda, good conduct has freedom from remorse as object and profit; freedom from remorse has joy; joy has rapture; rapture has calm; calm has happiness; happiness has concentration; concentration has seeing things as they really are; seeing things as they really are has revulsion and fading of interest; revulsion and fading of interest

---

[1] *Samādhi.*

have release by knowing and seeing as their object and profit. So you see, Ānanda, good conduct leads gradually up to the summit.'[1]

§ ii (2). *Thinking with intention.*

'Monks, for one who is virtuous, in full possession of virtue, there is no need for the purposeful thought:[2] May freedom from remorse arise in me. This, monks, is in accordance with nature—that for one who is virtuous, in full possession of virtue, freedom from remorse arises.

Monks, for one who is free from remorse there is no need for the purposeful thought: May joy arise in me. This, monks, is in accordance with nature[3]—that for one who is free from remorse joy arises.

Monks, for one who is joyous there is no need for the purposeful thought: May rapture arise in me. [3] This, monks, is in accordance with nature—that for one who is joyous rapture arises.

Monks, for one whose heart is enraptured[4] there is no need for the purposeful thought: May my body be calmed. This, monks, is in accordance with nature—that for one whose heart is enraptured the body is calmed.

Monks, for one whose body is calmed there is no need for the thought:[5] I feel happiness. This, monks, is in accordance with nature—that one whose body is calmed feels happiness.

Monks, for one who is happy there is no need for the thought: My mind is concentrated. It follows that the happy man's mind is concentrated.

---

[1] *Anupubbena aggāya parenti; cf. S.* ii, 20, *ucchedaŋ pareti;* below, pp. 139, 312 of text (*hānāya*). *Comy. arahattāya gacchanti. Cf.* with this sequence that in *K.S.* ii, 26 (XII, § 27), and p. viii.

[2] *Na cetanāya karaṇīyaŋ.* For *cetanā* (thinking with intention) see Mrs. Rhys Davids's note at *Buddh. Psych. Ethics, n.* to § 5. This section, equal to the first of the Elevens, is quoted at *Netti,* p. 144, with *cetanā karaṇīyā* and *jāyeyya* in each case for *uppajjatu* of our text; while all its verbs are in the optative mood.

[3] *Dhammatā esā.*

[4] *Pīti-manassa.*

[5] Up to this point, as noted above, the verbs are optative; the rest are in the indicative mood. I have therefore dropped the word 'purposeful' qualifying *cetanāya*.

Monks, for one who is concentrated there is no need for the thought: I know and see things as they really are. It follows naturally that one concentrated does so.[1]

Monks, for one who knows and sees things as they really are there is no need for the thought: I feel revulsion; interest fades in me. It follows naturally that such an one feels revulsion and fading interest.

Monks, for one who feels revulsion and fading interest there is no need for the thought: I realize release by knowing and seeing. It follows naturally that he who feels revulsion and fading interest realizes release by knowing and seeing.

So you see, monks, revulsion and fading of interest have release by knowing and seeing as object and profit; seeing and knowing (things) as they really are, have revulsion and fading interest as object and profit; concentration has knowing and seeing things as they really are as object and profit; happiness has concentration as object and profit; calm has happiness; rapture has calm; joy has rapture; freedom from remorse has joy; good conduct has freedom from remorse as its object, freedom from remorse as its profit. [4] Thus, monks, one state just causes another state to swell, one state just causes the fulfilment of another state,[2] for the sake of going from the not-beyond to the beyond.'[3]

§ iii (3). *Basis (a) (by the Teacher).*

'Monks, in the immoral man who has lost virtue his freedom from remorse lacks basis.[4] Freedom from remorse not exist-

---

[1] *Cf. Expositor*, 157.

[2] *Dhammā'va dhamme abhisandenti . . . paripūrenti*; *cf. D.* i, 73, *so imaŋ kāyaŋ vivekajena pīti-sukhena abhisandeti parisandeti paripūreti parippharati.*

[3] *Apārā pāraŋ gamanāya.* Here *Comy.* 'for the purpose of going from the this-side-become three-dimensioned round to the nibbāna-beyond.' *Cf. K.S.* v, 225, where this is mistranslated.

[4] *Hat'upaniso* (*Comy. hata-kāraṇo*); *cf. A.* i, 198, *sa-upanisa*=*G.S.* i, 179; *A.* iv, 99, where the same sequence of virtues begins with *hirottappa* and *indriya-saŋvara*, as 'bases' or connecting-links of virtue. *Comy., ad loc.*, has *jinna-paccayo.* [The word *upanisa* seems in Pāli to be rather connected with *upanissaya* (support) than with the idea of mystic or secret doctrine.]

ing, joy lacks basis in him who has lost freedom from remorse. Joy not existing, rapture lacks basis in him who has lost joy. Rapture not existing, calm lacks basis in him who has lost calm. Happiness not existing, right concentration[1] lacks basis in him who has lost happiness. Right concentration not existing, knowing and seeing (things) as they really are lacks basis in him who has lost right concentration. Knowing and seeing things as they really are not existing, revulsion-and-fading of interest lacks basis in him who has lost knowing and seeing things as they really are. Revulsion-and-fading of interest not existing, release by knowing and seeing lacks basis in him who has lost revulsion-and-fading of interest.

Suppose, monks, a tree[2] that has lost its branches and foliage; its sprouts also come not to full growth, its bark, softwood and core come not to full growth. In like manner, monks, in the immoral man who has lost virtue his freedom from remorse lacks basis; release by knowing and seeing lacks basis in him who has lost revulsion-and-fading of interest.

But, monks, in the virtuous man complete in virtue his freedom from remorse is fully based. Freedom from remorse existing, the joy of him who is complete in virtue is fully based. Joy existing, the rapture of him who is complete in joy is fully based. Rapture existing, the calm of him who is complete in rapture is fully based. Calm existing, the happiness of him who is complete in calm is fully based. Happiness existing, [5] the right concentration of him who is complete in happiness is fully based. Right concentration existing, the knowing and seeing (things) as they really are of him who is complete in right concentration is fully based. Knowing and seeing things as they really are existing, the revulsion-and-fading of interest of him who is complete in knowing and seeing things as they really are is fully based. Revulsion-and-fading of interest existing, the release by knowing and seeing of him who is complete in revulsion-and-fading of interest is fully based.

---

[1] Here *sammā* is added to the *samādhi* of previous sections.

[2] The simile is at *A*. iii, 20, 200, 360; iv, 336; below text 314-17.

Suppose, monks, a tree complete with branches and foliage; its sprouts also come to full growth, its bark, soft-wood and core come to full growth. In like manner, monks, in the virtuous man, complete in virtue, his freedom from remorse is fully based. . . .'

§ iv (4). *Basis* (*b*) (*by Sāriputta*).[1]

(*A repetition of* § iii.)

§ v (5). *Basis* (*c*) (*by Ānanda.*)

[6] (*A repetition of* § iii.)

§ vi (6). *Concentration* (*a*) (*by the Teacher*).[2]

[7] Now the venerable Ananda went to see the Exalted One, and on coming to him saluted him and sat down at one side. So seated he said this to the Exalted One:

'Pray sir, may it be that a monk's winning of concentration is of such a sort that in earth he is unaware of earth, in water unaware of water, in heat unaware of heat, in air unaware of it, in the sphere of unbounded space unaware of it, in the sphere of infinite intellection unaware of it, in the sphere of nothingness unaware of it, in the sphere of neither-perception-nor-non-perception unaware of it; that in this world he is unaware of this world, in the world beyond unaware of it—and yet at the same time does perceive ?'

'It may be so, Ānanda. A monk's winning of concentration may be of such a sort that in earth he is unaware of earth . . . in the world beyond unaware of it, and yet at the same time he may perceive.'

'But, sir, in what way may a monk's winning of concentration be of such a sort that still he does perceive ?' [8.]

Herein, Ānanda, a monk has this perception: This is the real, this is the best, namely, the calming of all activities, the rejection of all substrate, the ending of craving, the fading of

---

[1] The *uddāna* (summary of titles in verse) of this chapter arranges titles differently, probably for the sake of rhythm.

[2] Repeated in the Elevens with the addition of one item.

interest, stopping, nibbāna. In such a way, Ānanda, a monk's winning of concentration may be of such a sort that in earth he is unaware of earth . . . in this world unaware of this world, in the world beyond unaware of it—and yet at the same time he does perceive.'

§ vii (7). *Concentration* (*b*) (*by Sāriputta*).

Now the venerable Ānanda went to see the venerable Sāriputta, and on coming to him greeted him courteously, and after the exchange of greetings and reminiscent talk, sat down at one side. So seated the venerable Ānanda said this to the venerable Sāriputta:

'Pray, Sāriputta, your reverence, may it be that a monk's winning of concentration is of such a sort that in earth he is unaware of earth . . . (*the whole as above*) . . . and yet at the same time he does perceive ?'

[9] 'Yes, Ānanda, your reverence, a monk's winning of concentration may be of such a sort. . . .'

'Pray, Sāriputta, your reverence, in what way may that be ?'

'Once on a time, Ānanda, your reverence, I myself was staying near this same Sāvatthī in Dark Wood,[1] and on that occasion I attained to concentration of such a sort that in earth I was unaware of earth and the rest . . . in this world I was unaware of this world, in the world beyond I was unaware of it, and yet at the same time I did perceive.'

'Pray what did you perceive on that occasion, Sāriputta, your reverence ?'

'One perception arose in me: To end becoming is nibbāna. Another perception faded out in me: To end becoming[2] is nibbāna. Just as, your reverence, from a fire of splinters[3] one spark arises and another spark fades out, even so in me one perception arose: To end becoming is nibbāna, and another perception that to end becoming is nibbāna faded out in me. Yet at the same time, your reverence, I consciously perceived.'

---

[1] *Cf. Vin.* i, 298; *A.* iii, 359; *K.S.* i, 160 *n.*

[2] *I.e.* rebirth. [3] Simile at *M.* i, 259.

§ viii (8). *The believer.*[1]

[10] 'Monks, a monk may be a believer but yet not be virtuous. Thus in that respect he is incomplete. That defect must be remedied by the thought: How can I be both a believer and virtuous? But, monks, when a monk is both of these, he is complete in that respect.

Monks, a monk may be both a believer and virtuous yet not learned;[2] a believer, virtuous and learned, yet no dhamma-preacher; he may be a believer, virtuous, learned and a dhamma-preacher, yet not a frequenter of debates;[3] he may be all of these, yet not be confident[4] in expounding dhamma in a company; he may be all of these, yet not expert in discipline;[5] he may be all these, yet no forest-dweller, a lodger in solitude; he may be all these, yet not be one who attains at will, without difficulty and without trouble, the four musings[6] which belong to the higher thought, which even in this same visible state are blissful to abide in; nor does he, by destroying the cankers, in this same visible state comprehending it of himself, realize the heart's release, the release by insight, and attaining it abide therein. So in that respect he is incomplete.

That defect must be remedied by the thought: How can I be both a believer and virtuous, also learned, a dhamma-preacher, a frequenter of debates, and confident in expounding dhamma in a company, also expert in the discipline, a forest-dweller, a lodger in solitude, and one who attains at will . . . **[11]** and by destroying the cankers . . . realize the heart's release, the release by insight, and attaining it abide therein?

Then, monks, when he has attained each one of these ten things, he is complete in that respect.

[1] *Saddho* is defined in the Elevens as one who is sure *Iti pi so Bhagavā*, etc.

[2] *Bahussuta*, one who has heard much.

[3] *Parisâvacara*; *cf. K.S.* v, 60 *n.*

[4] *Visārada*; *cf.* below, § 22, *visārado paṭijānāmi dhammaŋ desetuŋ.*

[5] *Vinayadhara*, one who, like Upāli, knows by heart the rules of discipline.

[6] All these belong to the Ariyan Method (*ñāya*), see *G.S.* ii, 41.

Monks, if he be endowed with these ten qualities a monk is altogether[1] charming and complete in every attribute.'

§ ix (9). *The blissful.*

(*The same as the above down to* ' a lodger in solitude.' *Then follows :*)

'He may be all of these yet not be one who abides experiencing with body those blissful deliverances[2] in the formless, experienced by him who passes beyond objective forms; and he may not, by destroying the cankers in this same visible state . . . [**12**] realize the heart's release . . . and abide therein. So in that respect he is incomplete.

So that defect must be remedied by the thought: How can I be both a believer, virtuous, and . . . (*as above*) . . . a lodger in solitude, and abide experiencing with body these blissful deliverances in the formless, experienced by him who passes beyond objective forms, and likewise, by destroying the cankers in this same visible state . . . realize the heart's release . . . and abide therein ?

Then when a monk is a believer, virtuous, and the rest, he is complete in that respect.

Monks, if he be endowed with these ten qualities a monk is altogether charming and complete in every attribute.'

§ x (10). *By knowing.*[3]

[**13**] (*The same as the two previous suttas down to* ' expert in the discipline.' *Then follows :*)

' (He may be all of these) yet not be one who can recall his former dwelling in divers ways, thus: One birth, two

---

[1] *Samanta-pāsādiko.* The title (*etad-agga*) conferred on the monk Upasena because of his highly qualified following at *A.* i, 24=*G.S.* i, 19. It is also the name of the Vinaya Commentary.

[2] *Cf. A.* ii, 183. 'The eightfold deliverance is to be experienced with body.' These eight are given at *A.* iv, 306, etc.; *D.* ii, III; Numbers 1-7 are discussed at *Buddh. Psych. Eth.*, § 246 *ff.*; *Expositor* i, 255.

[3] The *uddāna* has *Vijjaya* (?) probably referring to the sentence about his former dwelling.

births. . .[1] Thus he calls to mind in all their specific details, in all their characteristics, in divers ways, his former dwelling; and he may not be one who with the deva-sight, purified and surpassing that of men, beholds beings deceasing and rising up again . . . and recognizes beings as gone (to weal or woe) according to their deeds; and he may not be one who, by destroying the cankers . . . realizes the heart's release . . . and abides therein. So in that respect he is incomplete.

That defect must be remedied by the thought: How can I be both a believer, virtuous, and learned and a dhamma-preacher, a frequenter of debates, confident in expounding dhamma in a company, also expert in the discipline, likewise one who can recall his former dwelling in divers ways **[14]** . . . likewise one who with the deva-sight . . . recognizes beings gone (to weal or woe) according to their deeds; likewise one who, by destroying the cankers. . . .

Then, monks, when a monk is a believer, virtuous, and the rest . . . he is complete in that respect.

Monks, if he be endowed with these ten qualities, a monk is altogether charming and complete in every attribute.'

Chapter II.—Things Making for Warding.[2]

§ i (11). *Lodging.*

[15] 'Complete in five factors, monks, a monk who follows after and resorts to the lodging-place[3] which is complete in five factors in no long time, by destroying the cankers, realizes in this same visible existence the heart's release, the release by insight, thoroughly comprehending it of himself, and having attained it abides therein. How is a monk complete in five factors?

Herein a monk is a believer; he believes: He that Exalted

[1] Text abbreviates this well-known passage occurring *e.g.* at *G.S.* i, 147, and later on in this volume, and by error repeats several sentences.

[2] *Nātha* at § 17; *cf.* the name *Anātha-piṇḍika*, 'feeder of the helpless.'

[3] *Cf. G.S.* i, 220.

One, Arahant, is a perfectly Enlightened One, perfect in knowledge and practice, a Welfarer, a world-knower, trainer unsurpassed of men to be trained, teacher of devas and mankind, Awakened One, Exalted One. Moreover he is little troubled by sickness and disease; he is furnished with digestive power[1] not too hot or too cold, but even and suitable for striving;[2] he is honest, no deceiver, he is one who shows himself as he really is to the Teacher, to his discerning co-mates in the brahma-life; he dwells resolute in energy, ever striving to abandon bad qualities, stout and strong to acquire good qualities, not shirking the burden in good qualities;[3] he is a man of insight, possessed of insight for tracing the rise and fall of things, insight that is Ariyan, penetrating, going on to the utter destruction of Ill.[4] In this way, monks, a monk is complete in five factors.

And how is one's lodging-place complete in five factors?

Herein, monks, a lodging-place is not too far and not too near (a village), but suitable for coming and going, by day not frequented, by night quiet and undisturbed by noise, not plagued with contact of flies, mosquitoes, wind, rain and creeping things. Moreover, for one dwelling in such a lodging-place the supply of robes and alms-food, of bed and lodging, comforts in sickness and medicaments comes about with little trouble; further in that lodging-place dwell elder monks who have heard much, who are versed in the sayings, who know the teachings thoroughly, [**16**] who know the discipline and summaries by heart.[5] Consorting with them from time to time he inquires of them and questions them

---

[1] *Sama-vepākiṇiyā gahaṇiyā ; cf. D.* ii, 177; iii, 166=*Dialog.* ii, 208 and *n.*; iii, 157 (in *Marks of the Superman*); *A.* iii, 65=*G.S.* iii, 54. Our *Comy.* has nothing to say about this *gahaṇī* or inner process or organ. According to *DA.* ii, 628, it is *kammaja-tejo-dhātu* (digestive heat). See note to *Dialog.* ii, 208.

[2] *Majjhimāya padhāna-kkhamāya.* So Mr. Hare at *G.S.* iii, 54. At *Dialog.* iii, 157, the quality is ascribed to the person himself (patience in exertion), but obviously it refers to the digestion.

[3] *Cf. K.S.* v, 173 (The Controlling Power of Energy).

[4] *Cf. K.S.* v, 175 (The Controlling Power of Insight).

[5] *Āgatâgamä ; cf. G.S.* i, 101; iii, 257.

thus: "How is this, your reverence? What is the meaning of this?" Those worthies then open up to him what was sealed, make clear what was obscure, and on divers doubtful points of doctrine they resolve his doubts. That, monks, is how one's lodging-place is complete in five factors.

Indeed, monks, complete in five factors, a monk who follows after and resorts to the lodging-place complete also in five factors in no long time, by destroying the cankers, realizes in this same visible existence the heart's release, the release by insight, thoroughly comprehending it of himself, and having attained it abides therein.'

§ ii (12). *Factors.*

'Monks, a monk who has given up five factors and is complete in five factors is called in this dhamma-discipline "all-proficient,[1] one who has lived the life, the best of men." And how is a monk one who has given up five factors?

Herein a monk's sensual desire is given up, malevolence, sloth-and-torpor, worry-and-flurry, doubt-and-wavering are given up. Thus is he one who has given up five factors. And how is he complete in five factors?

Herein a monk is complete in the sum total of a master's virtues, of a master's concentration,[2] in the sum total of a master's insight, release, the release by knowing and seeing. Thus is he complete in five factors.

Monks, a monk who has given up five and is complete in five factors is called in this dhamma-discipline "all-proficient, one who has lived the life, the best of men."

Not sensual desire, malevolence,
Nor sloth-and-torpor, worry-and-flurry at all,
Not doubt-and-wavering in a monk are seen.

---

[1] *Kevalī; cf. Itiv.* § 97, 'One lovely in virtue, nature and insight' (an 'all-rounder') is so called. *Comy. kevalehi guṇehi samannāgato; cf. VM.* i, 146: *KhA.* 115 (on *kevala-kappa*)=*SA.* i, 15, which quotes our passage, reading *kevalaŋ*. The word is also used for nibbāna; in Sankhya and Yoga works it means the complete absorption in the thought of the universal unity (*kaivalya*), or the complete isolation of the *purusha* after death of the body.

[2] *Samādhi-kkhandha ; cf. G.S.* ii, 51.

[17] Blest with a master's virtues, concentration,
Release and knowledge which belong to it,—
He surely, with five factors all complete,
Abandoning five factors, is thus called
" One all-proficient in this dhamma-discipline." '[1]

§ iii (13). *Fetters.*

' There are these ten fetters, monks. What ten ?

The five fetters pertaining to this world and the five pertaining to the higher world.[2] And what, monks, are the five pertaining to this world ?

The view of the individual-group, doubt-and-wavering, wrong handling of habit-and-ritual, sensual desire and malevolence. These are the five fetters pertaining to this world. And what are the five pertaining to the higher world ?

Lust of objective form, lust of the formless, conceit, excitement and ignorance. These are the five fetters pertaining to the higher world.'

§ iv (14). *Obstruction.*

' Monks, in whatsoever monk or nun five mental obstructions[3] are not abandoned and five bondages of the heart are not well rooted out, in such an one come night, come day, decline, not growth, in good states may be looked for. And in what sort[4] are the five mental obstructions not abandoned ?

Herein a monk has doubts and waverings about the Teacher. He is not drawn to him, he is not sure about him. In a monk who so doubts and wavers, who is not drawn to and is not sure about the Teacher, the mind of such an one inclines not to exertion, to application, to perseverance, to striving. In him

---

[1] Partly at *Thag. v.* 74 and *v.* 1010; *Thig. v.* 165.

[2] *Cf. K.S.* v, 49 *nn.*

[3] *Ceto-khilā ; cf. K.S.* v, 45; *G.S.* iii, 182 (without similes). The sutta is at *M.* i, 101; *Further Dialog.* i, 71. Lord Chalmers trans. ' the fallows of his heart are left untilled.' In *M.* our first simile is lacking, while the last one is of the hen hatching eggs.

[4] *Katamassa. M.* i, *ad loc.*, has *katam assa* throughout followed by *imassa.*

whose mind inclines not [18] to these things this first mental obstruction is not abandoned.

Again, monks, a monk has doubts about dhamma, about the order of monks, about the training . . . he is vexed with his co-mates in the brahma-life, displeased, troubled in mind, come to a stop. In a monk who is thus his mind inclines not to exertion . . . to striving. In him whose mind inclines not to these things this (last) is the fifth mental obstruction not abandoned. In this one the five mental obstructions are not abandoned.

And in what sort are the five bondages of the heart not well rooted out?

Herein a monk is not dispassionate in things sensual; desire, affections, thirsting, distress and craving have not gone from him. In a monk who is such the mind inclines not to exertion, to application, perseverance and striving. In him whose mind inclines not to these things, this first bondage of the heart is not well rooted out.

Again in body a monk is not dispassionate; he is not dispassionate in the matter of objective form; having eaten his bellyful[1] he lives given to the pleasure of lying down on back or side,[2] a prey to torpor; or he leads the brahma-life with a view to join some order of devas, with the thought: By virtue of this way of life or practice or austerity or brahma-life I shall become some deva or other. Whatsoever monk . . . has such an object in view, his mind inclines not to exertion [19], to application, to perseverance and striving. In him whose mind inclines not to these things, this fifth bondage of the heart is not well rooted out.

Monks, in whatsoever monk or nun these five mental obstructions are not abandoned and these five bondages of the heart are not well rooted out, in such an one, come night, come day, decline, not growth, in good states may be looked for.

---

[1] *Cf. A.* iv, 343.

[2] *Seyya-sukhaŋ passa-sukhaŋ; cf. G.S.* ii, 249 on postures; where the 'luxurious' are said to lie on the side.

Just as, monks, in the dark period of the moon,[1] come night, come day, it wanes in beauty, wanes in roundness, wanes in splendour, wanes in the height and compass of its orbit—even so in whatsoever monk or nun these five mental obstructions be not abandoned or these five bondages of the heart be not well rooted out, in such, come night, come day, decline, not growth, in good states may be looked for. But in whatsoever monk or nun . . . they are abandoned and rooted out . . . growth, not decline, in good states may be looked for.

And in what sort, monks, are the five mental obstructions abandoned?

Herein a monk has no doubts and waverings about the Teacher, he is drawn to him, he is sure of him. Whatsoever monk or nun has no doubts and waverings about the Teacher, but is sure of him, of such the mind inclines to exertion, to application, to perseverance, to striving. In him whose mind so inclines this is the first mental obstruction that is abandoned.

Again a monk doubts not dhamma . . . the order of monks . . . the training [20] . . . he is not vexed with his co-mates in the brahma-life, but is pleased and untroubled in mind, not come to a stop. In such an one this (last) is the fifth mental obstruction that is abandoned. In such the five mental obstructions are abandoned.

And in what sort, monks, are the five bondages of the heart well rooted out?

Herein a monk is dispassionate in things sensual. Desire. affections, thirsting, distress and craving are gone from him. In a monk who is such, his mind inclines to exertion, to application, to perseverance, to striving. In him whose mind so inclines this first bondage of the heart is well rooted out.

Again, in body a monk is dispassionate; he is dispassionate as to objective form; he does not eat his bellyful and live given to the pleasure of lying down on back or side, a prey to torpor. He leads not the brahma-life with a view to join some order of devas with the thought: By virtue of this way of life or practice or austerity or brahma-life I shall become some deva

---

[1] *Cf. S.* ii, 106=*K.S.* ii, 139; below, § 67.

or other. Whatsoever monk or nun has no such object in view, his mind inclines to exertion, to application, to perseverance, to striving. In him whose mind so inclines this (last) is the fifth bondage of the heart well rooted out.

In this one then the five bondages of the heart are well rooted out.

Monks, in whatsoever monk or nun these five mental obstructions are abandoned and these five bondages of the heart are well rooted out, in such an one, come night, come day, growth, not decline, in good states may be looked for. Just as in the bright period of the moon, come night, come day, it waxes in beauty, waxes in roundness, waxes in splendour, waxes in the height and compass of its orbit, even so in whatsoever monk or nun these five mental obstructions are abandoned and these five bondages of the heart are well rooted out, in such, come night, come day, growth not decline in good states may be looked for.'

§ v (15). *Seriousness.*

[21] 'Monks, as compared with creatures, whether footless, bipeds, quadrupeds, or those of many feet, with form or void of form, with sense or void of sense, or indeterminate in sense, a Wayfarer, an arahant, a fully enlightened one is reckoned chief of them, even so, monks, whatsoever good states there be, all of them are rooted in seriousness, unite in seriousness, of those states seriousness is reckoned chief.[1]

Just as, monks, of all the foot-characteristics of such creatures as roam about[2] are joined together in the foot of the elephant, and as the elephant's foot in size is reckoned chief, even so, whatsoever good states there be, all of them are rooted in seriousness, unite in seriousness, of those states seriousness is reckoned chief.

Just as, monks, in a peaked house all the rafters whatsoever go together to the roof-peak, slope to the roof-peak, are joined together in the roof-peak, and of them the roof-peak is

---

[1] *Cf. A.* ii, 34; iii, 35=*G.S.* ii, 38; iii, 26.

[2] Reading *jangamānaŋ* for text's *jangalānaŋ* ; *cf. K.S.* v, 34 *ff.* and notes.

reckoned chief, even so, monks, whatsoever good states there be, all of them are rooted in seriousness, unite in seriousness, of those states seriousness is reckoned chief.

[22] Just as, monks, of all root scents, black gum[1] is reckoned chief, even so whatsoever good states there be. . . . Just as of all wood scents red sandalwood is reckoned chief . . . Just as of all flower scents the jasmine is reckoned chief. . . . Just as all petty princes whatsoever follow in the train of the universal monarch and he is reckoned chief of them. . . . Just as of all starry bodies whatsoever the radiance does not equal one-sixteenth part of the radiance of the moon and the moon's radiance is reckoned chief of them. . . . Just as in the autumn season, when the sky is opened up and cleared of clouds, the sun leaping up into the firmament drives away all darkness and shines and burns and flashes forth. . . . Just as, monks, whatsoever great rivers there be,[2] such as Gangā, Yamunā, Aciravatī, Sarabhū and Mahī, all of them make for, flow to, slide and tend to the ocean, and the mighty ocean is reckoned chief of them, even so, monks, whatsoever good states there be, all of them are rooted in seriousness, of these states seriousness is reckoned chief.'

§ vi (16). *Worshipful.*

[23] 'Monks, these ten[3] persons are worthy of worship, worthy of reverence, worthy of gifts, worthy of salutations with clasped hands, a field of merit unsurpassed for the world. What ten persons?

A Wayfarer, arahant, a fully enlightened one, a Pacceka Buddha, one released in both respects, one released by insight, one who has testified (to the truth) in his own person,[4] one

---

[1] *Kāḷânusārī*. *P. Dict.* 'a fragrant black substance.' According to Benfey's *Sanskrit Dict.* (ref. to *Suçr.* ii, 94, 21) it is benzoin; 'gum-benjamin' is a thick juice flowing from cuts in the bark of a tree in Sumatra. Elsewhere I have wrongly translated (*K.S.* iii, 132; v, 35) as 'dark sandalwood.'

[2] *Cf. K.S.* v, 32, etc.

[3] At *G.S.* ii, 250, the first four are reckoned worthy of a cairn. At *A.* iv, 10, seven of these are worshipful.

[4] *Kāya-sakkhī*; *cf. G.S.* i, 69, 102, 103 *nn.*; ii, 99.

who has won view, one released by faith, and one who is a son by adoption.[1] These are the ten persons worthy of worship. . . .'

§ vii (17). *Warder* (*a*).

'Monks, do ye live warded,[2] not warderless. Sorrowfully dwells the warderless monk. Monks, there are these ten states that make for warding. What ten?

Herein a monk is virtuous, restrained with the restraint of the Obligation, well equipped in range of practice, seeing danger in minutest faults, and undertaking the precepts trains himself therein. In so far as a monk is such an one, this is a state that makes for warding.

Then again a monk has heard much; he bears in mind what he has heard, he stores up what he has heard. Whatsoever teachings, lovely at the beginning, lovely midway, lovely at the end (of life), in spirit and in letter do stress the brahma-life in its all-round fulness and utter purity, such teachings are much heard by him, borne in mind, repeated aloud, pondered and well penetrated by vision.[3] In so far as a monk is such an one, this is too a state that makes for warding.

[**24**] Then again a monk has a friendship with the lovely, fellowship with the lovely, companionship with the lovely. In so far as a monk has such friendship, this too is a state that makes for warding.

Again a monk is pleasant to speak to, he is blest with qualities that make him easy to speak to, he is patient and clever at grasping instruction given.[4] In so far as a monk is such, this too is a state that makes for warding.

Then again in all the undertakings of his co-mates in the

---

[1] *Gotrabhū*, 'become one of the clan,' 'converted,' 'one of the elect.' *Cf. A.* iv, 373; defined at *Pugg.* 12, 13; *VM.* 138; *Compendium of Philosophy*, 55, 215. Here *Comy.* has *sikhā-patta* (flame-, or crest-reached?) *vipassanā-bhūto* (insight-become) *nibbānârammaṇe gotrabhū-ñānena samannāgato.*

[2] At *D.* iii, 266. *Cf.* below, § 97; *K.S.* v. 149 and above, § 11; for *Sa-nātha, cf. Dhp. vv.* 160, 380, *attā hi attano nātho.*

[3] *Cf. G.S.* ii, 23, 24.

[4] *Cf. G.S.* ii, 152.

brahma-life, be they matters weighty or trivial, he is shrewd and energetic, possessing ability to give proper consideration thereto, as to what is the right thing to do and how to manage it.[1] In so far as a monk is such an one, this too is a state that makes for warding.

Then again a monk delights in dhamma, is pleasant to converse with,[2] rejoices exceedingly in further dhamma and further discipline.[3] In so far as a monk is such an one, this state also makes for warding.

Again a monk dwells resolute in energy for the abandonment of bad qualities, stout and strong to acquire good qualities, not shirking the burden in good qualities. In so far as a monk is such an one, this too is a state that makes for warding.

[25] Again a monk is content with whatsoever supply of robes, alms-food, lodging, comforts and medicaments for sickness he may get. In so far as a monk is such an one, this too is a state that makes for warding.

Again a monk is concentrated, possessed of mindful discrimination in the highest degree, able to call to mind and remember things done and said long ago . . . this too is a state that makes for warding.[4]

Once more, monks, a monk is possessed of insight; he has insight for tracing out the rise and fall of things, insight which is Ariyan, penetrating, going on to the utter destruction of Ill. In so far as a monk has all these ten qualities, this too is a state that makes for warding.

---

[1] *Cf. G.S.* ii, 40; iii, 89. In the first reference the qualities are those ascribed to a *mahāpurisa* by the brāhmin Vassakāra in conversation with the Master.

[2] Quoted *Milinda*, p. 344=trans. ii, 237. *Piyasamudâhāra. Comy.* explains 'listens attentively when another is talking, but likes to expound his own view to others.'

[3] *Abhidhamme abhivinaye.* As Rhys Davids notes in his trans., *Mil., loc. cit., abhidhamma* is *not* metaphysics, nor, it may be added, is it the so-called third division of the Piṭaka Collection (as *Comy.* makes out).

[4] Most of these faculties are described under the 'Five controlling Powers,' *K.S.* v, 169 *ff.*, 201.

Monks, do ye live warded, not warderless. Sorrowful dwells the warderless, monks.

These then are the ten states that make for warding.'

§ viii (18). *Warder* (*b*).

'Monks, do ye live warded, not warderless . . . (*as in* § vii).

Herein a monk is virtuous. . . . Saying, "Virtuous indeed is this monk, he lives restrained with the restraint of the Obligation . . . and trains himself therein," the senior monks consider him to be [**26**] one fit for encouragement; so likewise do the monks of middle standing and the novices. For him thus regarded with kindly feeling by senior monks, by those of middle standing and by novices alike, growth, not decline, in good states is to be looked for. This then is a state that makes for warding.

Then again a monk has heard much . . . such teachings . . . are pondered by him and well penetrated by vision. Saying, "This monk has indeed heard much . . ." the senior monks consider him to be one fit for encouragement. . . . This too is a state that makes for warding.

Then again a monk has friendship with the lovely . . . is pleasant to speak to . . . [**27**] in all the undertakings of his co-mates in the brahma-life . . . he is shrewd and energetic . . . he delights in dhamma . . . he dwells resolute in energy . . . [**28**] he is content with whatever supply of robes . . . he may get . . . he is concentrated . . . possessed of insight . . . and (in each case) the senior monks consider him to be one fit for encouragement; so likewise do the monks of middle standing and the novices also. [**29**] For him, thus regarded with kindly feeling . . . growth not decline in good states is to be looked for. This too is a state that makes for warding. Monks, do ye live warded, not warderless. Sorrowful dwells the warderless, monks.

These then are the ten states that make for warding.'

§ ix (19). *Ariyan living* (*a*).

'Monks, there are these ten ways of Ariyan living,[1] according to which Ariyans have lived, do live and shall live. What ten?

Herein a monk has abandoned five factors, is possessed of six factors, guards one factor, observes the four bases,[2] has shaken off individual[3] belief, has utterly given up longings, his thoughts are unclouded, his body-complex is tranquillized, he is well released in heart, he is well released by insight. These are the ten ways of Ariyan living, according to which Ariyans have lived, do live and shall live.'

§ x (20). *Ariyan living* (*b*).

[30] Once the Exalted One was staying among the Kurus at Kammāsadhamma,[4] a township of the Kurus. On that occasion the Exalted One addressed the monks, saying: 'Monks, there are these ten ways of Ariyan living, according to which Ariyans have lived, do live and shall live. What ten?

Herein a monk has abandoned five factors . . . (*as in previous sutta*). . . .

And how is a monk one who has abandoned five factors?

Herein a monk has abandoned sensual desires, malevolence, sloth-and-torpor, worry-and-flurry, doubt-and-wavering. Thus he is one who has abandoned five factors.

And how is a monk one who is possessed of six factors?

Herein a monk, seeing an object with the eye, is not elated or depressed, but lives indifferent, mindful and composed. Hearing a sound with the ear . . . smelling a scent with the

---

[1] This summary of qualities, detailed in the following sutta, is at *D.* iii, 269 = *Dialog.* iii, 247, where see Mrs. Rhys Davids' *Introduction* to *Sangīti-sutta* or recital, which refers to its being in Anguttara style. The list is recommended to the monks of Magadha by Asoka in the Bhabra Edict Rock-Inscription; *cf.* Vincent Smith's *Asoka*, pp. 31, 143; *Sakya*, p. 406 *ff.*

[2] *Catur-āpasseno* (= *apassaya*, a pillow or cushion, *Comy.*). *Cf. Dialog.* iii, 216 *n.*

[3] *Cf. G.S.* ii, 47.

[4] *Cf. D.* ii, 55; *M.* i, 532; Rhys Davids' *Buddhist India*, p. 27. *Comy.* = *DA.* iii, 1051.

nose . . . tasting a savour with the tongue . . . contacting an object with the body . . . with mind cognizing mental states, he is not elated nor depressed, but lives indifferent, mindful and composed. Thus is a monk possessed of six factors.

And how does a monk guard one factor ?

By guarding mindfulness he is composed in mind. Thus he guards one factor.

And how does a monk observe the four bases ?

Herein a monk deliberately[1] follows one thing, deliberately endures another thing; avoids one thing, suppresses another thing. Thus a monk observes the four bases.

[**31**] And how is a monk one who has shaken off individual beliefs ?

Herein, monks, whatsoever individual beliefs generally prevail among the generality of recluses and brāhmins, to wit: The world is eternal; the world is not; the world is finite; it is not; what life is, that is body: or, life is one thing, body another; or, a wayfarer exists beyond death, or, a wayfarer exists not beyond death; or, he both exists and yet exists not; or he neither exists nor exists not beyond death—all these beliefs are shaken off, put away, given up, let go, abandoned and dismissed. Thus is a monk one who has shaken off individual beliefs.

And how is a monk one who has utterly given up longings ?[2]

Herein in a monk longing for things sensual is abandoned, longing for becoming is abandoned, longing for the brahma-life has calmed down. Thus is a monk one who has utterly given up longings.

And how are a monk's thoughts unclouded ?

Herein a monk has abandoned thoughts sensual, thoughts malicious, thoughts of harming. Thus are his thoughts unclouded.

And how is a monk's body-complex tranquillized ?

Herein a monk, by abandoning pleasure and pain, by coming

---

[1] *Sankhāya*, gerund; *cf. G.S.* ii, 143. Here *eka*-is indefinite.

[2] *Samavaya-saṭṭhesano*=*samā-vissaṭṭha-sabba-esano, Comy.*; *cf. G.S.* ii, 48 *n.*

to an end of the ease and discomfort which he had before, attains and abides in a state of neither pain nor pleasure, an equanimity of utter purity which is the fourth musing. Thus his body-complex is tranquillized.

And how is a monk well released in heart?

Herein a monk's heart is released from passion, hate and delusion.

And how is a monk well released by insight?

[32] Herein a monk knows for certain: Passion is abandoned in me, cut off at the root, made like a palm-tree stump, made not to become again, of a nature not to arise again in future time. Hatred . . . delusion is abandoned in me . . . not to arise again in future time. Thus is a monk well released by insight.

Monks, whatsoever Ariyans have in past time lived according to the Ariyan living, all of them lived according to these ten ways of Ariyan living. Whatsoever Ariyans shall in future time so live . . . whatsoever Ariyans do now so live, all of them shall live and do live according to these ten ways of Ariyan living.

These, monks, are the ten ways of Ariyan living. . . .'

Chapter III.—The Great Chapter.

§ i (21). *The lion.*[1]

'Monks, the lion, king of beasts, at eventide comes forth from his lair. Having come forth from his lair he stretches himself. Having done so, he surveys the four quarters in all directions. Having done that he utters thrice his lion's roar. **[33]** Thrice having uttered his lion's roar he sallies forth in search of prey. What is the cause of that? (He roars with the idea:) Let me not cause[2] the destruction of tiny creatures wandering astray.

As for the word "lion," monks, this is a term for the Wayfarer who is arahant, a fully awakened one. Inasmuch as

---

[1] *Cf. G.S.* ii, 36; *K.S.* iii, 70.

[2] *Āpādesiṃ*, at *M.* i, 78 *āpādessaṃ*.

the Wayfarer teaches dhamma in the company, that is his lion's roar.

There are these ten Wayfarer's powers of the Wayfarer, monks, possessed of which powers the Wayfarer claims leadership, roars his lion's roar in the companies and sets rolling the Brahma-wheel. What are the ten ?

Herein, monks, the Wayfarer knows, as it really is, causal occasion (of a thing) as such,[1] and what is not causal occasion as such. Inasmuch as he so knows, this is a Wayfarer's power of the Wayfarer, because of which power he claims leadership, roars his lion's roar and sets rolling the Brahma-wheel.

Then again, monks, the Wayfarer knows, as it really is, the fruit of actions past, future and present, both in their causal occasion and in their conditions. Inasmuch as the Wayfarer so knows, this is a power of the Wayfarer, because of which power he claims leadership. . . .

Then again, monks, the Wayfarer knows every bourn-going faring-on,[2] as it really is. Inasmuch as he so knows, this is a Wayfarer's power of the Wayfarer, because of which power he claims leadership. . . .

[**34**] Then again, monks, the Wayfarer knows the world as it really is, in its divers shapes and forms. Inasmuch as he so knows, this is a Wayfarer's power of the Wayfarer, because of which power he claims leadership. . . .

Again, monks, the Wayfarer knows, as they really are, the divers characters of beings. Inasmuch as he knows, this is a Wayfarer's power. . . .

Again the Wayfarer knows, as they really are, the state of the faculties of other beings,[3] of other persons. Inasmuch as he so knows, this is. . . .

Again the Wayfarer knows as they really are the fault, the purification, and the emergence of attainments in musing,

---

[1] *Cf. G.S.* ii, 9; iii, 295.

[2] *Cf. K.S.* v, 270 and notes, where all these characteristics are claimed by Anuruddha through cultivating the four arisings of mindfulness. *Sabb'attha-gāmini-paṭipadaŋ=sabba-gati-gāminiñ ca maggaŋ, Comy.*

[3] *Indriya-paro-pariyattaŋ; cf. Vibh.* 340 *ff. VibhA.* 401 has *indriyānaŋ vuḍḍhiñ ca hāniñ ca.*

liberation and concentration. Inasmuch as he so knows, this is a Wayfarer's power. . . .

Again the Wayfarer can recall his manifold dwellings aforetime, thus: One birth, two births, three births and so on . . . [35] up to a hundred thousand births; likewise the divers folding up of æons, the divers unfolding of æons, the divers folding-unfolding of æons, (remembering): At that time I had such a name, was of such a family, of such complexion, was thus supported, thus and thus experienced weal and woe, had such and such span of life. As that one, I deceasing thence rose up again at that time; then too I had such a name, was of such a family. . . . As that one, I deceasing thence rose up again here. Thus with all details and characteristics he can recall his manifold dwellings aforetime. Inasmuch as the Wayfarer can do so, this is a Wayfarer's power of the Wayfarer, because of which power. . . .

Yet again, monks, the Wayfarer with the deva-sight, purified and surpassing that of men, beholds beings deceasing and rising up again; beings both mean and excellent, fair and foul, gone to a happy bourn, gone to an ill-bourn according to their deeds (so as to say): Alas, sirs, these beings,[1] given to the practice of evil deeds, of evil words, of evil thoughts, scoffing at the Ariyans, of perverted view and reaping the fruits of their perverted view—these beings, when body broke up, beyond death rose up again in the Waste, the Ill-bourn, the Downfall, in Purgatory! Or: Ah, sirs, these beings, given to the practice of good deeds, of good words, of good thoughts, not scoffing at the Ariyans, but of sound view and reaping the fruits of their sound view—these beings, when body broke up, beyond death rose up again in the Happy Bourn in the heaven world. Thus with the deva-sight . . . he beholds beings. . . . [36] Inasmuch as he thus sees, this is a Wayfarer's power.

Once more, monks, the Wayfarer, by destroying the cankers in this same visible existence, attains the heart's release, the release by insight, himself thoroughly comprehending it, and having realized it abides therein. In so far as the Wayfarer

---

[1] *Ime vata bhonto sattā; cf. G.S.* i, 148 *n.*

does so . . . this also is a Wayfarer's power of the Wayfarer, because of which he claims leadership, roars his lion's roar in the companies and sets rolling the Brahma-wheel.

These then, monks, are the Wayfarer's powers of the Wayfarer, possessed of which the Wayfarer claims leadership. . . .'

§ ii (22). *Statements of doctrine.*

Now the venerable Ānanda went to see the Exalted One . . . and the Exalted One said this to him:

'Whatsoever things, Ānanda, conduce to realizing the truth of this or that statement of doctrine,[1] confidently do I claim, after thorough comprehension of it, to teach dhamma about them in such a way that, when proficient, a man shall know of the real that it is, of the unreal that it is not; of the mean that it is mean, of the exalted that it is exalted; of that which has something beyond it, that it has something beyond it; of that which is unsurpassed, that it is unsurpassed. For there is the possibility[2] of his knowing or seeing or realizing [37] that which can be known, seen or realized. This, Ānanda, is knowledge unsurpassable, the knowledge of this or that thing as it really is. Than this knowledge, Ānanda, there is no other knowledge surpassing it or more excellent, I declare.

Ānanda, there are these ten Wayfarer's powers of the Wayfarer . . .' (*from this point the previous sutta is repeated, with* Ānanda *for* monks). [38.]

§ iii (23). *With body.*

[39] 'Monks, there are things to be abandoned with body, not with speech; there are things to be abandoned with speech, not body; things to be abandoned neither with body nor with speech, but by insight on seeing them. And what things are to be abandoned with body, not speech?

---

[1] Text and *uddāna* wrongly read *adhimutti-*, perhaps by confusion with that word in the sixth item of the previous sutta. Reading *adhivutti* (dogma); *cf. D.* i, 13; *DA.* i, 103; *M.* ii, 228; Trenckner-Andersen *P. Dict. s.v.* The comments agree with those of our *Comy.*: *adhivuttiyo ti diṭṭhiyo vuccanti, diṭṭhi-dīpakāni vacanāni*, adding that all Buddhas, past, future and present, do assert doctrinal views of this nature.

[2] *Ṭhānaŋ etaŋ vijjati.*

Herein a monk has committed a fault in a certain direction with body. His discreet co-mates in the brahma-life after investigation say thus: "Your reverence has committed a fault in a certain direction with body. It were well if your reverence were to give up wrong bodily practices and make good bodily practices to grow."

He then, thus spoken to by his discreet co-mates in the brahma-life after investigation, abandons wrong bodily practice and makes good bodily practice to grow. These, monks, are called "things to be abandoned with body, not speech."

And what sort of things, monks, are to be abandoned in speech, not body ?

Herein a monk has committed a fault in a certain direction with speech. Then his discreet co-mates in the brahma-life after investigation say this: "Your reverence has committed a fault . . . in speech. It were well if your reverence were to abandon wrong practice in speech and make good practice in speech to grow." He then, thus spoken to . . . abandons wrong practice in speech and makes good practice in speech to grow. These, monks, are called "things to be abandoned in speech, not body."

And what sort of things, monks, are to be abandoned neither with body nor in speech, but on seeing them with insight ?

Lust, monks, is to be so abandoned; malice . . . delusion . . . wrath . . . grudge . . . depreciation . . . spite . . . [**40**] selfishness . . . wrongful envy, monks, is to be abandoned neither with body nor in speech, but on seeing it by insight.

And of what sort, monks, is wrongful envy ?

Herein, monks, a housefather or housefather's son is affluent in wealth of grain or silver or gold. Then it occurs to some slave or underling:[1] O that affluence belonged not to this housefather or his son in wealth of grain or silver or gold ! Or suppose some recluse or brāhmin gets a good supply of robes and alms-food, lodging, medicines and requisites in

---

[1] *Upavāsa*. See remarks by Dr. E. H. Johnston in *J.R.A.S.*, July, 1931, p. 575. It appears to be used in Skt. in the sense of 'under-tenant of a field,' probably of the semi-servile class known as *ardhasītika*.

sickness. Then it occurs to some recluse or brāhmin: O that this reverend one had not a good supply of robes and alms-food! . . . This, monks, is called wrongful envy. That is to be abandoned neither with body nor in speech, but on seeing it by insight.

In like manner wrongful longing is to be abandoned. And of what sort is that?

Herein a certain unbeliever longs to be known for a believer; being immoral, to be known for one of virtue; being one who has heard little, to be known for one who has heard much; delighting in society, to be known as one given to seclusion; slothful, to be known as one of ardent energy; scatter-brained, to be known as one of concentrated mind; discomposed, to be known as composed; weak in wisdom, to be known as strong in wisdom; not having destroyed the cankers, he longs to be known as one who has done so. This is called wrongful longing. And it is to be abandoned by insight on seeing it.

[**41**] Now if lust overwhelms that monk and has its way . . . if malice, delusion, wrath, grudge, depreciation, spite, selfishness and wrongful envy overwhelm that monk and have their way, then he should be regarded thus: This venerable one understands not how lust ceases to be in him who understands. Thus does lust overwhelm his reverence and has its way. . . . If malice and the rest. . . . But if lust overwhelms not that monk and has not its way . . . if malice and the rest do likewise, then he should be regarded thus: This venerable one understands how lust ceases to be in him who understands. Thus it is that wrongful longing overwhelms him not, has not its way.'

§ iv (24). *Cunda the Great.*

Once the venerable Cunda the Great[1] was staying among the Cetī at Sahajāti.[2] On that occasion he addressed the monks, saying: 'Monks, your reverences.'

---

[1] For Cunda, see also *M.* i, 40; iii, 78; *Brethren* 119; *K.S.* iv, 30. At *S.* v, 81 he is healed of a sickness by the Master. He was Sāriputta's younger brother.

[2] *Cf. K.S.* v, 369 *n.* (*Sahajāta*); *G.S.* iii, 252 *n.* below, § 84 (as here).

'Yes, your reverence,' replied those monks to the venerable Cunda the Great, who then said this:

[42] 'Your reverences, suppose a monk utters talk about knowing, saying, "I know this dhamma, I see this dhamma." Yet if lust has overwhelmed that monk and persists; if malice, delusion, wrath, grudge, depreciation, spite, selfishness, wrongful envy, if wrongful longing overwhelm him and persist, then he should be regarded thus: This venerable one understands not how lust exists not in him who understands. Thus it is that lust overwhelms this venerable one and persists. He understands not how malice . . . and the rest exist not in him who understands. Thus it is that wrongful desire . . . and the rest overwhelm this venerable one and persist.

Suppose, your reverences, a monk prates of making-to-grow, saying: "I am one who has made body, virtue, thought and insight to grow." Yet if lust overwhelm that monk and persist, if malice, delusion and the rest overwhelm him, then he should be regarded thus: This venerable one understands not how lust exists not, how malice and the rest exist not in him who understands.

Suppose a monk prates of knowing and making-to-grow, saying: "I am one who has made body, virtue, thought and insight to grow." Yet if lust, malice and the rest overwhelm that monk and persist, then he should be regarded thus: **[43]** This venerable one understands not how lust, malice and the rest exist not in him who understands.

Just as if, your reverences, a man quite poor should prate of wealth; as if one lacking possessions should prate of possessions; as if one without property should prate of property; then, when occasion for producing[1] wealth arises, when occasion to produce property or grain or silver or gold arises, he fails to do so. Folk say of such an one: "This worthy, though quite poor, prates of his wealth; this worthy, though lacking possessions, prates thereof, being without

---

[1] *Upanīhātuŋ* (not in P. Dicts.). *Comy. nīharitvā dātuŋ*, 'pay down.'

property." Why do they say that ? Because, when occasion for producing such arises, he fails to do so.

Just in the same way, your reverences, a monk prates of knowing and making-to-grow. . . . Yet, if lust, malice, delusion and the rest overwhelm that monk and persist, then he should be regarded thus: This venerable one understands not how lust, malice and delusion and the rest exist not in him who understands.

[**44**] Monks, if a monk prates of knowing, or of making-to-grow, if he prates of both knowing and making-to-grow, yet if lust, malice and delusion and the rest overwhelm him not and persist not . . . then he should be regarded thus: This venerable one understands how lust exists not in one who understands, [**45**] thus lust exists not in this venerable one and persists not . . . thus wrongful longing overwhelms him not and persists not.

Just as if, your reverences, a man quite rich should prate of his wealth, as if a man of possessions should prate of his possessions, as if a man of property should prate of his property; then, when occasion for producing it arises, he would be able to produce his property or grain or silver or gold. Then folk would say of him: "This worthy, being rich, (may well) prate of his wealth; having possessions, may well prate of his possessions; owning property, may well prate of his property." Why do they say that ? Because, when occasion to produce wealth arises, he is able to produce property or grain or silver or gold.

Just in the same way a monk prates of knowing and making-to-grow, saying: "I know this dhamma, I see this dhamma, I am one who makes body to grow, virtue to grow, mind to grow, insight to grow." Then, if lust, malice, delusion and the rest overwhelm not that monk and persist not, he should be regarded thus: This venerable one understands how lust and the rest exist not in him who understands . . . thus wrongful longing overwhelms not this venerable one and persists not.'

§ v (25). *The devices.*

[46] 'Monks, there are these ten ranges of the devices.[1] What ten?

One person perceives the earth-device as above, below, across, undivided, immeasurable. Another person perceives the water-device . . . another the heat-device . . . another the air-device . . . another the blue-green . . . yellow . . . red . . . white . . . another the space-device; another perceives the intellection-device as above, below, across, as undivided, as immeasurable. These are the ten ranges of the devices.'

§ vi (26). *Kālī.*

Once the venerable Kaccāna the Great[2] was staying among the Avantī[3] at Kuraraghara (Ospreys' Haunt) on a sheer mountain crag.[4]

On that occasion the lay-follower Kālī[5] came to see the venerable Kaccāna the Great, and on coming to him she saluted him and sat down at one side. So seated she said this to him:

---

[1] *Kasiṇâyatanāni*, ranges, spheres or applications of the physical appliances or objects of concentration to induce self-hypnotism, during which the higher senses are called into action. See *A.* i, 41 = *G.S.* i, 37; *D.* iii, 268, 290; *Path of Purity*, ii, 138 *ff.*; *Manual of a Mystic*, passim. It would appear that the different methods were suited to different psychic temperaments. See the next sutta. The last two differ in some passages; *cf. VM. trans.* p. 202. The space-device appears to refer to feats in four-dimensional matter. *VM.* and our *Comy.* (as noted at *AA.* i, 77) do not discuss *viññāṇa-kasiṇa*, but probably it refers to a mental image (*anantaŋ viññāṇan ti ārammaṇaŋ katvā esa viññāṇañ câyatana-samāpattiŋ bhāvento viññāṇa-kasiṇaŋ bhāveti ti vuccati*). See *Expositor* i, 248.

[2] *Cf. Vin.* i, 194; *G.S.* i, 17, 61 *ff.*; iii, 214, 224, 227; *K.S.* iii, 10, 14; iv, 72.

[3] Our *Comy.* is silent on these names, but *SA.* ii, 258, on *S.* iv, 115 may be consulted.

[4] Our Text has *pavatte pabbate*, but at the other refs. cited *papāte pabbate*, acc. to which I trans.

[5] *Cf. G.S.* i, 25 *n.* She is named 'chief of those who believe even from hearsay.'

'Sir, this was said by the Exalted One in *The Maiden's Questions*:[1]

On winning of my weal, my peace of heart,
(Routing the host of sweet and pleasant shapes)
Musing alone I have attained to bliss.
Therefore I make no friendship with the folk.
Friendship with anyone is not for me.

[47] Pray, sir, how is the full meaning of this briefly put saying of the Exalted One to be viewed?'

'Some recluses and brāhmins, sister, highly expert in the attainments of the earth-device, have wrought their weal thereby. But the Exalted One has thoroughly comprehended to its utmost reach excellence in the attainment of the earth-device. By thus thoroughly comprehending it the Exalted One saw origination, saw the danger, saw the escape, saw the knowledge and insight into Way and Not-way.

Some recluses and brāhmins, sister, highly expert in the attainment of the water-device . . . the heat-device . . . the air-device . . . the blue-green . . . the yellow . . . the red- . . . the white- . . . the space-device . . . the intellection-device, have wrought their weal thereby.[2] But the Exalted One has thoroughly comprehended to its utmost reach excellence in the attainment of the intellection-device; thus thoroughly comprehending he saw the origination, saw the danger, saw the escape, saw the knowledge and insight into Way and Not-way.[3] As a result of so seeing, the attainment of his weal and peace of heart were seen by him. Thus, sister, as to what was said by the Exalted One in *The Maiden's Questions*:

On winning of my weal, my peace of heart . . .
Friendship with anyone is not for me—

---

[1] Answer to the question 'Why makest thou no friends among the folk?' of the personified Taṇhā at *S.* i, 126=*K.S.* i, 158. In i, 3 *S.* has *jhāyaŋ* for our *jhāyī*, but should read *anubodhiŋ*=*anubujjhiŋ*.

[2] *Atthâbhinibbattesuŋ*; *v.l. attâbhi-*, which would mean 'have attained rebirth' (acc. to *Niddesa* i, 49), or (?) 'have achieved selfhood.'

[3] The four truths. *Comy. samudaya-dukkha-nirodha-magga-saccaŋ.*

[48] this is how the full meaning of the Exalted One's briefly put saying is to be viewed.'

§ vii (27). *The Great Questions*[1] (*a*).

Once the Exalted One was staying near Sāvatthī at Jeta Grove in Anāthapiṇḍika's Park. Then a great number of monks, robing themselves in the forenoon and taking bowl and robe, set out for Sāvatthī questing for alms-food. Now it occurred to those monks thus: It is full early yet to range Sāvatthī for alms-food. Suppose we visit the park of the Wanderers holding other views. Accordingly they did so,

---

[1] At *K.S.* iv, 207 the housefather Citta puts these questions (*Kumāra-pañhā*) to the Nigaṇṭha, Nāta's son, and he cannot answer. See Mrs. Rhys Davids' *Introduction* to her trans. of *Khuddaka-pāṭha* (*S.B.* of *B. Series*), p. xlix *ff.*, where their origin and real ancient meaning is discussed. In the sutta following, the Kajangalan nun gives a list different in some respects. All three lists agree in the first three and ninth items. I give here a comparative table:

I (*KhP.*).	II (*A.* v, 50).	III (*The Nun*, p. 56).
I. All beings persist by food	The same.	The same.
II. Name and visible body-complex	The same.	The same.
III. Three knowings by sensation	The same.	The same.
IV. The four truths	Four sustenances.	Four satipaṭṭhānā.
V. Five grasping-groups	The same.	Five faculties.
VI. Six spheres in the self	The same.	Six elements of deliverance.
VII. Seven limbs of wisdom	Seven stations of consciousness.	Seven limbs of wisdom.
VIII. The eightfold Way	Eight world-conditions (*A.* iv, 156).	The eightfold Way
IX. Nine abodes of beings	The same.	The same.
X. Arahant's ten qualities	Good-action-paths.	Arahant's ten qualities.

At *A.* v, 58 the Master approves of the nun's version. In *Paṭisambhidā* i, 22 again we find another variation of ten things—viz.: No. 1, contact with cankers leading to grasping; Nos. 2 to 9 as here; No. 10, the ten *āyatana*'s.

and on getting there greeted them courteously, and, after the exchange of greetings and reminiscent talk, sat down at one side. So seated those Wanderers of other views said this to them:

'Your reverences, Gotama the recluse thus teaches dhamma: Come ye, monks, do ye thoroughly grasp all dhamma, do ye dwell ever and always thoroughly grasping all dhamma. Now, your reverences, we also thus teach dhamma to our followers: Come, your reverences, do ye thoroughly grasp all dhamma; do ye ever and always dwell thoroughly grasping all dhamma. Herein, your reverences, pray what is the distinction, what is the specific feature, what is the difference between Gotama the recluse and ourselves **[49]**, that is, between his teaching of dhamma and ours, or his way of instruction and ours?'

Thereupon those monks made no reply, either of approval or of disapproval to those Wanderers holding other views; but without expressing either approval or disapproval they rose up and went away, saying: 'We will learn the meaning of this saying in the company of the Exalted One.'

So those monks, after ranging Sāvatthī for alms-food, on returning from their alms-round and after eating their meal, went to see the Exalted One, and on coming to him saluted him and sat down at one side. So seated they said this to the Exalted One:

'Sir, here in the forenoon we robed ourselves . . .' and they related the incident and how they went away without answering the Wanderers. **[50.]**

'Monks, when Wanderers holding other views speak thus, they should be thus spoken to: "The one question, the one statement, the one explanation; the two . . . three . . . the ten questions, the ten statements, the ten explanations." Thus questioned, monks, the Wanderers holding other views will fail to answer, and further will come to discomfiture. Why so? Because, monks, that is beyond their scope.[1] Monks, I behold not in the world with its Devas, its Māras,

---

[1] *Cf. K.S.* iv, 16, 39.

its Brahmās, its host of recluses and brāhmins, together with its devas and mankind, I behold not one who could convince the mind with an explanation of these questions save only the Wayfarer or one of his disciples, or one who had heard it from that source.

As to the saying: "The one question, the one statement, the one explanation," owing to what was it said?

Monks, if in one thing a monk rightly feel revulsion, rightly feel fading interest (in the world), rightly be released, rightly have sight to the furthest bounds and rightly comprehend the meaning of things, then in this same visible state he makes an end of Ill.[1] In what one thing? In this, namely: All beings are persisters by food. **[51]** In this one thing, monks, if a monk rightly feel revulsion . . . he makes an end of Ill. "The one question, the one statement, the one explanation" was said because of this.

As to the saying: "The two questions, the two statements, the two explanations," owing to what was it said?

Monks, if in two things a monk rightly feel revulsion . . . then in this same visible state he makes an end of Ill. In what two things? Both in name-and-visible-body-complex. In these two things if a monk rightly feel revulsion . . . he makes an end of Ill. "The two questions, the two statements, the two explanations" was said because of this.

As to the saying: "The three questions, the three statements, the three explanations," owing to what was it said?

Monks, if in three things a monk rightly feel revulsion . . . he makes an end of Ill. In what three things? The three knowings (by sensation). In these three things if a monk rightly feel revulsion . . . he makes an end of Ill. "The three questions . . ." was said because of this.

As to the saying: "The four questions, the four statements, the four explanations," owing to what was it said?

[52] Monks, if in four things a monk rightly feel revulsion . . . he makes an end of Ill. In what four things? The four

---

[1] This paragraph, according to *Comy.*, forms the *uddesa* or statement. The words 'all beings,' etc., are the *veyyâkaraṇaŋ* or explanation.

sustenances.[1] If in these four things a monk rightly feel revulsion . . . he makes an end of Ill. "The four questions . . ." was said because of this.

As to the saying: "The five questions, the five statements, the five explanations," owing to what was it said?

Monks, if in five things a monk rightly feel revulsion . . . he makes an end of Ill. What five things? The five grasping-heaps. If in these five things a monk rightly feel revulsion . . . he makes an end of Ill. "The five questions, the five statements, the five explanations" was said because of this.

As to the saying: "The six questions, the six statements, the six explanations," owing to what was it said?

Monks, if in six things a monk rightly feel revulsion . . . he makes an end of Ill. What six things? The six spheres in the self. If in these six things a monk rightly feel revulsion . . . he makes an end of Ill. "The six questions . . ." was said because of this.

[53] As to the saying: "The seven questions,. the seven statements, the seven explanations," owing to what was it said?

Monks, if in seven things a monk rightly feel revulsion . . . he makes an end of Ill. What seven things? The seven stations of consciousness.[2] If in these seven things a monk rightly feel revulsion . . . he makes an end of Ill. "The seven questions . . ." was said because of this.

As to the saying: "The eight questions, the eight statements, the eight explanations," owing to what was it said?

Monks, if in eight things a monk rightly feel revulsion . . . he makes an end of Ill. What eight things? The eight worldly matters.[3] If in these eight things a monk rightly feel revulsion . . . he makes an end of Ill. "The eight questions . . ." was said because of this.

---

[1] *I.e.* solid food, contact (of sense), work of mind, consciousness (or as we should say 'the conscious self').

[2] Described at *A.* iv, 39, but is the same as the first seven of the Nine Abodes of Beings.

[3] *Cf. A.* iv, 156, gain and not gain, repute and not-repute, blame and praise, pleasure and pain.

[54] As to the saying: "The nine questions, the nine statements, the nine explanations," owing to what was it said?

Monks, if in nine things a monk rightly feel revulsion . . . he makes an end of Ill. What nine things? The nine abodes of beings.[1] If in the nine things a monk rightly feel revulsion . . . he makes an end of Ill. "The nine questions . . ." was said because of this.

As to the saying: "The ten questions, the ten statements, the ten explanations," owing to what was it said?

Monks, if in ten things a monk rightly feel revulsion, rightly feel fading interest (in the world), rightly be released, rightly have sight to the furthest bounds and rightly comprehend the meaning of things, then in this same visible state he makes an end of Ill. What ten things? The ten wrong ways of action.[2] If in these ten things a monk rightly feel revulsion . . . in this same visible state he makes an end of Ill. "The ten questions, the ten statements, the ten explanations" was said because of this.'

§ viii (28). *The Great Questions* (*b*).

Once the Exalted One was staying at Kajangalā[3] in Bamboo Grove. Now a great number of lay followers of Kajangalā came to see the nun of Kajangalā, and on coming to her saluted her and sat down at one side. So seated those lay followers of Kajangalā said this to the nun of Kajangalā:

'This was said, lady, by the Exalted One in *The Great Questions*: "The one question, the one statement, the one explanation . . . [55] . . . The ten questions, the ten statements, the ten explanations." Pray, lady, how should this that was said in brief by the Exalted One be regarded in full?'

'Well, worthy sirs, I have not heard it or gathered it face to face with the Exalted One, nor yet from the monks who

---

[1] The seven of No. 7, with two spheres of unconsciousness.

[2] The wrong actions of the first four precepts, with three of speech, coveting, harmfulness and wrong view. *Cf. Netti*, 43.

[3] *Cf. Sisters*, p. xxxvi; *Gotama the Man*, 147, 156.

make the mind to grow.[1] Nevertheless do ye listen how it appears to me. Pay attention carefully and I will speak.'

'We will, lady,' replied those lay followers to the nun of Kajangalā, who then said this:

'"The one question, the one statement, the one explanation": this was said by the Exalted One. Owing to what was it said? *(Here she repeats the first three items of the previous sutta.)*

[56] "The four questions, the four statements, the four explanations" was said by the Exalted One. Owing to what was it said?

If in four things, worthy sirs, a monk has rightly made good growth of mind, if rightly he have sight to the furthest bounds and rightly comprehend the aim[2] (in things), then in this same visible state he makes an end of Ill. In what four things? In the four arisings of mindfulness. If in these four things a monk has rightly made good growth of mind . . . he makes an end of Ill. "The four questions . . ." was said because of this.

"The five questions, the five statements, the five explanations" was said by the Exalted One. Owing to what was it said?

If in five things, worthy sirs, a monk has rightly made good growth of mind . . . he makes an end of Ill. What five things? In the five faculties. If in these five things a monk has rightly made good growth of mind . . . he makes an end of Ill. "The five questions . . ." was said because of this.

[57] "The six questions, the six statements, the six explanations" was said by the Exalted One. Owing to what was it said?

If in six things, worthy sirs, a monk has made good growth of mind . . . he makes an end of Ill. What six things? The

---

[1] *Mano-bhāvanīyānaŋ*. I trans. this wrongly at *K.S.* iii, 1. See Mrs. Rhys Davids' remarks in her *Introduction* to *Gradual Sayings* iii, p. xii, and *Sakya*, 245. Compare the use of *subhāvita-citto* in the nun's reply.

[2] *Attha-*.

six elements of deliverance.[1] If in these six things a monk . . . he makes an end of Ill. "The six questions . . ." was said because of this.

"The seven questions, the seven statements, the seven explanations" was said by the Exalted One. Owing to what was it said?

If in seven things, worthy sirs, a monk has rightly made good growth of mind . . . he makes an end of Ill. In what seven things? The seven limbs of wisdom.[2] If in these seven things a monk . . . he makes an end of Ill. "The seven questions . . ." was said owing to this.

"The eight questions, the eight statements, the eight explanations" was said by the Exalted One. Owing to what was it said?

If in eight things, worthy sirs, a monk has rightly made good growth of mind . . . he makes an end of Ill. In what eight things? The Ariyan Eightfold Way. If in these eight things . . . he makes an end of Ill. "The eight questions . . ." was said owing to this.

"The nine questions, the nine statements, the nine explanations" was said by the Exalted One. Owing to what was it said?

If in nine things, worthy sirs, a monk rightly feel revulsion . . . he makes an end of Ill. In what nine things? The nine abodes of beings. If in these nine things, worthy sirs, a monk rightly feel revulsion . . . he makes an end of Ill. "The nine questions . . ." was said owing to this.

"The ten questions, the ten statements, the ten explanations" was said by the Exalted One. Owing to what was it said?

If in ten things, worthy sirs, a monk has rightly made good

---

[1] *Chasu nissaraṇīyesu dhātūsu.* Three are at *Itivuttaka*, p. 61 (deliverance from the *kāmā*, by *nekkhamma, āruppaŋ, nirodha*); five at *A.*iii, 245=*G.S.* iii, 179 (from *kāma, vyāpāda, vihesa, rūpa* and *sakkāya*); but six at *D.* iii, 247 (*mettā, karuṇā, muditā, upekhā, animitta-ceto-vimutti* and *asmī ti māna-samugghāta*, which are probably those referred to here.

[2] *Cf. K.S.* v, 51 *ff.*

growth of mind, if rightly he have sight to the furthest bounds if he rightly comprehend the aim (in things), then in this same visible state he makes an end of Ill. In what ten things? The ten right ways of action.[1] If in these ten things a monk has rightly made good growth of mind . . . he makes an end of Ill. "The ten questions, the ten statements, the ten explanations" was said owing to this.

[**58**] Thus, worthy sirs, as to the words of the Exalted One: "The one question, the one statement, the one explanation . . . the ten explanations" uttered in brief, thus do I understand the meaning of them in full. However, if you, worthy sirs, wish to do so, you can go to see the Exalted One himself and ask him about the meaning of this. As the Exalted One expounds it,[2] so do you bear it in mind.'

'We will, lady,' replied those lay followers to the Kajangalan nun, and after praising her reply and returning thanks, they rose up and saluting the Kajangalan nun by keeping the right side towards her, went away to see the Exalted One; and on coming to him, saluted him and sat down at one side. As they sat thus they told him all their talk with the Kajangalan nun. The Exalted One said this:

'It is well! It is well, housefathers! A wise woman is the Kajangalan nun. If you, housefathers, were to come to me and ask about the meaning of this [**59**] I should give just the same explanation as that given by the Kajangalan nun. Indeed that is the meaning of it, and so should ye bear it in mind.'

§ ix (29). *The Kosalan (a).*

'Monks, as far as the Kāsi Kosalans extend, as far as the rule of Pasenadi the Kosalan rājā extends, therein Pasenadi the Kosalan rājā is reckoned chief. Yet, monks, even for Pasenadi the Kosalan rājā there is change and reverse. So seeing the learned Ariyan disciple feels revulsion; on feeling

---

[1] The nun improves on the ten negatives of the previous answer. In § 176 below these *kamma-pathā* are called *dhaṃma-pathā* (3 *sīlas* of *kāya*, 4 of *vācā*, and 3 of *mano*). *Cf. D.* iii, 71, 269, 290; *K.S.* ii, 111.

[2] Reading *v.l. naŋ* for *vo*.

revulsion his interest in the topmost fades, not to speak of the low.

Monks, as far as the moon and sun move in their course and light up all[1] quarters with their radiance, so far extends the thousandfold world-system. Therein are a thousand moons, a thousand suns, a thousand Sinerus lords of mountains; therein are a thousand Rose-apple Lands,[2] a thousand Western Ox-wains, a thousand Northern Kurūs, a thousand Eastern Videhas; four thousand mighty oceans, four thousand Mighty Rulers, four thousand Four-Great-Rulers; a thousand Heavens of the Thirty-three, one thousand Yama-worlds, one thousand Heavens of the Devas of Delight, one thousand Heavens of the Devas who delight in creation, one thousand of those Devas who delight in others' creations, and one thousand Brahma-worlds.

As far, monks, as the thousandfold world-system extends [**60**], therein the Great Brahmā is reckoned chief. Yet even for the Great Brahmā, monks, there is change and reverse. So seeing the learned Ariyan disciple feels revulsion; in him so feeling revulsion interest in the topmost fades, not to speak of the low.

There comes a time, monks, when this world rolls up.[3] As the world rolls up, beings are generally reborn as Radiant Ones.[4] There they are made as if of mind, feeding on joy, self-radiant, faring through the sky, in splendour abiding, for a long, long time they stand fast. Monks, when the world rolls up, it is the Radiant Devas who are reckoned chief. Yet for the Radiant Devas there is change and reverse. So seeing the learned Ariyan disciple feels revulsion . . . interest in the topmost fades, not to speak of the low.

Monks, there are these ten ranges of the devices. What ten ?[5]

One person perceives the earth-device as above, below,

---

[1] At *A.* i, 227=*G.S.* i, 207, where see notes.

[2] *Jambudīpa*, name for India, is really the earth.

[3] *Saṃvaṭṭati* (involution) as opposed to *vivaṭṭati* (evolution); *cf. G.S.* ii, 145 and *D.* i, 17 (where text § 2 has wrongly *loke saṃvaṭṭamāno*).

[4] Text *Ābhassara-vattanikā*, but *D.*, *loc. cit.*, has *-saṃvaṭṭanikā*.

[5] Repeated from § 5 above.

across, undivided, immeasurable. Another person perceives the water-device . . . another the heat-device . . . another the air-device . . . another the blue-green . . . yellow . . . red . . . white . . . another the space-device; another perceives the intellection-device as above, below, across, as undivided, immeasurable. These are the ten ranges of the devices.

Of these ten ranges of the devices this is the topmost, when a person perceives the intellection-device as above, below, across, undivided, immeasurable. There are indeed, monks, persons who thus perceive. Yet to persons thus perceiving there is change and reverse. **[61]** So seeing the learned Ariyan disciple feels revulsion. In him thus feeling revulsion his interest in the topmost fades, not to speak of the low.

Monks, there are these eight stations of mastery.[1] What eight?

A certain one, being conscious of material quality, in his own person, sees objects external to himself to be limited, fair or foul. Having mastered them[2] with the thought: I know, I see, he is thus conscious (of knowing and seeing, and so enters the musings). This is the first station of mastery.

A certain one, being conscious of material quality in his own person, sees objects external to himself to be immeasurable, fair or foul. Having mastered them . . . he is conscious. . . . This is the second station of mastery.

A certain one, being unconscious of material quality in his own person, sees objects external to himself to be limited, fair or foul . . . to be immeasurable, fair or foul. Having

---

[1] *Abhibhâyatanāni.* Six at *K.S.* iv, 46 (or 'of the conqueror'). *Cf. D.* ii, 110=*Dialog.* ii, 118; *M.* ii, 13=*Further Dialog.* ii, 8; *G.S.* i, 36; *Dhammasangaṇi* § 223; *Expositor* i, 252 *ff.*, where *n.* has '*abhibhâyatana* is *jhāna* with an overpowering (*abhibhū*) preamble, or knowledge, as cause (*āyatana*); or *jhāna* with an abode or locus (*āyatana*) called "the object to be overpowered" (*abhibhāvitabbaṃ*).'

[2] Our *Comy.* has nothing here, but *cf. Expositor, loc. cit.*, 'a person of transcendent and clear knowledge masters the device-objects and attains *jhāna* . . . he produces ecstasy together with the production of the image of the mark (*nimitta*) in this limited object.'

mastered them . . . he is conscious. . . . These are the third and fourth stations of mastery.

A certain one, being unconscious of material quality in his own person, sees objects external to himself to be blue-green, of the colour blue-green, blue-green to look at (as a whole), blue-green as a shimmering mass. Just as for instance the flower of flax is blue-green, of the colour blue-green, blue-green to look at, a shimmering mass of blue-green; or just as Benares muslin, smooth on both sides, is blue-green . . . so blue-green are the external objects that he sees. Having mastered them . . . he is thus conscious. This is the fifth station of mastery.

A certain one, being unconscious of material quality in his own person, sees objects external to himself as yellow, of the colour yellow, yellow to look at, a shimmering mass of yellow. Just as for instance the *kaṇikāra* flower is yellow . . . or just as that Benares muslin, smooth on both sides, is yellow **[62]** . . . so yellow are the external objects that he sees. Having mastered them . . . he is thus conscious. This is the sixth station of mastery.

A certain one, being unconscious of material quality in his own person, sees objects external to himself to be blood-red, of colour blood-red, blood-red to look at, a shimmering mass of blood-red. Just as the *bandhu-jīvaka* flower is blood-red . . . or that Benares muslin is blood-red . . . so are the external objects that he sees blood-red. Having mastered them . . . he is thus conscious. This is the seventh station of mastery.

A certain one, being unconscious of material quality in his own person, sees objects external to himself to be white, white in colour, white to look at, a shimmering mass of white. Just as, for instance, the star of healing[1] is white, white in colour, white to look at, a shimmering mass of white; or just as that Benares muslin, smooth on both sides, is white . . . even so white are the external objects that he sees. Having mastered them with the thought: I know, I see, he is thus conscious (of

---

[1] *Osadhī-tāraka*, probably Venus. See *Itiv.* 20 *n.*

knowing and seeing, and so enters the musings). This is the eighth station of mastery.

These, monks, are the eight stations of mastery.

Now, monks, of these eight stations of mastery the topmost is that in which a certain one, being unconscious of material qualities in his own person, sees objects external to himself to be white, white in colour, white to look at, a shimmering mass of white; and having mastered them with the thought: I know, I see, is thus conscious (of knowing and seeing). Indeed, monks, there are beings thus conscious. Yet for beings thus conscious **[63]** there is change and reverse. So seeing the learned Ariyan disciple feels revulsion; so feeling revulsion his interest in the topmost fades, not to speak of the low.

Monks, there are these four modes of progress.[1] What four?

The painful mode of progress with sluggish intuition; the painful mode of progress with swift intuition; the pleasant mode of progress with sluggish intuition; the pleasant mode with swift intuition. These are the four.

Now, monks, of these four modes of progress the topmost is the pleasant mode with swift intuition. There are indeed beings who have thus progressed. Yet for beings who have thus progressed there is change and reverse. So seeing, monks, the learned Ariyan disciple feels revulsion . . . his interest in the topmost fades, not to speak of the low.

Monks, there are these four modes of perception. What four?

A certain one perceives the limited, another the extensive, another the immeasurable, and another perceives: There is nothing at all, the sphere of nothingness. These are the four.

Now, monks, of these four the topmost is the perception: There is nothing at all, the sphere of nothingness. There are indeed beings who thus perceive, yet for such there is change and reverse. So seeing the learned Ariyan disciple feels revulsion. . . .

---

[1] *Paṭipadā.* At *G.S.* ii, 153; Dhs. §§ 176-9; *cf. Netti* 113.

Monks, of outsiders[1] who hold views, this view:

> Were I not then, it would not now be mine;
> I'll not become, 'twill not become in me—[2]

is the topmost. Of one who holds this view, monks, this may be looked for—that feeling of no-disgust in becoming will not become for him, and that feeling of disgust at ending becoming will not become for him. [**64**] Indeed, monks, there are beings who hold this view. Yet for such beings . . . there is change and reverse. So seeing the learned Ariyan disciple feels revulsion. . . .

Monks, there are some recluses and brāhmins who proclaim purification as the greatest blessing. Of those who do so topmost is he who, passing beyond the sphere of nothingness, attains the sphere of neither-consciousness-nor-not-consciousness and so abides. They teach dhamma for the thorough comprehension of that, for the realization of that. Indeed, monks, there are beings who make this claim. Yet for those who do so there is change and reverse. So seeing, the learned Ariyan disciple feels revulsion. . . .

Monks, there are some recluses and brāhmins who proclaim as chief nibbāna in this visible state. Of those who so proclaim the topmost achievement is the release-without-grasping, by seeing as it really is the arising and the ceasing, the attraction and the danger of, the escape from the six spheres of contact.[3] I, monks, am one who make this claim and announcement, and

---

[1] *Bāhirakā*, 'outside the *sāsana*,' *Comy.*

[2] *No c'assaŋ no ca me siyā*
Na bhavissāmi na me bhavissati.

Cf. K.S. iii, 48 *n.*, 152; *SA.* ii, 275. At *Ud.* 66, *na câhu na bhavissati na c'etarahi vijjati*; *Ud.* 78, *na bhavissati na ca me bhavissati*, where see my note in the translation. *Not a view of outsiders*, however, for it is a view ascribed to the Master and praised by him when held by Kaccāyana, as the determination to end the round of rebirth. The *SA.* comment is in brief, 'If it were not for my past karma, my present body-person would not exist. Here our *Comy.* has 'if in future time I shall not become, no obstacle (*palibodha*) whatever shall become in me.'

[3] *Cf. D.* i, 22, 38.

some recluses and brāhmins accuse me of unreality, hollowness, falsehood and untruth therein, saying: "Gotama the recluse proclaims not the full comprehension of passions, proclaims not the full comprehension of objective forms, proclaims not the full comprehension of feelings." [65] But, monks, it is just of passions that I do proclaim full comprehension, it is just of objective forms, of feelings that I do proclaim full comprehension. In this same visible state hungering no more, waned,[1] grown cool, do I proclaim the full nibbāna without grasping.

§ x (30). *The Kosalan* (*b*).

Once on a time the Exalted One was staying near Sāvatthī at Jeta Grove in Anāthapiṇḍika's Park. On that occasion the rājā Pasenadi of Kosala had just returned from a sham[2] fight, having being victorious, and attained his object. Then the rājā turned in the direction of the Park. So far as the cart-road went he rode in his chariot, and then got down and reached the residence.

Now at that time a number of monks were walking up and down in the open air. Then Pasenadi the rājā of Kosala went towards those monks, and on reaching them thus accosted them:

'Pray, your reverences, where now is the Exalted One staying, that arahant, the fully enlightened one? I long to behold that Exalted One.'

'Yonder is his lodging, mahārājā, with the door shut. Do you go up quietly without nervousness, enter the verandah, cough and rattle the door-bar. The Exalted One will open the door to you.'

So the rājā Pasenadi of Kosala went up to the lodging as he was told, coughed and rattled the door-bar. And the Exalted One opened the door.[3]

Then Pasenadi entered the lodging, fell with his head at the

---

[1] *Cf. S.* iv, 204, *vedanānaŋ khayā bhikkhu nicchāto parinibbuto.*

[2] *Uyyodhikā.* Our *Comy.* takes it as a real fight with *Ajātasattu.*

[3] *Comy.* will not allow that the Great Man stooped to open the door himself: 'He just willed it to open.' *Cf. Majjhima,* Sutta 89.

feet of the Exalted One, kissed his feet and stroked them with his hands, and announced his name,[1] saying, 'Sir, I am Pasenadi, the rājā of Kosala, Pasenadi the rājā of Kosala am I.'

[66] 'But, mahārājā, seeing what significance therein do you show me this profound humility and pay such affectionate obeisance to this body of mine?'

'To show my gratitude,[2] sir, to show my thankfulness to the Exalted One do I show this profound humility and pay such affectionate obeisance. For the Exalted One, sir, is one who is set on the profit, on the happiness of many folk, he is one who establishes many folk in the Ariyan method, that is, conformity with whatsoever is lovely and goodly. Inasmuch as the Exalted One is such an one, that, sir, is why I show my gratitude, my thankfulness in this way.

Then again, sir, the Exalted One is virtuous, he has the Buddha-virtues, the Ariyan, the goodly virtues, he is possessed of the goodly virtues. That is another reason for my showing this profound humility. . . .

Again, sir, the Exalted One has for many a day been a forest-dweller, a haunter of forest solitudes **[67]**, resorting to the solitary lodging of the forest. That is another reason. . . .

Yet again, sir, the Exalted One is well content with whatsoever offerings of robes and alms-food, lodging and bed, supply of medicines and requisites in sickness he may receive. That is another reason. . . .

And he is worshipful, worthy of honour, worthy of offerings, of salutations with clasped hands, he is a field of merit unsurpassed for the world. That, sir, is another reason. . . .

Yet again, sir, as regards talk[3] that is serious, fit for opening

---

[1] Hardly necessary to do so. But see a similar case at *Ud.* vi, 2, where he announces himself to the wandering informers in the same words.

[2] Literally 'seeing the significance of gratitude.' *Comy.* thinks this refers to the cure of his habitual gluttony by the Master, *K.S.* i, 108. Here the rājā is made to recite the qualities ascribed to virtuous monks, together with their occult attainments, with which he would hardly be acquainted. Moreover, who recorded this private conversation?

[3] *Cf. G.S.* iii, 91; *Ud.* 36.

up the heart, that is to say, talk about wanting little, about contentment, about solitude, avoiding society, putting forth energy; talk about virtue, concentration of mind, wisdom, release, knowledge and insight of release—such talk as this the Exalted One gets at pleasure, without pain and without stint. Since the Exalted One does this, that is a further reason. . . .

Then again, sir, the Exalted One wins at pleasure, without pain and without stint, the four musings which are of the clear consciousness[1] [**68**], which are concerned with the happy life in this same visible state. Since the Exalted One does this, that is a further reason. . . .

Again, sir, the Exalted One can recall his manifold dwelling aforetime,[2] thus: one birth, two births, three . . . ten . . . up to a hundred thousand births; likewise the divers foldings up of æons, the divers unfoldings of æons, the divers folding-and-unfolding of æons (remembering): At that time I had such a name, was of such a family, of such complexion, so supported, thus and thus experiencing weal and woe, of such and such a span of life. I, as that one, thence deceasing, rose up again at that time. There too I had such a name, was of such a family, of such complexion. . . . I, as that one, thence deceasing, rose up again here. Thus with all detail and characteristics he can recall his manifold dwelling aforetime. Since the Exalted One does this, that is another reason. . . .

And again, sir, the Exalted One with the deva-sight, purified and surpassing that of men, beholds beings deceasing and rising up again; beings both mean and excellent, fair and foul, gone to a happy bourn, gone to an ill-bourn according to their deeds (so as to say): Alas, sirs ! these beings, given to the practice of evil deeds [**69**], of evil words, of evil thoughts, scoffing at the Ariyans, of perverted view and reaping the fruit of their perverted view—these beings, when body broke up beyond death rose up again in the Waste, the Ill-bourn, the Downfall, in Purgatory. Or, Ah, sirs ! these beings, given to the practice of good deeds, of good words, of good thoughts,

---

[1] *Cf. G.S.* ii, 24.

[2] As above III, i (21).

not scoffing at the Ariyans, but of sound view and reaping the fruit of their sound view—these beings, when body broke up beyond death rose up again in the Happy Bourn, in the Heaven World. Thus with the deva-sight, purified and surpassing that of men, he beholds beings. . . . Since the Exalted One does this, that is another reason. . . .

Yet again, sir, by the destruction of the cankers the Exalted One in this same visible state attains the heart's release, the insight of release, himself acquiring it by his own comprehension, and realizing it abides the rein. Since the Exalted One does so, seeing this significance do I thus show this profound humility and pay such affectionate obeisance to the Exalted One.

Well now, sir, we must be going. We are busy folk and have much to do.'

'Do what seems good to you, mahārājā.'

So Pasenadi the rājā of Kosala, rising from his seat, saluted the Exalted One by keeping his right side towards him and departed.

Chapter IV.—Upāli and Ānanda.

§ i (31). *Upāli and the Obligation.*[1]

[70] Now the venerable Upāli came to see the Exalted One, and on coming to him saluted him and sat down at one side. So seated, he said this to the Exalted One:

'Pray, sir, with what object in view was the training enjoined on the disciples of the Wayfarer and the obligation pronounced ?'

'It was done with ten objects in view, Upāli. What ten ? For the excellence of the Order, for the well-being of the Order; for the control of ill-conditioned monks and the comfort of well-behaved[2] monks; for the restraint of the cankers[3] in this same visible state; for protection against the cankers in a future life; to give confidence to those of little faith;[4] for the betterment of the faithful; to establish true dhamma, and to support the discipline.

These, Upāli, are the ten objects in view of which the training was enjoined on the Wayfarer's disciples and the obligation pronounced.'

'Pray, sir, what is the nature of the suspension of the obligation ?'[5]

'The suspension of the obligation, Upāli, is of ten sorts. What ten ?

When a transgressor is seated in that company; when

---

[1] *Pāṭimokkha, cf.* in detail *G.S.* i, 83 *ff.* *Vin.* i, 103 gives the supposed derivation of the word; *pāṭimokkhan ti ādiŋ etaŋ, mukhaŋ etaŋ, pamukhaŋ etaŋ kusalānaŋ dhammānaŋ, tena vuccati p.*; *cf. Vin.* ii, 196; *A.* i, 98; *G.S.* i, 83; *Netti* 50 ; Rhys Davids in *E.R.E.* art., 'Pātimokkha.'

[2] *Pesalānaŋ* (of dear virtue).

[3] At *A.* i, 98 (for the restraint of) the cankers of guilt, faults, fears and unprofitable states.

[4] Wrong at *G.S.* i, 83.

[5] *Ṭhapana; cf. Vin.* ii, 241, 243; *UdA.* 299.

debate[1] about a transgressor is unfinished; [71] when a person not fully ordained is seated in that company; when debate about such an one is unfinished; when one who has renounced the training is seated in that company; when debate on that subject is unfinished; when a eunuch[2] is seated in that company; when debate about such is unfinished; when one who has defiled a nun[3] is seated in that company; when debate about such is unfinished. These are the ten suspensions of the obligation.'

§ ii (32). *Passing sentence.*

'Pray, sir (asked Upāli), what ten qualities should a monk possess in order to be considered fit for passing sentence?'[4]

'He should possess ten qualities, Upāli, for such a purpose. What ten?

Herein, Upāli, a monk is virtuous, restrained with the restraint of the obligation, proficient in following the practice of right conduct, seeing cause for fear in the slightest faults, he takes up and trains himself in the rules of morality. Then he has heard much, bears in mind what he has heard, he hoards up what he has heard. Those teachings which are alike lovely at the beginning, lovely in the middle, lovely at the end (of life), proclaim in the spirit and the letter the all-fulfilled, the utterly purified brahma-life—suchlike are the teachings he has much heard, borne in mind, practised in speech, pondered in the heart, rightly penetrated by view.

By him both of the obligations[5] in full are thoroughly learned by heart, well analysed, with thorough knowledge of the meaning, clearly divided sutta by sutta and in minute

---

[1] *Pārājika-kathā vippakatā hoti.* *Comy.* 'Has such an one fallen into transgression or not?' when such talk has started and is left unfinished; so with the other cases.

[2] *Cf. Vin.* i, 85. Such might not be fully ordained. If discovered he must be unfrocked.

[3] *M.* i, 67.

[4] *Ubbāhikāya* (as a member of council) about expulsion of a monk. *Cf. Vin.* ii, 95.

[5] *Vin.* i, 65, 68; ii, 249; *A.* iv, 140. To be recited in full twice monthly; in brief only when there was some hindrance. *Vin.* i, 113; below, § 98.

detail. Moreover he is established in the discipline, immovable therein. He is competent to make both parties in a dispute understand, to win them over, to make them see, to reconcile them. **[72]** He is skilled in the rise and settlement of disputes,[1] he knows the matter at issue, he knows the cause of its rise, he knows the way to end it, he knows the procedure leading to the ending of it.

Possessing these ten qualities a monk is to be considered fit for passing sentence.'

§ iii (33). *Full ordination.*

'Pray, sir, how must a monk be qualified in order to give full ordination ?'

'He must possess ten qualities, Upāli, in order to do so. Herein a monk is virtuous . . . (*as in previous sutta*) . . . rightly penetrated by view. By him the obligation in full is thoroughly learned by heart. . . . He is competent to attend to the sick or to cause such attendance. He is competent to calm discontent or cause it to be calmed. He is competent to restrain bad conduct in accordance with dhamma (lawfully) (or to see that it is done),[2] to dissuade the adoption of theories (or to see that it is done),[2] to establish one in the higher virtue, in the higher thought, in the higher insight.

One must possess these ten qualities, Upāli, in order to give full ordination.'

§ iv (34). *Tutelage.*

[73] 'Pray, sir, by a monk how qualified should tutelage[3] be assigned . . . and a novice provided for ?'

---

[1] *Su-ppavattīni* (well-flowing, fluently). *Comy.* at *A.* iv, 140 has *āvajjanâvajjana-ṭṭhāne suṭṭhu pavattāni, daḷha-paguṇāni.* In next sutta, *suppavattaŋ.*

[2] *Cf. Vin.* ii, 74 (words bracketed omitted in our text). For waiting on sick, *Vin.* i, 64.

[3] *Nissaya. Cf. Vin.* i, 49 (*Comy.* on *A.* i, 99 *bālassa avyattassa* [?] *seyyasakassa bhikkhuno* [wrong at *G.S.* i, 84 *n.*: apparently the name (*Seyyasaka*) of a monk, according to *Words in S.* by Prof. Dines Andersen, *J.P.T.S.*, 1909] *niyassa-kamma* [read *nissaya-*; so also at *A.* i, 99 and *Pv.* iv, i], an act of a chapter of monks appointing a tutor to unreliable students). The *upaṭṭhāka* has charge of a novice. For *sāmaṇera upaṭṭhāpetabbo* see *Vin.* i, 64 *ff.*

'He must possess ten qualities, Upāli, in order to assign tutelage and provide for a novice. What ten?

Herein a monk is virtuous . . .' (*as in previous suttas*).

§ v (35). *Schism in the Order* (*a*).[1]

'As to the words: Schism in the Order, schism in the Order, sir—pray, sir, to what extent can the Order be disunited?'

'Herein, Upāli, monks proclaim not-dhamma as dhamma and dhamma as not-dhamma; monks proclaim not-discipline as discipline and discipline as not-discipline; **[74]** proclaim what was not said, not uttered by the Wayfarer as being his words and utterance; proclaim his words and utterance as not said, not uttered; proclaim what was not practised by the Wayfarer as his practice, and the reverse; proclaim what was not ordained by the Wayfarer as ordained by him, and the reverse.

On these ten grounds they break up and separate (the Order),[2] they pass separate ordinances and proclaim a separate obligation.[3]

To this extent, Upāli, the Order is disunited.'

§ vi (36). *Harmony in the Order* (*a*).[4]

'As to the words: Harmony in the Order, harmony in the Order, sir—pray, sir, to what extent can the Order be in harmony?'

'Herein, Upāli, monks proclaim not-dhamma as not-dhamma, and dhamma as dhamma; not-discipline as not-discipline, and discipline as such; proclaim what was not said, not uttered by the Wayfarer as not his words and utterance, and the reverse; proclaim his ordinances and practices as such and the reverse.

---

[1] *Cf. Vin.* ii, 203.

[2] Text *avakassanti vavakassanti*, which *Comy.* interprets 'pull down, disintegrate the company, set it aside.' Text *Vin.* ii, 203 reads *apakasanti avapakasanti* with the next words different. *Cf. A.* iii, 145.

[3] *Āveni. Comy. visuŋ* (separate). At *Ud.* 60 of Devadatta.

[4] Continued at *Vin.* ii, 204.

On these ten grounds they break not up and separate (the Order), and proclaim no separate obligation. To this extent, Upāli, there is harmony in the Order.'

§ vii (37). *Schism in the Order* (*b*).

[75] (*Ānanda asks the same question as in* § v *and gets the same reply.*)

§ viii (38). *Fruits of causing schism.*

'But pray, sir, by breaking up the harmonious Order what does that man get?'

'He gets demerit, Ānanda, lasting for the æon.'

'Pray, sir, what is demerit lasting for the æon?'

'For the æon, Ānanda, he ripens[1] in purgatory.'

[76] Doomed to the Waste, to purgatorial woe
For age-long penalties, provoking schism,
Of discord fain, fixed in unrighteousness,
From peace-from-bondage doth he fall away.
Breaking the concord of the Company—
Age-long in purgat'ry he waxeth ripe.[2]

§ ix (39). *Harmony in the Order* (*b*).

(*Ānanda asks the same question as in* § vi *and gets the same reply.*)

§ x (40). *Fruits of causing harmony in the Order.*

'Pray, sir, by making the Order harmonious what does that man get?'

'He gets Brahma-merit, Ānanda, lasting for the æon.'

'But, sir, what is Brahma-merit lasting for the æon?'

'For the æon, Ānanda, he rejoices in heaven.'

[77] A blessed thing is concord of the Order.
The friend of those who are in harmony,
Of concord fain, and fixed in righteousness,
From peace-from-bondage he falls not away.
Making the concord of the Company—
Age-long doth he rejoice i' the heaven-world.

---

[1] *Paccati,* literally 'is cooked.'

[2] *Vin.* ii, 198; *Itiv.* II and *gāthās.*

CHAPTER V.—REVILING.

§ i (41). *Quarrels.*

Now the venerable Upāli went to see the Exalted One . . . and said this:

'Pray, sir, what is the reason, what is the cause why disputes and uproar, strife and quarrels arise in the Order and monks live not happily?'

'Herein, Upāli, monks proclaim not-dhamma as dhamma . . . (*as in* § vi *above*). [78] That is the reason why . . .'

§ ii (42). *Roots of quarrels* (*a*) and § iii (43) (*b*).[1]

'Pray, sir, what are the roots of quarrels?'

'Ten, Upāli, are the roots of quarrels. What ten?

Herein monks point to what is no offence as an offence,[2] to an offence as no offence; to a trivial offence as a grievous one, to a grievous offence as a trivial one; to an offence against chastity as no offence, to what is no offence against chastity as an offence; to a partial offence as a complete [79] offence, to a complete offence as a partial one; they point to a pardonable offence as unpardonable and the reverse. These are the ten roots of quarrels.'

§ iv (44). *At Kusinārā.*

Once the Exalted One was staying at Kusinārā in the Wood of Offerings.[3] On that occasion the Exalted One addressed the monks saying: 'Monks.'

'Yes, sir,' replied those monks to the Exalted One, who said this:

---

[1] *Vin.* ii, 88. (*a*) repeats answer to § i. [2] At *G.S.* i, 14.

[3] *Cf. G.S.* i, 251 *n.*, *Bali-haraṇe vanasaṇḍe.* A *bali* ceremony, as still practised in India and Ceylon, is a sort of devil-dancing to appease local 'deities' by offerings. When there is no ceremony, fruit and flowers are offered to the devas.

'Monks, a monk who desires to admonish another[1] should do so after investigation of five conditions in his own self, after setting up five conditions in his own self. What are the five conditions he should investigate in his own self?

A monk who desires to admonish another must thus investigate: Am I or am I not one who practises utter purity in body; am I or am I not possessed of utter purity in body flawless and untainted? Is this quality manifest in me or is it not? If he be not so, there are found folk who say to him: "Come now, let your reverence practise conduct as to body." Folk are found to speak thus.

Again, monks, a monk who desires to admonish another should thus investigate: Am I or am I not one who practises utter purity in speech, flawless and untainted? Is this quality manifest in me or is it not? If he be not so, there are found folk who say to him: "Come now, let your reverence practise conduct as to speech." Folk are found to speak thus.

[**80**] Again, monks, a monk who desires to admonish another should thus investigate: Is a heart of goodwill free from malice established in me towards my fellows in the Brahma-life? Is this quality manifest in me or is it not? If it be not so, there are found folk to say to him: "Come now, let your reverence practise the heart of goodwill." Folk are found to speak thus.

Then again, monks, a monk who desires to admonish another should thus investigate: Am I or am I not one who has heard much, who bears in mind what he has heard, who hoards up what he has heard? Those teachings which, lovely alike at the beginning, the middle and the end (of life) proclaim in the spirit and in the letter the all-fulfilled, utterly purified Brahma-life—have such teachings been much heard by me, borne in mind, practised in speech, pondered in the heart and rightly penetrated by view? Is this quality manifest in me or is it not? Then, monks, if he be not one who has heard much . . . if those teachings have not . . . been rightly penetrated by view, then folk are found to say to him:

---

[1] At *Vin.* ii, 248, addressed to Upāli.

"Come now, let your reverence complete knowledge of the Sayings."[1] Folk are found to speak thus.

Again, monks, a monk who desires to admonish another should thus investigate: Are the obligations in full thoroughly learned by heart, well analysed with thorough knowledge of the meaning, clearly divided sutta by sutta and in minute detail by me? Is this condition manifest in me or is it not? For if not [**81**] there are found folk to say to him: "But where was this said by the Exalted One, your reverence?" When thus questioned he cannot explain. Then there will be those who say: "Come now, let your reverence train himself in the discipline." There will be found folk to speak thus.

These five conditions must be investigated in his own self.

And what five conditions must be set up in his own self?[2]

(He considers:) Do I speak in season or not? Do I speak of facts or not, gently or harshly, do I speak words fraught with profit or not, with a kindly heart or inwardly malicious? These five conditions he must set up in his own self.

Monks, these five conditions are to be investigated in his own self, and these other five conditions are to be set up in his own self by a monk who desires to admonish another.'

§ v (45). *Entering the royal court.*

'Monks, there are these ten disadvantages of entering the royal court. What ten?

In this connexion, monks, suppose the rājā is seated with his favourite wife. Then in comes a monk. The wife, on seeing the monk, smiles, or else the monk smiles on seeing her. Then the rājā thinks: Surely these two are guilty or will be guilty. This is the first disadvantage of entering the royal court.

Then again, suppose the rājā, his mind being much occupied with business, has intercourse with a certain woman and for-

---

[1] *Āgama.* The āgamas are usually the Four Great Nikāyas. One who knows these is called *āgatâgamo.* This evidently refers to the two recognized 'collected sayings' of ancient times, the *āgama* and the *vinaya* (*-pāṭimokkha*) as in next §.

[2] At *G.S.* iii, 144 *ff.*

gets about it. Thereby she becomes pregnant. Then the rājā thinks: [82] No one but a home-leaver[1] enters here. Maybe it is the work of a home-leaver. This is the second disadvantage of entering the royal court.

Again, perhaps some gem is missing in the royal court. Then the rājā thinks: No one but a home-leaver enters here. Maybe it is the work of a home-leaver. This is the third disadvantage of entering the royal court.

Again, the secret plans[2] within the royal court, by being divulged abroad, are spoiled. Then the rājā thinks as before. . . . This is the fourth disadvantage of entering the royal court.

Again, in the royal court a father aspires for a son[3] or a son aspires for a father. Then they think: No one but a home-leaver enters here. It must be the work of a home-leaver. This is the fifth disadvantage. . . .

Again, monks, a rājā sets up a man of low estate in a high place. Those to whom this is displeasing think thus: The rājā is intimate with the home-leaver. This must be the work of the home-leaver. This is the sixth disadvantage of entering the royal court.

Again, the rājā puts a man of high estate in a low place. Those to whom this is displeasing think as before. . . . This is the seventh disadvantage. . . .

Again, the rājā musters the host unseasonably. Those to whom this is displeasing think thus: The rājā is intimate with the home-leaver. This must be the work of the home-leaver. This is the eighth disadvantage. . . .

Again, the rājā, after mustering the host at the proper time,

---

[1] *Pabbajita*, 'gone-forth' is not necessarily a monk or *bhikkhu* of the Order.

[2] *Antepure guyha-mantā* (*Comy. guyhitabba-mantā*) *bahiddhā sambhedaŋ gacchanti.* *Cf. A.* iii, 129 (*G.S.* iii, 99), where in a similar phrase Mr. Hare seems to take *mantā* as equal to *manta(r)*. *Mantā* here is 'secret,' formulas, charms, or decisions.

[3] *Pitā vā puttaŋ pattheti, putto vā pitaraŋ pattheti.* As far as I can see, this can only refer to the uncertainty of parentage in a royal harem. *Comy.* merely has the strange comment *māretuŋ icchati* (longs to kill)! The mendicant friar is suspected of causing the confusion.

sends it back from the highroad. Those to whom this is displeasing [83] think as before. This is the ninth disadvantage. . . .

Once more, monks, the rājā's court is crowded[1] with elephants, horses and chariots; objects, sounds, scents and savours that are defiling have to be encountered, such as are not suited to one who has given up (the world).[2] This, monks, is the tenth disadvantage of entering the rājā's court.

So, monks, these are the ten disadvantages of entering the rājā's court.'

§ vi (46) *Sakyans.*

Once the Exalted One was staying among the Sakyans at Kapilavatthu in Banyan Park.

At that time a number of Sakyan lay-followers, that day being the sabbath, came to visit the Exalted One, and on coming to him saluted him and sat down at one side. So seated the Exalted One said this to those Sakyan lay-followers:

'Pray, Sakyans, are you keeping the sabbath complete in its eight parts?'[3]

'Sometimes, sir, we do so, but maybe sometimes we don't.'

'Well, Sakyans, in those matters it is no gain to you, it is ill gotten by you, since, in a life thus conjoined to fear of grief, in a life thus conjoined to fear of death, ye sometimes do and sometimes maybe do not keep the sabbath complete in its eight parts.

What think ye, Sakyans? Suppose a man here, without meeting an unlucky day, were to earn[4] half a *kahāpaṇa*[5] in

---

[1] Text quite unsuitably reads *sammada* (drowsiness), but with *v.l.* *sammadda*: so also *Comy.*, which explains as equal to *sambādha*. *Cf.* the passage at *K.S.* v, 303 *ff.*, where the chamberlains Isidatta and Purāṇa complain of the difficulties of official life at court.

[2] Here I take *pabbajitena* to mean a bhikkhu.

[3] The *aṭṭhanga-sīlāni* or eight precepts are kept on full-, half-, and sometimes quarter-moon days, from sunrise of the *uposatha*-day to that of next day, the devotees being dressed in white.

[4] *Nibbiseyya.*

[5] Reckoned to be worth about a florin of our times, but often rendered by 'farthing.' *Cf.* Rhys Davids' *Buddhist India*, p. 100 *ff.*, 'a square copper coin weighing about 146 grains, and guaranteed as to weight and fineness by punch-marks made by private individuals.'

some business or other. Might not folk well say of him: [**84**] " A clever fellow, full of energy !" '

'Yes, sir, they might.'

'What think ye, Sakyans, suppose a man here, without meeting an unlucky day, were to earn a *kahāpaṇa* . . . or two or more . . . up to fifty *kahāpaṇas* in some business or other, might not folk well say of him: " A clever fellow, full of energy !" '

'Yes, sir, they might.'

'Now, what think ye, Sakyans ? Suppose that man, day by day earning a hundred, a thousand *kahāpaṇas,* and hoarding up what he got, were to reach a hundred years, were to live a hundred years, would not he amass great wealth ?'

'He would, sir.'

'Well, Sakyans, what think ye ? Would that man, because of his wealth, on account of his wealth, in consequence of his wealth—would that man for a single night or a single day, or even half a night or half a day, live in the enjoyment of utter happiness.'

'Surely not, sir.'

'And why not ?'

'Because, sir, lusts are impermanent, hollow, false, of the nature of falsehood.'

'Now, Sakyans, suppose here a follower of mine, living serious, ardent and resolved, were to live faring onward as I have advised for ten years, he would spend a hundred years, a hundred times a hundred years [**85**], a hundred times a thousand years, a hundred times a hundred thousand years enjoying utter happiness. And he would be a once-returner, or a not-returner, or a winner of surety, a stream-winner.

Let alone ten years, Sakyans, suppose here a follower of mine were to live faring onwards as I have advised for nine eight, seven, six . . . for a single year, he would live a hundred years . . . a hundred times a hundred thousand years enjoying utter happiness. And he would be a once-returner, or a not-returner, or at any rate[1] a stream-winner.

---

[1] *Apaṇṇakaŋ.* See *A.* i, 113=*G.S.* i, 97 *n.* where it is equal to *ekaŋsikaŋ* (as *Comy.* here), but *SA.* iii, on *S.* iv, 253, takes it as meaning 'incommunicable.' See Trenckner-Andersen-Smith, *P.D.* i, 6, *s.v.*

Let alone a single year, Sakyans, suppose here a follower of mine, living serious, ardent and resolved, were to live faring onward as I have advised, for ten months, for nine, eight . . . a single month, half a month . . . ten nights and days . . . [**86**] for seven, six, five . . . if he were to live this for a single night and day, he would spend a hundred years, a hundred times a hundred years, a hundred times a thousand years, a hundred times a hundred thousand years enjoying utter happiness. And he would be a once-returner, or a not-returner, or a winner of surety, a stream-winner.

In those matters, Sakyans, it is no gain to you, it is ill-gotten by you, since in a life thus conjoined to fear of grief, in a life thus conjoined to fear of death, ye sometimes do and sometimes do not keep the sabbath complete in its eight parts.'

'Then, sir, from this day forth we here will observe the sabbath complete in its eight parts.'

§ vii (47). *Mahāli.*

Once the Exalted One was staying near Vesālī in Great Wood, at the House of the Peaked Roof. Then Mahāli the Licchavite[1] came to see the Exalted One . . . and said this to him:

'Pray, sir, what is the reason, what is the cause of doing an evil deed, of committing an evil deed ?'

'Lust, Mahāli, is the reason, lust is the cause of doing an evil deed, of committing an evil deed; malice, Mahāli, is the reason and cause . . . delusion is the reason and cause . . . not paying proper attention . . . [**87**] wrongly directed thought, these are the reasons, these are the causes of doing an evil deed, of committing an evil deed.'

'Pray, sir, what is the reason, what is the cause of doing a lovely deed, of committing a lovely deed ?'

'Not lusting, Mahāli, is the reason, not lusting is the cause . . . not-malice, not-delusion . . . paying proper attention,

---

[1] At *K.S.* i, 295 at the same place he asks about *Sakka*. According to *Apadāna*, p. 540, v. 28, he was father of Sīvalīthera. At *K.S.* iii, 60 he asks about purity.

rightly directed thought, Mahāli, is the reason and the cause of doing a lovely deed, of committing a lovely deed. These are the reason and the cause of it.

Moreover, Mahāli, if[1] these ten qualities were not found existing in the world, there would be here no proclaiming of wrong living and crooked living, or of right living and straight living. But since, Mahāli, these ten qualities are found existing in the world, therefore is there proclaiming of wrong and crooked living, of right and straight living.'

§ viii (48). *Conditions.*

'Monks, these ten conditions must again and again be contemplated by one who has gone forth (from the home). What ten?

He must again and again contemplate this fact: I am now come to a state of being an outcast.[2] And this: My very life is dependent on others. And this: I must now [**88**] behave myself differently. And this: Does the self[3] upbraid me for (lapse from) virtue, or does it not? And this: Do my discerning fellows in the Brahma-life, after testing me, upbraid me for (lapse from) virtue, or do they not? And this: In all things dear and delightful to me there is change and separation. And this: I myself am responsible for my deed,[4] I am the heir to my deed, the womb of my deed, the kinsman of my deed, I am he to whom my deed comes home.[5] Whatever deed I shall do, be it good or bad, of that shall I be the heir. The nights and days flit by for me—who have grown[6] to what? And this: In my void dwelling do I take delight or not? And this: Have I come by any superhuman experience,[7] any excellence of truly Ariyan knowledge and

---

[1] Reading *ce* for *ca*.

[2] As below § 101; quoted *Netti* 185.

[3] *Cf. G.S.* i, 125; ii, 116. According to *Comy. attā=cittaŋ*.

[4] *Kammassako'mhi.*

[5] *Kamma-paṭisaraṇo. M.* iii, 203; *Mil. Pañh.* 65 adds *kammaŋ satte vibhajati* (differentiates).

[6] Quoted *Mil. Pañh.* 392.

[7] *K.S.* iv, 208; *G.S.* i, 7.

insight, whereon when questioned in my latter days[1] by my fellows in the Brahma-life I shall not be confounded ?

These, monks, are the ten conditions to be again and again contemplated by one who has gone forth (from the home).'

§ ix (49). *Inherent in body.*

'These ten conditions, monks, are inherent in body.[2] What ten ?

Cold and heat, hunger and thirst, evacuation and urination, restraint of body, restraint of speech, restraint of living, and the again-becoming becoming-aggregate.[3] These ten conditions are inherent in body.'

§ x (50). *Strife.*

Once the Exalted One was staying near Sāvatthī at Jeta Grove in Anāthapiṇḍika's Park.

On that occasion a number of monks [**89**] after returning from their alms-round and eating their meal, as they sat assembled together in the service-hall, remained in strife and uproar and dispute, abusing each other with the weapons of the tongue.

Now the Exalted One at eventide, rising from his solitude, approached the service-hall, and on reaching it sat down on a seat made ready. When he had sat down the Exalted One addressed the monks, saying:

'Pray, monks, in what talk were ye engaged as ye sit here, and what was the topic of your talk left unfinished ?'

'Here, sir, after returning from our alms-round and eating our meal, we sat assembled together in the service-hall and remained in strife, uproar and dispute, abusing each other with the weapons of the tongue.'

'Monks, it is not seemly for you clansmen, who in faith went forth from home to the homeless, thus to abide in strife, uproar and dispute, abusing each other with the weapons of the tongue. Monks, there are these ten conditions to be re-

---

1 *Pacchime kāle=maraṇa-kāle, Comy.*

2 *Sarīra-ṭṭhā.*

3 *Bhava-sankhāro.*

membered,[1] which, as they make for affection and respect, do conduce to fellow-feeling, to not-quarrelling, to concord and unity. What ten?

Herein a monk is virtuous,[2] restrained with the restraint of the obligation, proficient in following the practice of right conduct, seeing ground for fear in the minutest faults, and takes upon him and trains himself in the rules of morality. In so far as a monk is virtuous and so forth . . . and so trains himself, this is a condition to be remembered, which, as it makes for affection and respect, does conduce to fellow-feeling, to not-quarrelling, to concord and unity.

Then again, a monk has heard much, he bears in mind what he has heard, he hoards up what he has heard. Those teachings which, alike lovely at the beginning, midway and at the end (of life), proclaim in spirit and in letter the all-fulfilled, utterly purified Brahma-life—suchlike are the teachings he has much heard, borne in mind, practised in speech, [90] pondered in the heart and rightly penetrated by view. In so far as he has heard much . . . this is a condition to be remembered, which . . . does conduce . . . to unity and concord.

Again, a monk has a lovely friend, a lovely comrade, a lovely intimate. In so far as he is such . . . this is a condition to be remembered.

Again, a monk is easy to speak to,[3] possessed of qualities which make him easy to speak to; he is tractable, capable of being instructed. In so far as he is such . . . this is a condition to be remembered.

Then again, in all the undertakings of his fellows in the Brahma-life, be they matters weighty or trivial, he is shrewd and energetic, having ability to give proper consideration

---

[1] *Sārāṇīya dhammā* (*MA*. i, 394=*AA* on *A*. iii, 288)=*saritabba-yuttā* . . . *na pamussitabbā* (never-to-be-forgotten). Translated by Lord Chalmers and Mr. Hare respectively (*loc. cit.*), 'states of consciousness' and 'ways of being considerate.' Following *Comy.*, I translate as above: thus also *sārāṇīya-kathā* is 'reminiscent talk' (about things remembered in common). Six others at *D*. iii, 245=*Dial.* iii, 231; *A*. iii, 288=*G.S.* iii, 208.

[2] *Cf.* above No. 17.

[3] *A*. ii, 148; iii, 180.

thereto, as to what is the right thing to do and how to manage it. In so far as a monk is such . . . this is a condition. . . .

Again, a monk delights in dhamma, is pleasant to converse with, rejoices exceedingly in further dhamma, in further discipline. In so far as a monk is such . . . this is a condition to be remembered.

Again, a monk dwells resolute in energy for the abandoning of bad qualities, stout and strong to acquire good qualities. **[91]** In so far as a monk is such . . . this is a condition to be remembered.

Then again, a monk is content with whatsoever supply of robes, alms-food, bed and lodging, comforts and necessaries in sickness he may get. In so far as a monk is such . . . this is a condition to be remembered.

Again, a monk is concentrated, possessed of mindful discrimination in the highest degree, able to call to mind and remember a thing done and said long ago. In so far as a monk is such . . . this is a condition to be remembered.

Lastly, a monk is possessed of insight; he has insight for tracing out the rise and fall of things, insight which is Ariyan, penetrating, going on to the utter destruction of Ill. In so far as a monk has such insight . . . this also is a condition to be remembered, which, as it makes for affection and respect, does conduce to fellow-feeling, to not-quarrelling, to concord and unity.

These, monks, are the ten conditions to be remembered . . . which conduce . . . to concord and unity.'

CHAPTER VI.—ONE'S OWN THOUGHTS.

§ i (51). *One's own heart.* (*a*) *By the Master.*

[92] Once the Exalted One was staying near Sāvatthī at Jeta Grove in Anāthapiṇḍika's Park. On that occasion the Exalted One addressed the monks, saying:

'Monks, though a monk be not skilled in the habit of others' thoughts, at least he can resolve: I will be skilled in the habit of my own thought.[1] Thus, monks, should ye train yourselves.

And how is a monk skilled in the habit of his own thought?

Just as if, monks, a woman or man or a young lad fond of self-adornment, examining the reflection of his own face in a bright clean mirror or bowl of clear water, should see therein a stain or speck and strive for the removal of that stain or speck; and when he no longer sees it there is pleased and satisfied thereat,[2] thinking: A gain it is to me that I am clean—even so a monk's introspection is most fruitful in good conditions, thus: Do I or do I not generally live covetous? [93] Do I or do I not generally live malevolent in heart? Do I or do I not generally live possessed by sloth-and-torpor? Do I or do I not generally live excited in mind?[3] Do I generally live in doubt-and-wavering, or have I crossed beyond it? . . . wrathful or not? . . . with soiled thoughts or clean thoughts? . . . with body passionate or not? . . . sluggish or full of energy? . . . Do I generally live uncontrolled or well-controlled?

---

[1] *Sa-citta-pariyāya-kusalo,* literally 'skilled in own-heart-habit'; but *Comy.* exp. *attano citt'ovāda-kusalo* (self-exhortation-skilled).

[2] *Paripuṇṇa-sankappo, cf. M.* iii, 276.

[3] At *S.* v, 112=*K.S.* v, 95 the two extremes of a sluggish and elated mind are bars to tranquillity.

Monks, if on self-examination a monk finds thus: I generally live covetous, malevolent in heart, possessed by sloth-and-torpor, excited in mind, doubtful and wavering, wrathful, with soiled thoughts, with body passionate, sluggish and uncontrolled—then that monk must put forth extra desire, effort, endeavour, exertion, impulse, mindfulness and attention for the abandoning of those wicked, unprofitable states.[1]

Just as, monks, when one's turban or head is ablaze, for the extinguishing thereof one must put forth extra desire, effort, endeavour, exertion, unflagging mindfulness and attention, even so for the abandoning of those wicked, unprofitable states . . . one must do the same.

[94] But if on self-examination a monk finds thus: I do not generally live covetous . . . uncontrolled, then that monk should make an effort[2] to establish just those profitable states and further to destroy the cankers.'

§ ii (52). *One's own heart.* (*b*) *By Sāriputta.*

Thereafter the venerable Sāriputta addressed the monks, saying: 'Monks.'

'Yes, your reverence,' replied those monks to the venerable Sāriputta, who said: (*he repeats the previous sutta*). [95.]

§ iii (53). *Standing still.*

[96] 'Monks, I praise not standing still, not to speak of waning,[3] in good conditions. I praise growth in good conditions, monks, not standing still, not waning. And how is there waning, not standing still, not growth ?

Herein a monk is a striver[4] in faith, virtue, lore, giving up,

---

[1] As at *S.* v, 440=*K.S.* v, 372.

[2] *Yogo, cf. A.* ii, 94=*G.S.* ii, 104.

[3] Text misprints as *pārihāniŋ*.

[4] *Yattako*, not in *Indexes*, *Dicts.* or *Comy.* It seems equal to *yatta* (*yatati*).

insight and ready speech.[1] Yet his conditions neither stand still nor make growth. This I call "waning in good conditions," monks, not standing still, not growth.

Thus there is waning in good conditions, not standing still, not growth.

And how is there standing still, not waning, not growth in good conditions?

Herein a monk is a striver in faith, virtue, lore, giving up, insight and ready speech. But his conditions wane not nor wax. This I call standing still. . . . Thus there is standing still, not waning, not growth in good conditions.

And how is there growth in good conditions, not standing still, not waning?

Herein a monk is a striver in faith, virtue and the rest. But his conditions stand not still nor wane. This I call growth in good conditions. Thus there is growth not standing still, not waning in good conditions.

Monks, though a monk be not skilled in the habit of others' thoughts,[2] at least he can resolve: I will be skilled in the habit of my own thought. Thus must ye train yourselves. And how is a monk skilled in the habit of his own thought?'

[97] (*The rest is as in the previous sutta.*)

§ iv (54). *Peace of heart.*

[98] 'Though a monk be not skilled in the habit of others' thoughts . . . just as if, monks, a woman or a man or young lad fond of self-adornment . . . (*as in former sutta, with this change*): . . . even so a monk's introspection is most fruitful in good conditions, thus: Am I or am I not a winner of peace of heart in my own self? Am I or am I not a winner of insight of the higher and insight into dhamma?

If, monks, on self-examination a monk knows thus: I am a winner of peace of heart in my own self, but not a winner of wisdom of the higher and insight into dhamma—then he

---

[1] Growth in the first five of these constitutes the Ariyan growth at *S.* iv, 250; *A.* iii, 80. The last (*paṭibhāna*) is explained by *Comy.* as *vacana-santhana.*

[2] Here text misprints as *paricitta-*.

must put forth effort to establish peace of heart in his own self and acquire insight of the higher and insight into dhamma. Then on some later occasion he is a winner of both alike.

If, however, on self-examination a monk knows thus: I am a winner of insight of the higher and insight into dhamma, but not of peace of heart in my own self—then he must make an effort to establish the one and acquire the other. Then on some later occasion he is winner of both alike.

But if on self-examination a monk knows thus: I am not a winner of either quality, then he must put forth extra desire, effort, endeavour, exertion, unflagging mindfulness and attention for the acquiring of those profitable conditions.

Just as, monks, when one's turban or head is ablaze,[1] for the extinguishing thereof one must put forth extra desire, effort . . . even so for the acquiring of those profitable conditions one must put forth extra desire, effort . . . then **[100]** at some future time he is a winner both of peace of heart in his own self and insight of the higher and insight into dhamma.

If, however, on self-examination a monk finds that he has both qualities, then he must make an effort to establish just those profitable conditions, and further to destroy the cankers.

As to the robe, monks, I declare that it is to be sought after or not sought after in a twofold way. I say the same of alms-food, bed and lodging, village and township, of countryside and district, also of a person.

Now I spoke of the robe being sought after or not sought after in a twofold way. Why was this said?

In this matter if one know: By seeking after this sort of robe[2] unprofitable states wax in me and profitable states wane in me—then such a robe is not to be sought after. But if one know: By seeking after this robe unprofitable states wane in me and profitable states wax in me—such robe should be sought after. That, monks, is why I said this about the robe.

[101] And the same is to be said of alms-food, bed and lodging, village and township, countryside and district . . . **[102]** and of the person.'

---

[1] *Cf. K.S.* i, 19; 136.

[2] This § occurs at *A.* iv, 366 *ff.*

§ v (55). *Waning.*

Thereupon the venerable Sāriputta addressed the monks, saying: 'Monks, your reverences.'

'Yes, your reverence,' replied those monks to the venerable Sāriputta, who then said:

'Your reverences, there is the frequent saying "A person whose nature is to wane." Now to what extent has a person been called by the Exalted One "a person whose nature is to wane," and to what extent has a person been called "of a nature to wax"?'

'We would come from far, your reverence, to know the meaning of this in the presence of the venerable Sāriputta. It were well if the meaning of this saying were to occur to the venerable Sāriputta. **[103]** Hearing it from the venerable Sāriputta the monks would bear it in mind.'

'Then, your reverences, do ye listen. Pay attention carefully and I will speak.'

'We will, your reverence,' replied those monks to the venerable Sāriputta, who then said:

'Now to what extent was a person called "of a nature to wane" by the Exalted One? Herein, your reverences, a monk listens not to a teaching not heard before, while the teachings he has heard go to confusion; those teachings formerly contacted by thought[1] no longer occur to him, and he understands not what is unintelligible. To this extent was a person called "one of a nature to wane" by the Exalted One.

And to what extent was a person called "of a nature to wax"?

(*Herein the words are applied when just the opposite is the case.*)

Though a monk be not skilled in the habit of others' hearts, yet he can resolve: I will be skilled in the habit of my own heart. That, your reverences, is how ye must train yourselves. And how is a monk skilled in the habit of his own heart?

[1] *Cf. K.S.* iv, 60.

(*All is repeated from previous suttas with this difference: after each self-examination, he asks himself*:) **[104.]**

Is this condition to be seen in me or not? Are my thoughts soiled or are they not? Is this condition to be seen in me or not? Am I a winner of delight in dhamma?[1] Is this condition to be seen in me or not? Am I a winner of peace of heart in my own self? Is this condition to be seen in me or not? Am I a winner of insight in the higher and insight into dhamma? Is this condition to be seen in me or not?

If, however, your reverences, a monk on self-examination finds: All these profitable conditions are not in my self—then for the acquiring of all these profitable conditions he must put forth extra desire, effort, endeavour, exertion, impulse, mindfulness and attention. Just as when one's turban or head is ablaze, for the extinguishing thereof he must put forth . . . even so for the acquiring of all these profitable conditions he must put forth extra desire . . . mindfulness and attention.

If, however, your reverences, on self-examination a monk finds some profitable conditions in himself, but not others **[105]**, then, for the establishment of those profitable conditions he sees in himself and for the acquiring of those which he sees not in himself, he must put forth extra desire. . . .

Just as when one's turban or head is ablaze . . . even so must he do.

If again on self-examination a monk finds: All these profitable conditions are to be found in my own self, then, your reverences, he must make an effort to establish just those profitable conditions and further to destroy the cankers.'

§ vi (56). *Ideas (a).*

'Monks, these ten ideas, if made to grow and made much of, are of great fruit, of great profit for plunging into the deathless, for ending up in the deathless. What ten ideas?

The idea of the foul, of death, of the repulsiveness in food, of distaste for all the world, the idea of impermanence, of

[1] This is an addition to the former items.

ill in impermanence, of not-self in Ill, the idea of abandoning, of fading, of ending.

These ten ideas, monks, if made to grow . . . are of great profit for plunging into the deathless,[1] for ending up in the deathless.'

§ vii (57). *Ideas* (*b*).

(*Another set of ten.*)

[106] '. . . The idea of impermanence, of not-self, of death, of the repulsiveness in food, of distaste for all the world, the idea of the bony (skeleton), of worms, of the discoloured (corpse), the fissured (corpse), of the swollen (corpse).

These ideas, if made to grow . . . are of great profit. . . .'

§ viii (58). *Rooted in the Exalted One.*

'If, monks, the Wanderers holding other views should thus question you: "Rooted in what, your reverences, are all things, compounded of what, arising from what, conjoined in what, headed by what, ruled over by what, having what as ultimate, of what essence, into what plunging, ending up in what are all things?" Thus questioned, what explanation would ye give to those Wanderers holding other views?'

'Rooted in the Exalted One, sir, are things for us, having the Exalted One as guide, having the Exalted One for resort.[2] Well for us, sir, if the meaning of this that is said by the Exalted One should occur to him. Hearing it from the Exalted One the monks will bear it in mind.'

'Then, monks, do ye listen. Pay attention carefully, and I will speak.'

'We will, sir,' replied those monks to the Exalted One, who then said: **[107]** 'If the Wanderers holding other views should thus question you, being thus questioned, monks, ye should thus explain to them: "Rooted in desire, your reverences, are all things, compounded of thinking are all things,

---

[1] *Amat'ogadhā.* We find also *nibbāna-*, *jagatą-* and *brahmacariya-ogadha*. *Cf. A.* i, 168; ii, 26; *S.* v, 344.

[2] *Cf. K.S.* ii, 56; iv, 149, etc.

originating from contact, conjoined in sensation, headed by concentration, ruled over by mindfulness, having wisdom as ultimate are all things, having release for their essence, plunging into the deathless, with nibbāna for their conclusion are all things.''

Thus questioned, monks, thus should ye reply to the Wanderers holding other views.'

§ ix (59). *Forthgoing.*

'Wherefore, monks, thus must ye train yourselves:

Our thought shall be compassed about as it was when we went forth (from home);[1] evil, unprofitable states arising shall not overpower our thought and abide therein; compassed about with the idea of impermanence shall our thought become; compassed about with the idea of the not-self, with the idea of the foul, with the idea of the danger (in things) shall our thought become; learning the straight way and the crooked way in the world[2] our thought shall be compassed about by the idea of that; learning the composition and decomposition of the world our thought shall be compassed about with that idea; knowing the origin and the ending of the world our thought shall be compassed about by that idea; with the idea of abandoning, of fading interest, of making it to cease shall our thoughts be compassed about.

Thus, monks, must ye train yourselves.

[108] And when a monk's thought is thus compassed about at his forthgoing, and when evil, unprofitable states arising overpower not his thought and abide therein, and when his thought is compassed about . . . in all these ways . . . one of two fruits is to be looked for in him—either gnosis in this same visible state or, if there be any remnant, the fruit of not-returning.'

---

[1] *Yāthā-pabbajjā-paricitaŋ=vaḍḍhitaŋ, Comy. UdA.* 323 equal to *samantato citā* (heaped up all round), *suvaḍḍhita.* At *A.* iv, 402, *paññāya cittaŋ paricitaŋ=cittâcāra-pariyāyena cito vaḍḍhito, Comy.*

[2] *Lokassa samañ ca visamañ ca=satta-lokassa sucarita-duccaritāni, Comy.*

§ x (60). *Girimānanda.*[1]

Once the Exalted One was staying near Sāvatthī at Jeta Grove in Anāthapiṇḍika's Park. Now on that occasion the venerable Girimānanda was sick, suffering, stricken with a sore disease. And the venerable Ānanda came to see the Exalted One . . . and said this to him:

'Sir, the venerable Girimānanda is sick, suffering, stricken with a sore disease. It were well, sir, if the Exalted One were to visit him, out of compassion for him.'

'If you, Ānanda, were to visit the monk Girimānanda and recite to him the Ten Ideas, there are grounds for supposing that when he hears them that sickness will be allayed there and then.[2] What are the Ten Ideas ?[3]

[109] The idea of permanence, of not-self, of the foul, of the disadvantage, abandoning, revulsion, fading, distaste for all the world, of impermanence in all compounds, of concentration on in-breathing and out-breathing.

And what, Ānanda, is the idea of impermanence ?

Herein a monk who has gone to the forest or the root of a tree or a lonely place thus contemplates: Impermanent is objective form, impermanent are feelings, ideas, compounded things, impermanent is consciousness. Thus he abides seeing impermanence in the five grasping-heaps. This is called "the idea of impermanence."

And what, Ānanda, is the idea of not-self ?

Herein a monk who has gone to the forest . . . thus contemplates: The eye is not the self, objective form is not the self, the ear and sounds . . . nose and scents . . . tongue and tastes . . . body and tangibles . . . mind and mind-states are not the self. Thus he abides not seeing the self in those six outer and inner spheres. This, Ānanda, is called "the idea of not-self."[4]

---

[1] The prefix *giri-* is common and may refer to hillmen. This Girimānanda, or one of that name, has verses at *Apadāna* i, 330. There are several instances of sick men 'rising up' on hearing similar 'comfortable words'—*e.g.*, Kassapa at *K.S.* v, 66; *cf. ibid.* 350.

[2] *Ṭhānaso,* for this use *cf. K.S.* v, 40 ('on the spot').

[3] *Cf.* those at § vi above and another ten at *K.S.* v, 112.

[4] All these are not the self, but they do not constitute denial of its existence.

And what, Ānanda, is the idea of the foul?

Herein a monk examines just this body,[1] upwards from the soles of the feet, downwards from the top of the head, enclosed by skin, full of manifold impurities (and concludes): There are in this body hair of the head, hair of the body, nails, skin, teeth, flesh, nerves, bones, marrow, kidneys, heart, liver, pleura, spleen, lungs, intestines, bowels, stomach, fæces, bile, phlegm, pus, blood, sweat, fat, tears, serum, spittle, mucus, nose-mucus, synovial fluid, urine.[2] Thus he abides observant of the foul in body. This, Ānanda, is called "the idea of the foul."

And what, Ānanda, is the idea of the disadvantage?

Herein a monk who has gone to the forest . . . thus contemplates: [110] This body has many ills, many disadvantages. Thus, in this body arise divers diseases, such as:[3] disease of eyesight and hearing, of nose, tongue, trunk, head, ear, mouth, teeth; there is cough, asthma, catarrh, fever, decrepitude, belly-ache, swooning, dysentery, griping, cholera, leprosy, imposthume, eczema, phthisis, epilepsy; skin-disease, itch, scab, tetter,[4] scabies; bile-in-the-blood (jaundice),[5] diabetes, piles, boils, ulcers; diseases[6] arising from bile, from phlegm, from wind, from the union of bodily humours, from changes of the seasons, from stress of circumstances,[7] or from the ripeness of one's karma; also cold and heat, hunger and thirst, evacuation and urination. Thus he abides observant

---

[1] *Cf. K.S.* iv, 69. Explained at *VM.*, p. 241 *ff.*=*Path of Purity*, ii, 276.

[2] So also at *S.* v, 279, but *Khp.* 3 has *matthalungaŋ* (brain in head) as the last item. A similar catalogue is at *Maitr. Upan.* i, 3; 3, 4; *Ātm. Upan.* i.

[3] *Cf. Vin.* ii, 271; *Nidd.*[2] 166.

[4] Texts *rakhasā* (not in *Dicts.*). *Comy.* explains the *v.l. nakhasā* as 'a disease at the place scratched by the nails.'

[5] *Lohita-pitta* (not in *Dicts.*). *Comy.* has nothing. The conjecture is mine.

[6] At *S.* iv, 230=*K.S.* iv, 155 (quoted at *Mil. Pañh.* 134) and *A.* ii, 87=*G.S.* ii, 97.

[7] *Visama-parihāra-jā.* *Comy.* (as on *A.* ii), 'from sitting or standing too long.'

of the disadvantages in this body. This, Ānanda, is called "the idea of the disadvantage."

And what, Ānanda, is the idea of abandoning?

Herein a monk admits not sensual thinking that has arisen,[1] but abandons, restrains, makes an end of it, forces it not to recur. He admits not malicious thinking . . . harmful thinking . . . evil, unprofitable states that arise from time to time, but abandons, restrains, makes an end of them, forces them not to recur. This, Ānanda, is called "the idea of abandoning."

And what, Ānanda, is the idea of revulsion?

Herein a monk who has gone to the forest . . . thus contemplates: This is the real, this is the excellent, namely, the calming of all the activities, the casting off of every basis, the destruction of craving, revulsion, nibbāna. This, Ānanda, is called "the idea of revulsion."

And what is the idea of ending?

Herein a monk who has gone to the forest . . . thus contemplates: **[111]** This is the real, this is the excellent . . . the destruction of craving, ending, nibbāna. This, Ānanda, is called "the idea of ending."

And what, Ānanda, is the idea of distaste?

Herein a monk, by abandoning, by not clinging to those graspings of systems,[2] those mental standpoints and dogmatic bias that are in the world, delights not therein. This is called "the idea of distaste."

And what, Ānanda, is the idea of impermanence?

Herein a monk is troubled by, ashamed of and disgusted[3] with all compounded things. This is called "the idea of impermanence."

And what, Ānanda, is the idea of concentration on in-breathing and out-breathing?

Herein a monk who has gone to the forest[4] or the root of

---

[1] *G.S.* ii, 121.

[2] At *S.* ii, 17=*K.S.* ii, 13 (system and dogmas). *Cf. Sn.* 170 *kissa loko upādāya? Katamaŋ taŋ upādānaŋ yattha loko vihaññati.* The answer is *pañca kāmaguṇā* (with mind as sixth), things sensual which mislead the mind to form views.

[3] *Cf. K.S.* iii, 129.

[4] *Cf. S.* v, 309=*K.S.* v, 275 and notes.

a tree or a lonely place, sits down crosslegged, holding the body upright and setting mindfulness in front of him. He breathes in mindfully and mindfully breathes out. As he draws in a long breath he knows: A long breath I draw in. As he breathes out a long breath he knows: A long breath I breathe out.[1] As he draws in a short breath he knows: A short breath I draw in. As he breathes out a short breath he knows: A short breath I breathe out.

He puts into practice the intention: I shall breathe in, feeling it go through the whole body. Feeling it go through the whole body I shall breathe out. Calming down the body-aggregate I shall breathe in. Calming down the body-aggregate I shall breathe out.

He puts into practice the intention: Feeling the thrill of zest I shall breathe in and out; feeling the sense of ease I shall breathe in and out. Aware of all mental factors I shall breathe in and out. Calming down the mental factors I shall breathe in and out.

[112] He puts into practice the intention: Gladdening my mind I shall breathe in and out. Composing my mind . . . detaching my mind I shall breathe in and out.

He puts into practice the intention: Contemplating impermanence . . . dispassion . . . ending . . . contemplating renunciation I shall breathe in and out.

This, Ānanda, is called "the idea of concentration on in-breathing and out-breathing."

Now, Ānanda, if you were to visit the monk Girimānaṇda and recite to him these Ten Ideas, there is ground for supposing that on his hearing them that sickness of his will straightway be allayed.'

Thereupon the venerable Ānanda having got by heart these Ten Ideas in the presence of the Exalted One, visited the venerable Girimānanda and recited them. On his hearing them that sickness of the venerable Girimānanda was straightway allayed, and he rose up from that sickness. And in this way that sickness was banished from the venerable Girimānanda.

---

[1] Omitted in my translation referred to above.

Chapter VII.—The Pairs.

§ i (61). *Ignorance.*

[113] 'Monks, the extreme point of ignorance[1] is not apparent, so that one may say: "Ignorance was not before; it has since come to be." And this statement, monks, is made. Nevertheless, this thing is apparent: Ignorance is conditioned by this or that.[2]

Ignorance, I declare, monks, has its nutriment.[3] It is not without nutriment. And what is the nutriment of ignorance? "The five hindrances" should be the reply. I declare, monks, that the five hindrances have their nutriment, are not without nutriment. And what is the nutriment of the five hindrances? "The three wrong ways of practice" should be the reply. They too have their nutriment. What? "Not-restraint of the sense-faculties" should be the reply. They too have their nutriment. What? "Lack of mindfulness and self-composure" should be the reply. That too has its nutriment, I declare. What? "Lack of thorough work of mind" should be the reply. And what is the nutriment of that? "Lack of faith" should be the reply. What is the nutriment of that? Not listening to true dhamma.[4] I declare, monks, that not listening to true dhamma has its nutriment, is not without nutriment. And what is the

---

[1] The essence of this and following sutta is at *K.S.* ii, 118 *ff.* Quoted *VM.* 525=*Path of Purity,* iii, 625; *UdA.* 176; *Expositor,* 13 (in stating that ignorance is caused by the cankers). For *koṭi saŋsārassa, cf. K.S.* ii, 119, etc.

[2] *Idappaccayā.*

[3] *Sâhāraŋ=sappaccayaŋ, Comy.*

[4] Here *saddhamma* may mean, as I have pointed out at *G.S.* ii, 21 *n.*, 'the voice of conscience' (*saka-dhamma*).

nutriment of not listening to true dhamma? "Not following after the very man"[1] should be the reply.

Thus, monks, the act of not following after the very man, when complete, completes not listening to true dhamma; not listening to true dhamma, when complete, completes lack of faith; lack of faith completes lack of thorough work of mind; [**114**] lack of thorough work of mind, when complete, completes lack of mindfulness and self-composure; and that, not-restraint of the sense-faculties; and that, the three wrong ways of practice; and that, the five hindrances;[2] the five hindrances, when complete, complete ignorance. Such is the nutriment of this ignorance, and such is its fulfilment.

Just as when, monks, on a mountain[3] the rain falls in heavy drops, that water flowing onwards according to the slope fills up the mountain-clefts and rifts and gullies, and they when filled fill up the little pools, and the little pools in turn fill up the big pools, and they in turn fill up the small rivers; they fill the large rivers, and the large rivers in turn fill up the sea, the mighty ocean—thus is the nutriment of the mighty ocean and thus its fulfilment—in the same way, monks, not following after the very man, when complete, completes not listening to true dhamma . . . and the five hindrances, when complete, complete ignorance. Thus is the nutriment of this ignorance and thus its fulfilment.

Release by knowledge, monks, I declare has its nutriment, it is not without nutriment. And what is nutriment of release by knowledge? "The seven limbs of wisdom" should be the reply. The seven limbs of wisdom, I declare, have their nutriment. What? "The four arisings of mindfulness" should be the reply. They too have their nutriment, the three

---

[1] For *sappurisa* in this connexion see *Dhp.* v, 208 (Mrs. Rhys Davids' trans.), *taŋ tādisaŋ sappurisaŋ sumedhaŋ bhajetha.* At *G.S.* ii, 251, four states conduce to growth in wisdom—viz., association with the very man, hearing true dhamma, thorough work of mind and living according to dhamma.

[2] *Pañca nīvaraṇāni*; ; sensuality, ill-will, sloth-and-torpor, flurry-and-worry, doubt-and-wavering.

[3] For the simile *cf. K.S.* v, 339; *G.S.* i, 223.

right ways of practice. And they, [115] control of the faculties of sense. The nutriment of these is mindfulness and self-possession. Their nutriment is thorough work of mind. Of that the nutriment is faith. The nutriment of faith is listening to true dhamma. And what is the nutriment of listening to true dhamma? "Following after the very man" should be the reply.

Thus, monks, following after the very man, when complete, completes listening to true dhamma; listening to true dhamma completes faith; faith completes thorough work of mind; and that, mindfulness and self-possession; that, control of the sense-faculties; that, the three right ways of practice; that, the four arisings of mindfulness; and that, the seven limbs of wisdom; while the seven limbs of wisdom, when complete, complete release by knowledge.

Thus is the nutriment of release by knowledge, and thus is its fulfilment. Just as when, monks, on a mountain the rain falls in heavy drops . . . thus is the nutriment of the sea, the mighty ocean . . . [116] even so does following after the very man complete listening to true dhamma . . . and the seven limbs of wisdom, being complete, complete release by knowledge.

Thus is the fulfilment of release by knowledge and thus its fulfilment.'

§ ii (62). *Craving.*

'Monks, the extreme point of craving-to-become is not apparent, so that one may say: "Craving-to-become was not before; it has since come to be." And, monks, this statement is made. Nevertheless this thing is apparent: Craving-to-become is conditioned by this or that.

I declare, monks, that craving-to-become has its nutriment; it is not without nutriment. And what is the nutriment of craving-to-become? "Ignorance" should be the reply. Ignorance, I declare, has its nutriment. . . . What? The five hindrances . . . (*all the rest as in previous sutta*) [117-9]. . . . Thus is the nutriment of release by knowledge, and thus its fulfilment.

§ iii (63). *The goal.*

'Monks, whosoever have come to the goal in me,[1] all of them are endowed with (right) view.

Of five such endowed with (right) view their goal is won here (on earth). Of other such five their goal is won on leaving here (this earth).[2]

Of which five is the goal won here?

[120] Of him who has but seven more births at most, of him who is reborn in a good family,[3] of the one-seeder, and of him who in this same visible state is arahant. Of such the goal is won here.

And of which five is the goal won on leaving here?

Of him who attains release midway, of him who attains release by reduction of his time, or without much trouble, or with some little trouble, and of the up-streamer who goes to the Elders.[4] Of such the goal is won on leaving here.

Whosoever, monks, have come to the goal in me, all of them are endowed with (right) view. Of five such the goal is won here; of other such five the goal is won after leaving here.'

§ iv (64). *Unwavering.*

'Monks, whosoever have unwavering faith in me, all of them are stream-winners. Of those who are stream-winners

---

[1] *Mayi niṭṭhangatā=nibbematikā* (unanimous), *Comy. Cf. A.* i, 275; ii, 144. On this and § iv. *cf. M.* i, 142.

[2] *Comy.* by *parinibbāna* here on earth or *Brahmaloka* after death.

[3] *Kolankola*, 'One who goes from family to family.' *Cf. G.S.* i, 213, 'such an one, by destroying three fetters, is reborn in a good family,' according to *PuggA.* p. 196 (*J.P.T.S.* 1914); *S.* v, 69, 205; but I am not sure whether my translation is right. It is not a matter of caste, but seems something of the nature of *gotra-bhū* (defined elsewhere). The subject is discussed at *Pts. of Controversy*, 77, 269, where it is called 'salvation by rank.' Perhaps it means 'one of the elect.' *Netti Comy.* p. 247, has *Yo pana dve vā tīṇi vā kulāni sandhāvitvā saŋsaritvā dukkhass' antaŋ karoti, ayaŋ kolankolo.*

[4] *Akaniṭṭha-devā* ('no youngsters there,' *Comy.*), the home of the Four Great Brahmās. At *G.S.* i, 213 I wrongly translated 'Pure Abodes.' 'Not the course of the ordinary man,' says *Comy.*

the goal of five is won here (on earth); of five others the goal is won on leaving here. Of which five is the goal won here?

Of him who has but seven more births at most, of him who is reborn in a good family, of the one-seeder, and of him who in this same visible state is arahant. Of such the goal is won here (on earth).

And of which five is the goal won on leaving here?

Of him who attains release midway, of him who does so by reduction of his time, or who does so without much trouble, or with some little trouble, and of the up-streamer who goes to the Elders. Of such the goal is won on leaving here.

Whosoever have unwavering faith in me, all of them are stream-winners.'

§ v (65). *Weal and woe* (*a*).

Once the venerable Sāriputta was staying among the Magadhese at Nālakagāmaka.[1]

[**121**] Now the Wanderer Sāmandakāni[2] came to see the venerable Sāriputta, and on coming to him greeted him courteously and, after the exchange of courtesies and reminiscent talk, sat down at one side. So seated he said:

'Pray, Sāriputta, your reverence, what is weal and what is woe?'

'Your reverence, rebirth[3] is woe, not-rebirth is weal. Where there is rebirth, this woe may be looked for: Cold and heat; hunger and thirst; evacuation and urination; contact with fire, the rod, the spear; even one's own relatives and friends abuse one, when they meet or gather together. Where there is rebirth, your reverence, this woe may be looked for.

But where there is no rebirth this weal may be looked for: No cold and heat; no hunger and thirst; no evacuation and urination; no contact with fire, rod and spear; nor do one's

---

1 Also Nālakagāma—*e.g.*, *K.S.* iv, 170. It was his native village and he died there, *S.* v. 161, etc.

2 At *S.* iv, 261 *Sāmaṇḍaka*, but Sinh. texts and *Comy*. *Sāmañcakāni*. *Cf. Brethren*, 40.

3 *Abhinibbatti*.

friends abuse one when they meet or gather together. Where there is not rebirth, your reverence, this woe is not to be looked for.'

§ vi (66). *Weal and woe* (*b*).

Once the venerable Sāriputta was staying among the Magadhese at Nālakagāmaka. Now the Wanderer Sāmandakāni came to see him and said:

'Pray, Sāriputta, your reverence, in this dhamma-discipline what is weal and what is woe?'

'Your reverence, when there is discontent this woe may be looked for: Whether one goes, stands, sits, or lies, he reaches not happiness and pleasure; whether he has gone to the forest, to the root of a tree, to a lonely place, to life in the open air, to life amid the monks, he reaches not happiness and pleasure. Where there is discontent, this woe may be looked for.

Where there is content, your reverence, this weal may be looked for: Whether one goes, stands, sits or lies, he reaches happiness and pleasure. Whether he has gone to the forest, to the root of a tree, to a lonely place, to a life in the open air or life amid the monks, he reaches happiness and pleasure.

Where there is content, your reverence, this weal may be looked for.'

§ vii (67). *At Naḷakapāna* (*a*).

Once the Exalted One was going his rounds among the Kosalans together with a number of monks, and came to Naḷakapāna,[1] a Kosalan township of that name. There the Exalted One resided at Judas-Tree Grove.

Now on that occasion the Exalted One was seated surrounded by monks, the day being the sabbath. And when the Exalted One for much of the night had instructed, stirred, fired, and gladdened the monks with a talk about dhamma, on looking round and seeing that the order of monks was perfectly silent,[2] he called to the venerable Sāriputta, saying: 'Sāri-

[1] *Cf. M.* i, 462 (*Naḷakapāna-sutta*, 'cane-drink'), where *Comy.* refers to *JA.* 20. The Bodhisattva, as a monkey, taught his followers to drink water through hollow reeds; hence the name.

[2] *Tuṇhī-bhūtaŋ tuṇhī-bhūtaŋ.*

putta, the order of monks [123] has banished sloth-and-torpor. Let some dhamma-talk occur to you. My back aches. I will ease it.'[1]

'Very well, sir,' replied the venerable Sāriputta to the Exalted One.

Then the Exalted One had his robe spread fourfold, and lying on his right side he took up the lion-posture, resting foot on foot, mindful and composed, fixing his thoughts on rising up again.

Thereupon the venerable Sāriputta called to the monks, saying: 'Monks, your reverences.'

'Yes, Sāriputta, your reverence,' replied those monks to the venerable Sāriputta, who said:

'Your reverences, whosoever hath not faith in good states, whosoever hath not modesty and self-respect, energy and wisdom in good states, for such an one, come night, come day, waning not waxing in good states is to be looked for.

Just as, your reverences, in the dark period of the moon, come night, come day, it wanes in beauty, wanes in roundness, in splendour, wanes in the height and compass of its orbit, even so, your reverences, in whomsoever there is not faith in good states . . . waning not waxing in good states is to be looked for.

To say "a man, a person, is faithless," this implies waning. To say "a man, a person, is immodest," this implies waning. To say "a man, a person, is without self-respect, sluggish, weak in wisdom, wrathful, grudging, of evil desires, evil friends, of wrong view," this, your reverences, constitutes waning.

But in whomsoever there is faith in good states, modesty, self-respect, energy, [124] wisdom in good states—in such, come night, come day, growth in good states is to be looked for, not waning.

Just as, your reverences, in the bright period of the moon, come night, come day, it waxes in beauty, waxes in roundness,

---

[1] *Āyamissāmi*, literally 'stretch it,' an incident which occurs several times. On such occasions the instruction was handed over to Sāriputta, Moggallāna or Ānanda—*e.g.*, *K.S.* iv, 118.

waxes in splendour, in the height and compass of its orbit, even so, in whomsoever there is faith in good states . . . growth in good states, not waning, is to be looked for. To say "a man, a person, is faithful," this constitutes not-waning; to say he is modest, self-respecting, stoutly energetic, strong in wisdom, this constitutes not-waning. To say "a man, a person, is without wrath, grudging, of small desires"; that he has a lovely friend, has right view—this, your reverences, constitutes not-waning.'

Thereupon the Exalted One, rising up again, called to the venerable Sāriputta, saying:

'Well said! Well said, Sāriputta! In whomsoever there is not faith in good states . . . wisdom in good states, in such an one, come night, come day, waning, not growth in good states, is to be looked for. Just as in the dark period of the moon . . . even so [**125**] waning, not growth in good states is to be looked for. To say "a man, a person, is faithless . . . of wrong view," this, Sāriputta, constitutes waning. But in whomsoever there is faith in good states . . . just as in the bright period of the moon . . . growth in good states is to be looked for. To say "a man, a person, is faithful," this constitutes growth in good states, not waning.'

§ viii (68). *Naḷakapāna* (*b*).

Once the Exalted One was staying at Naḷakapāna in Judas-tree Grove. On that occasion the Exalted One was seated surrounded by monks, the day being the sabbath. Then the Exalted One, when for much of the night he had instructed, stirred, fired and gladdened the monks with a talk about dhamma . . . (*as in previous sutta*) called to the venerable Sāriputta, saying:

'Sāriputta, the order of monks has banished sloth-and-torpor. Let some dhamma-talk occur to you. My back aches, I will ease it.'

'Very well, sir,' replied the venerable Sāriputta to the Exalted One.

[**126**] Then the Exalted One lay down . . . and the venerable Sāriputta addressed the monks, saying: . .

'Your reverences, in whomsoever there is not faith in good states, nor modesty and self-respect, nor energy nor attention[1] to what he hears, nor bearing dhamma in mind, nor examination of meaning, nor behaviour according to dhamma, nor seriousness in good states—in such an one, come night, come day, waning, not growth, in good states is to be looked for.

Just as in the dark period of the moon . . . it wanes in the height and compass of its orbit, even so in whomsoever there is not faith in good states . . . waning, not growth, in good states is to be looked for.

But in whomsoever there is faith in good states . . . and the rest . . . growth, not waning, in good states is to be looked for.

Just as in the bright period of the moon . . . it waxes in the height and compass of its orbit **[127]**, even so in whomsoever there is faith in good states . . . growth, not waning, in good states is to be looked for.'

Thereupon the Exalted One rising up again called to the venerable Sāriputta: 'Well said, Sāriputta! Well said, Sāriputta! In whomsoever there is not faith in good states . . .' (*and he repeated all that S. had said*). **[128.]**

§ ix (69). *Topics of talk* (*a*).

Once the Exalted One was staying near Sāvatthī at Jeta Grove in Anāthapiṇḍika's Park.

On that occasion a number of monks, after returning from their alms-round and eating their meal, had gathered and sat down in the service-hall. There they stayed indulging in divers sorts of aimless talk about such things as: Rājahs,[2]

---

[1] *Avadhāna* (not in *P. Dicts.*), but *cf. Sn.* 322; *MP.* 21; *UdA.* 17; *A.* i, 198.

[2] *Comy.* instances Mahāsammata and Mandhāta (rājās of the first *kalpa*); then forgetting his history says, 'talk about Dharmasoka.' A similar comment is on *Petavatthu* iv, 3 *s.v. Moriya*, where *Comy.* has, 'Here he is speaking of Dharmasoka.' *Petav.* and *Vimāna-vatthu* both seem of late date anyhow. This would point to the likelihood that the Piṭakas were not finally put in order till *after* Asoka's Council, and may have been added to still later.

robbers and great ministers; talk of armies, panic and battle; talk of food and 'animal talk,'[1] drink, clothes, beds, flowers, garlands and perfumes; talk of relatives, vehicles, villages, townships, cities and districts; talk about women and champions, about streets and gossip at the well; ghost-stories,[2] desultory talk and fables about (the origin of) land and sea; and talk of becoming and not-becoming.[3]

Then the Exalted One rising from his solitude at eventide went towards the service-hall, and on reaching it sat down on a seat made ready. Being seated the Exalted One addressed the monks, saying:

'Pray, monks, on what subjects were ye conversing gathered together here, and what was the nature of the talk left unfinished by you?'

'Sir, after returning from our alms-round and eating our meal we gathered and sat down here in the service-hall and so stayed indulging in divers sorts of pointless talk, such as: Rājahs, . . . of becoming and not-becoming.'

'Monks, it is not seemly that ye clansmen **[129]** who in faith have gone forth from the home to the homeless should indulge in such talk.[4] There are these ten topics of talk. What ten?

Talk about wanting little, about contentment, seclusion, solitude, energetic striving, virtue, concentration, insight, release, release by knowing and seeing. These, monks, are the ten topics of talk.

Monks, if ye should engage again and again in talk on these ten topics, ye would outshine in brilliance even the brilliance of moon and sun, which are of such mighty power and majesty—not to speak of the brilliance of the Wanderers who hold other views.'[5]

---

[1] *Tiracchāna-kathā*; *cf. K.S.* v, 355, and *Comy.* there as at *DA.* i, 89, 'Talk not conducive to heaven, release and the Way'; generally translated 'animal-talk' (not of course *about* animals), 'childish talk'; but I think the emphasis is on the idea of *close to the ground* (*cf.* 'pedestrian' muse) as opposed to the upright human posture or, as in Skt., 'oblique, awry.'

[2] *Pubba-peta-kathā*, 'deceased relatives,' *Comy.*

[3] *Bhavâbhava* may also mean 'all sorts of becomings.'

[4] A frequent form of rebuke. *Cf. Ud.* 11.

[5] *Cf. Ud.* vi, 10.

§ x (70). *Topics of talk* (*b*).

'Monks, there are these ten praiseworthy examples. What ten? **[130.]**

In this connexion, monks, a monk, as regards himself, is one who wants little, and he is one who makes wanting little a topic of talk among the monks. Both a monk who wants little and a monk who makes others talk about wanting little are praiseworthy examples. Also a monk is contented . . . fond of seclusion . . . of solitude . . . of energetic striving . . . is virtuous . . . proficient in concentration, insight, release, release by knowing and seeing. In each of these cases, monks, both he who has the quality and he who makes such quality a topic of talk among the monks is a praiseworthy example.' [1]

---

[1] *Cf. M.* i, 214.

Chapter VIII.—On Wishes.

§ i (71). *Wishing.*

[131] Once the Exalted One was staying near Sāvatthī at Jeta Grove in Anāthapiṇḍika's Park. On that occasion the Exalted One addressed the monks, saying: 'Monks.'

'Yes, sir,' replied those monks to the Exalted One, who said this:

'Monks, do ye dwell proficient in virtue, proficient in the Obligation, do ye dwell restrained with the restraint of the Obligation, proficient in the practice of good conduct, seeing grounds for fear in minutest faults; do ye undertake and train yourselves in the training of the precepts.

If a monk should wish: O that I were dear and charming to my fellows in the Brahma-life, that I were esteemed and sought after by them!—then let him be a fulfiller of the virtues, in his own self let him be given to peace of mind, not rejecting musing,[1] possessed of insight, fostering resort to lonely spots.

If a monk should wish: O that I were the winner of supplies of robe and alms-food, of bed and lodging, of medicines and necessaries for sickness!—then let him be a fulfiller of the virtues . . . fostering resort to lonely spots.

If a monk should wish: O may the services of those whose[2] offerings of robe and alms-food . . . and necessaries for sickness which I make use of be of great fruit and profit to them!—then let him be a fulfiller of the virtues.

[132] If a monk should wish: O may that piety of mine,[3]

---

[1] *Cf. Itiv.* 39.

[2] Text has *yesâhaŋ* for *yesam ahaŋ*.

[3] *Cf. Khp.* § 7 and *Petavâtthu.* The pitris, fathers, are supposed to be in heaven, but the petas (*pretas*), referred to here, are in purgatory, sometimes translated as 'ghosts,' and supposed to be conscious of offerings made to them by the living.

remembered by those kinsmen and blood-relations (dead and) gone before,[1] be of great fruit and profit !

If a monk should wish: May I be content with any supply of robe and alms-food and the rest that I may get !—then let him be a fulfiller of the virtues.

If a monk should wish: May I endure cold and heat,[2] hunger and thirst, the bite of flies and mosquitoes, the contact of wind and sun and creeping things; may I endure abusive, pain-causing ways of speech and painful bodily feelings, grievous, sharp, racking, distracting and discomforting, that drain the life away—then let him be a fulfiller of the virtues.

If a monk should wish: May I overcome likes and dislikes, may not likes and dislikes overcome me, but may I abide ever and again vanquishing likes and dislikes as they arise—then let him be a fulfiller of the virtues. . . .

If a monk should wish: May I overcome fear and dread, may not fear and dread overcome me, but may I abide ever and again vanquishing fear and dread as they arise, let him be a fulfiller of the virtues. . . .

If a monk should wish: May I win easily and without effort the four stages of musing which are of the clear consciousness,[3] which are concerned with the happy life in this same visible state, let him be a fulfiller of the virtues. . . .

If a monk should wish: By destroying the cankers may I attain in this same visible state, of myself realizing it by comprehension, the cankerless heart's release, the release by insight, and so abide—then let him be a fulfiller of the virtues, in his own self given to peace of mind, not rejecting musing, possessed of insight and fostering resort to lonely spots.

Monks, do ye dwell proficient in virtue, proficient in the Obligation, do ye dwell restrained with the restraint of the

---

[1] *Cf. Khp.* v. 10, *petānaŋ dakkhiṇaŋ dajjā pubbe kataŋ anussaraŋ.* Here text reads *pasanna-cittā*, agreeing with *petā* ; but *Comy. pasanna-cittaŋ*, referred to by *taŋ* following, and explains as I have translated.

[2] As at *G.S.* ii, 122.

[3] *Abhicetasika ; cf. G.S.* ii, 24. According to *Comy.* it is *abhikkanta-visuddha-cittaŋ.*

Obligation, proficient in the practice of good conduct, seeing grounds for fear in minutest faults; do ye undertake and train yourselves in the training of the precepts.'

§ ii (72). *The thorn (in the flesh).*

[**133**] Once the Exalted One was staying near Vesālī in Great Grove, at the House with the Peaked Roof, together with a number of senior monks who were his disciples—namely, the venerable Cāla, Upacāla, Kakkaṭa, Kaḷimbha, Nikaṭa, and Kaṭissaha and other notable monks.[1]

Now on that occasion a crowd of notable Licchavites, riding in their splendid cars in rivalry[2] with din and uproar, were dashing into Great Wood to see the Exalted One.

Then those venerable ones thought: 'Here is a crowd of notable Licchavites . . . dashing into Great Wood to see the Exalted One. Now it has been said by the Exalted One that noise is a thorn to musing. Suppose we retreat to Gosinga Wood where is the sāl grove[3] [**134**]; there we can stay pleasantly, free from noise and crowds.'

So those venerable ones retreated to Gosinga Wood, where is the sāl grove, and there they stayed pleasantly, free from noise and crowds. Later on the Exalted One called to the monks, saying: 'Monks, where is Cāla, where is Upacāla, where are Kakkaṭa, Kaḷimbha, Nikaṭa and Kaṭissaha? Where are those monks, my senior disciples, gone?'

---

[1] *Comy.* has nothing about these elders. There are nuns Cālā and Upacālā at *S.* i, 133; monks of these names at *Brethren* 46. Kakkaṭa, Nikaṭa and Kaṭissaha are upāsakas who died at *S.* v, 358. One Cāla and one Upacāla are called nephews of Sāriputta, *Pss. of the Brethren*, 46.

[2] Text's *carapurāya*, as P. Dict. points out, should perhaps be *param parāya*, 'one after the other'; *Comy.* explains *cara*=the rear (but the word is not so used), and *pura*=the van or front part; and says the one behind tried to pass the one in front, *mahā-puri-vārenā ti attho*. *Cf. Vin.* i, 231; *D.* ii, 96, for the Licchavī and their splendid equipages and rivalry.

[3] For *Gosinga-vana-sāla-dāya cf. M.* i, 205. *MA., ad loc.*, states that on one of the ancient trees there grew a fork resembling cow's horns; hence the name. But a pair of horns on a tree are said to mark a watering-place.

'As to that, sir, it occurred to those venerable ones: Here is a crowd of notable Licchavites, riding in their splendid cars in rivalry with din and uproar, dashing into Great Wood to see the Exalted One. Now it has been said by the Exalted One that noise is a thorn to musing. Suppose we retreat to Gosinga Wood, where is the sāl grove; there we can stay pleasantly, free from noise and crowds. So, sir, those venerable ones are gone there. There they are staying pleasantly, free from noise and crowds.'

'Well said! Well said, monks! Those who should assert what those great disciples have asserted would rightly do so. Indeed, monks, I have said that noise is a thorn to musing. There are these ten thorns. What ten?

To one who delights in seclusion delight in society is a thorn. To one devoted to concentration on the mark of the foul concentration on the mark of the fair is a thorn. To one guarding the doors of the sense-faculties the sight of shows[1] is a thorn. To the Brahma-life consorting with womenfolk is a thorn. **[135]** To the first musing sound is a thorn; to the second musing thought directed and sustained; to the third zest; to the fourth musing in-breathing and out-breathing is a thorn. To the attainment of the ending of awareness-and-feeling awareness-and-feeling are a thorn. Lust, malice and delusion are thorns.

So, monks, do ye abide thornless, do ye abide thorn-removers, do ye abide thornless thorn-removers. Monks, the thornless are arahants, the thornless thorn-removers are arahants.'

§ iii (73). *Desirable.*

'Monks, these ten things are desirable, dear, charming, hard to win in the world. What ten?

Wealth is desirable . . . beauty . . . health . . . virtues . . . the Brahma-life . . . friends . . . much knowledge . . . wisdom . . . teachings . . . the heaven worlds[2] are desirable,

---

[1] *Visūka-dassanaŋ*; *cf. K.S.* v, 394, where *Comy.* as at *DA.* i, 77, explains as *paṭāni-bhūtā* (probably 'with scenery of painted cloth'). Here *Comy.* simply has *visūka-bhūtaŋ dassanaŋ*.

[2] Burmese MSS. have *maggā*; Sinh. *sattā*. *Comy.* does not notice. The tenth item in next would indicate *maggā* as the more likely reading.

dear, charming, hard to win in the world. These are the ten.

[**136**] Monks, to these ten things desirable, dear . . . ten things are obstacles.

Sloth and non-exertion is an obstacle to wealth. Lack of finery and adornment is an obstacle to beauty. Acting unseasonably is an obstacle to health. Friendship with the wicked is an obstacle to virtues. Non-restraint of the sense-faculties is an obstacle to the Brahma-life. Quarrelling is an obstacle to friends. Failure to repeat (what one has heard) is an obstacle to much knowledge. Not to lend an ear[1] and ask questions is an obstacle to wisdom. Lack of study and examination is an obstacle to teachings. Wrong faring[2] is an obstacle to (gaining) the heavens. These are the ten obstacles to these ten things which are desirable, dear, charming, hard to win in the world.

Monks, ten things are helps[3] to these ten things which are desirable. . . .

Energy and exertion are helps to getting wealth. Finery and adornment are helps to beauty. Seasonable action is a help to health. A lovely friendship is a help to virtues. Restraint of the sense-faculties is a help to the Brahma-life. Not quarrelling is a help to friendship. Repetition is a help to much knowledge. Lending an ear and asking questions are helps to wisdom. Study and examination are helps to teachings. Right faring is a help to the heaven worlds.

These are the ten helps to these ten things which are desirable, dear, charming, hard to win in the world.'

§ iv (74). *Growth.*

[**137**] 'Monks, by increasing in ten growths the Ariyan disciple grows in the Ariyan growth, takes hold of the essential, takes hold of the best for his[4] person. What ten?[5]

---

[1] Read *asussūsā* for text's *asussusā*, and so below.

[2] *Micchā-paṭipatti* (*cf. paṭipanno*, one who fares on a way).

[3] *Āhāra* is nutriment or food.

[4] *Kāyassa*. Text gives *v.l. kāyassa bhedā*. *Comy.* has nothing.

[5] Five at *K.S.* iv, 168.

He grows in landed property, in wealth and granary, in child and wife, in slaves and folk who work for him, in four-footed beasts; he grows in faith and virtue, in love, generosity and wisdom. In these ten growths the Ariyan disciple grows. . . .

> Whoso in this world grows in wealth and store,
> In sons and wives and in fourfooted beasts,
> Hath fame and worship as a man of means
> From relatives and friends and those who rule.
>
> But whoso in this world in faith and virtue,[1]
> In wisdom, generosity and lore
> Alike makes growth,—a very man like this,[2]
> Keen-eyed, in this life grows alike in both.'

§ v (75). *Migasālā.*[3]

Once the Exalted One was staying near Sāvatthī at Jeta Grove in Anāthapiṇḍika's Park. On that occasion the venerable Ānanda, robing himself in the forenoon and taking robe and bowl, went to the dwelling of the woman disciple Migasālā, and on reaching it sat down on a seat made ready.

Then the woman disciple Migasālā came to where the venerable Ānanda was, and on coming to him saluted him and sat down at one side. So seated she said this to the venerable Ānanda:

'Pray, Ānanda, your reverence, how[4] should this teaching given by the Exalted One be understood? [**138**] It is that one who lives the Brahma-life and one who does not so live alike reach the same bourn in the life to come.

Now, sir, my father Purāṇa lived the Brahma-life, lived apart (from evil), abstained from sexual intercourse, from dealings

---

[1] The latter part of these gāthās occurs at *S.* iv, 250; at *A.* iii, 80= *G.S.* iii, 66, where *Comy. varâdāyī=uttamassa varassa ādāyako.* The first part resembles those at *D.* iii, 165.

[2] *Tādiso sappuriso ; cf.* above, § 61.

[3] The first part of this sutta is at *A.* iii, 347=*G.S.* iii, 246-7.

[4] Text *kathankathā ; v.l. kathaŋ kathaŋ. Comy. kathaŋ=kena kāraṇena.*

with women. He when he died was pronounced by the Exalted One to be a once-returner, one reborn in the Company of Delight. But, sir, my father's brother Isidatta was not a liver of the Brahma-life, he took pleasure in his wife. Yet he too was pronounced by the Exalted One to be a once-returner, reborn in the Company of Delight. Pray, sir, how should this teaching of the Exalted One be understood, namely, that one who lives the Brahma-life and one who does not shall both alike reach the same bourn in the life to come?'

'Sister, it is to be understood just as the Exalted One declared.'

Thereupon the venerable Ānanda, after receiving his alms-food at the hands of the woman disciple Migasālā, rose up from his seat and departed.

Then, after returning from his alms-round and eating his meal, he went to see the Exalted One, and on coming to him saluted him and sat down at one side. So seated he said this to the Exalted One:

'Here, sir, I robed myself in the forenoon, and taking bowl and robe went to the dwelling of the woman disciple Migasālā (and he related her talk). **[139]** Whereupon, sir, I said to her: "Sister, it is to be understood just as the Exalted One declared."'

'But, Ānanda, in the knowledge of the destiny of others who is the woman disciple Migasālā—just a foolish, witless, female woman, with just a woman's wit—and who are the individuals, the male men[1] (who have this knowledge)?

---

[1] I read with *v.ll.* of text *ke ca purisa-puggalā paro-pariya-ñāṇe*, instead of all as one word, as text and *Comy.* and Mr. Hare at *G.S.* iii, 246. This form of comparison is not uncommon, as below in § 99. If it be not so taken there is no noun to agree with *ke*. Text has *ambhakā* for *ambakā* ; *v.l.* at *G.S.* iii is *amma*. I believe the word is not found elsewhere, and would read *ammakā* (' mummyish '). I take *purisa-puggalā* as emphatic male as opposed to the other. *Paro-pariya-ñāṇa* is used of clairvoyant insight into others' conditions. Elsewhere *purisa-puggalā* (*par excellence*) are the eight sets of beings on the eight stages of the Fourfold Path (*yadidaŋ cattāri purisa-yugāni aṭṭha purisa-puggalā, esa Bhagavato sāvaka-sangho*). In this case the *purisa-puggala* who knows is himself (*ahaŋ, yo vā mādiso*).

Ānanda, these ten persons are found existing in the world. What ten ?

In this connexion a certain person is immoral and comprehends not that release of the mind, that release by insight, as it really is, wherein that immorality of his utterly ceases without remainder. He has neglected to lend an ear, he has done nothing by way of deep learning, he has not penetrated by (right) view, he wins not even temporary release.[1] When body breaks up, beyond death, he tends to waning, not to excellence; he is one who goes on to waning, he goes not on to excellence.

Herein again, Ānanda, a certain person is immoral, but he does comprehend that mind-release, that release by insight, as it really is, [**140**] wherein that immorality of his ceases without remainder. He has given ear, he has used deep knowledge, he has penetrated by view, he wins temporary release. When body breaks up, beyond death, he tends to excellence, not waning; he goes on to excellence, he goes not on to waning.

Thereupon, Ānanda, those who measure thus measure:[2] These qualities are both in this man and in the other. Why then is the one of them mean and the other exalted ? Such judgment is for them to their loss and pain for many a day. For of the two the one is immoral, but does comprehend that mind-release, that release by insight, as it really is, wherein that immorality of his ceases without remainder; for he has given ear, he has used deep knowledge, he has penetrated by view, he wins temporary release—this person, Ānanda, is more goodly and excellent than that other person. Why so ? Because the ear of dhamma[3] saves this person. Who save the Wayfarer could know the cause herein ?

---

[1] *Sāmāyikaŋ*, occurring variously as *sāmādhika*, *sāmayika*, *samāyika*; *cf. K.S.* i, 150 *n.* (where text has *sāmādhikaŋ*), and *SA.* i, 182, *ad loc.*; *M.* iii, 110. Here *Comy.* explains 'he does not win *pīti-pāmojjaŋ* through seasonably hearing dhamma.'

[2] For *pamāṇikā pamiṇanti*, *cf. A.* ii, 70.

[3] *Dhamma-sota nibbahati.* This seems '*ear* for dhamma' (which I take to mean 'hearing the voice of conscience'), but is translated

Wherefore, Ananda, be ye not measurers of persons, take not the measure of persons. A person is ruined,[1] Ānanda, by taking the measure of other persons. But I myself, Ānanda, and whoso is like unto me, could take the measure of persons.

[141] Again in this connexion a certain person is virtuous, but he comprehends not that mind-release, that release by insight, as it really is, wherein that virtue of his ceases without remainder. Moreover he has neglected to lend an ear, he has neglected deep learning, he has not penetrated by view, nor does he win temporary release. When body breaks up, beyond death, he tends to waning, he goes not on to excellence.

Again in this connexion a certain person is virtuous, but he does not comprehend that mind-release . . . he has not neglected to lend an ear . . . he does win temporary release. When body breaks up . . . he goes on to excellence, not waning.

Thereupon, Ānanda, those who measure thus measure: These qualities are both in this man and in the other. Why then is the one of them mean and the other exalted ? This judgment is for them to their loss and pain (*as above*). Wherefore, Ānanda, be ye not measurers in persons; take not the measure of persons . . . I myself and whoso is like unto me could take the measure of persons.

Again in this connexion a certain person has keen passions, and comprehends not that mind-release . . . wherein that passion of his ceases without remainder. Moreover he has neglected to lend an ear, he has neglected deep learning, he

---

'stream' at *K.S.* ii, 33, 42 (*sotaŋ samāpanno*), and at *G.S.* iii, 248, but I have nowhere seen *dhamma-sota* in this sense. The reference is to *dhamma-savaṇa* just above. *Comy.* 'as he is a champion, it draws out (*nibbahati*) the knowledge-and-insight existing in him and makes him reach the Ariyan ground.' (However, for *soto* as *magga*, see *S.* v, 247; *UdA.* 290; and *SA.* on *S.* ii, quoted above.) It occurs again at § 12 of the Elevens. Reading with *G.S.* iii, and *Comy. tadantaraŋ*= *kāraṇaŋ*. Text has *tadanantaraŋ* ('what follows immediately').

[1] *Khaññati* (pass. of *khaṇati*); *cf. M.* i, 132, *attānaŋ khaṇasi*.

has not penetrated by view, nor does he win even temporary release. When body breaks up, beyond death, . . . he goes on to waning, not excellence.

On the other hand, a person has keen passions, but does comprehend that mind-release . . . he has not neglected to lend an ear . . . he has penetrated by view. . . . When body breaks up . . . **[142]** he tends to excellence, not waning. . . .

Yet again in this connexion a person is wrathful . . . of muddled wits, and comprehends not that mind-release . . . (and the other person is the same, but does comprehend). . . . He goes to excellence not waning.

[143] Thereupon, Ānanda, those who measure thus measure: These qualities exist both in this man and the other. Why then is the one of them mean and the other exalted ? This judgment is for them to their loss and pain for many a day. For of the two the one is of muddled wits, but does comprehend that mind-release, the release by insight, wherein that muddled state of mind ceases without remainder. He has not neglected to lend an ear, he has not neglected deep knowledge, he has penetrated (things) by view and he wins temporary release. This person, Ānanda, is more goodly and excellent than that other. Why so ? The ear of dhamma saves this person. Who but the Wayfarer could know the cause herein ?

Wherefore, Ānanda, be ye not measurers in persons, take not the measure of persons. One is ruined, Ānanda, by taking the measure of persons. But I myself, Ānanda, and whoso is like unto me, could take the measure of persons.

In the knowledge of the destiny of others, Ānanda, who is the woman disciple Migasālā—just a foolish, witless female woman, with just a woman's wit—and who are the individuals, the male men (who have this knowledge) ?

So, Ānanda, these ten persons are found existing in the world.

With whatsoever virtue Purāṇa was endowed, with that same virtue Isidatta might be endowed. Yet herein Purāṇa will not know the bourn of Isidatta, the bourn of someone else.[1]

With whatsoever insight Isidatta was endowed, with that same insight Purāṇa might be endowed [**144**]. Yet herein Isidatta will not know the bourn of Purāṇa, the bourn of some-one else. Thus you see, Ānanda, these persons in both cases are mean in one quality.'

§ vi (76). *Unable to grow.*

'Monks, were not three states found existing in the world, the Wayfarer would not arise in the world, an arahant rightly enlightened; nor would the dhamma-discipline proclaimed by the Wayfarer be shown in the world. What are the three states? Birth, decay and death. Were not these three states found existing in the world, the Wayfarer would not arise in the world. . . . But since these three states are found therefore the Wayfarer does arise in the world, an arahant rightly enlightened, and the dhamma-discipline proclaimed by the Wayfarer is shown in the world.

By not abandoning three states one is unable to grow[2] so as to abandon rebirth, to abandon decay, to abandon death. What three states? By not abandoning lust . . . malice . . . delusion one is unable to grow so as to abandon rebirth, decay and death.

By not abandoning three states one is unable to grow so as to abandon lust, malice and delusion. What three?

The view of the individual-group, doubt-and-wavering, wrong handling of habit and rite. By not abandoning these three one is unable to grow so as to abandon lust, malice and delusion.

[**145**] By not abandoning three states . . . lack of giving thorough attention, following the wrong way, sluggishness

---

[1] The text here is incomplete—viz., *na-y-idha Purāṇo Isidattassa gatim pi aññassa*. There is no verb to account for the case of *gati* (*Comy.* =*ñāṇagatiŋ*). I conclude that *aññassati* (future of *jānāti*) has been mutilated by confusion with *aññassa*; or else originally there was no *aññassa*, only *gatim pi aññassati*.

[2] *Abhabbo.*

of mind . . . one is unable to grow so as to abandon the view of the individual-group, doubt-and-wavering and wrong handling of habit and rite.

By not abandoning three states . . . forgetfulness, discomposure, mental derangement . . . one is unable to abandon lack of giving thorough attention, following of the wrong way[1] and sluggishness of mind.

By not abandoning three states . . . distaste for seeing the Ariyans, distaste for hearing Ariyan dhamma, a carping disposition[2] . . . one is unable to grow so as to abandon forgetfulness, discomposure, mental derangement.

By not abandoning three states . . . flurry, lack of self-control and immorality one is unable to grow so as to abandon distaste for seeing the Ariyans, distaste for hearing Ariyan dhamma, and a carping disposition.

[146] By not abandoning three states . . . lack of faith, stinginess and indolence . . . one is unable . . . to abandon flurry, lack of self-control, immorality.

By not abandoning three states . . . disregard, stubbornness, friendship with the wicked . . . one is unable . . . to abandon lack of faith, stinginess, indolence.

By not abandoning three states . . . shamelessness, recklessness, lack of seriousness . . . one is unable . . . to abandon disregard, stubbornness, friendship with the wicked.

Suppose, monks, this one is shameless, reckless and lacks seriousness. Being thus without seriousness he cannot grow so as to abandon disregard, so as to abandon stubbornness, so as to abandon friendship with the wicked. Having wicked friends he cannot . . . abandon lack of faith, stinginess and indolence. Being indolent he cannot . . . abandon flurry, lack of self-control and immorality. Being immoral he cannot . . . abandon distaste for seeing the Ariyans, distaste for hearing Ariyan dhamma, and a carping disposition. Having a carping disposition he cannot . . . abandon forgetfulness, discomposure and mental derangement.

---

[1] *Kummagga ; cf. A.* ii, 14; iii, 418.

[2] *Upārambha-cittatā ; cf. A.* iv, 175, conjoined with *randha-gavesī* (looking for flaws).

[147] Being mentally deranged he cannot . . . abandon lack of giving thorough attention, following the wrong way and sluggishness of mind. Being sluggish of mind he cannot . . . . abandon view of the individual-group, doubt-and-wavering and wrong handling of habit and rite. Doubtful-and-wavering he cannot . . . abandon lust, malice and delusion. Not abandoning lust, malice and delusion, he cannot grow so as to abandon rebirth, decay and death. **[148.]**

But, monks, by abandoning three states one can grow so as to abandon rebirth, decay and death. What three ?

By abandoning lust, malice and delusion. By abandoning these three states one can grow so as to abandon rebirth, decay and death.'

[149] (*And so on in reverse order of the previous qualities.*)

§ vii (77). *The crow.*

'Monks, the crow is possessed of ten qualities contrary to dhamma. What ten ?

It is truculent[1] and pushing, greedy and a gross feeder, cruel and pitiless, clumsy,[2] of harsh voice,[3] muddle-headed and a hoarder of treasure.[4] A crow is possessed of these ten qualities contrary to dhamma.

In like manner a wicked monk is possessed of ten qualities contrary to dhamma. What ten ?'

(*The same as those of the crow.*)

§ viii (78). *The Unclothed.*[5]

[150] 'Monks, the Unclothed are possessed of these ten qualities contrary to dhamma. What ten ?

The Unclothed are unbelievers, immoral, shameless, reckless, they are no comrades of the very man,[6] they exalt self and depreciate others.

---

[1] *Dhaṃsī ; cf. Dhp.* 244 *kāka-sūrena, dhaṃsinā . . . pagabbhena.*

[2] *Dubbala* in its usual sense of 'feeble' cannot be applied to a crow.

[3] *Oravitā=orava-yutto, oravanto carati, Comy.* The word seems to occur nowhere else. *P. Dict.* doubts derivation, but suggests *ora-vitarati.* But it is evidently a lengthened form of *avaravati,* to croak.

[4] *Necayiko=nicaya-karo, Comy.*

[5] The Jains or naked ascetics, of whom the chief was Nātaputta.

[6] *Sappurisa; cf.* p. 79 *n.*

The Unclothed wrongly handle things temporal,[1] they tightly grip and refuse to let go of them. The Unclothed are rogues, monks, of evil desires, of perverse views.

These are the ten qualities contrary to dhamma possessed by the Unclothed.'

§ ix (79). *Occasions of ill-will.*

'Monks, there are these ten occasions of ill-will.[2] What ten?

One conceives ill-will at the thought: So-and-so has done me harm; he is doing me harm; he is going to do me harm.[3] One conceives ill-will at the thought: So-and-so has done harm to one dear and precious to me; he is doing harm, he is going to do harm to one dear and precious to me. One conceives ill-will at the thought: So-and-so has done good to one not dear and precious to me: he is doing good, he is going to do good to one not dear and precious to me. Thus one is groundlessly annoyed.

These are the ten occasions of ill-will.'

§ x (80). *Ways of checking ill-will.*

'Monks, there are these ten ways of checking ill-will. What ten?

One checks ill-will at the thought: So-and-so has done me harm. But how can that be?[4] **[151]** He is doing, he will do me harm. But how can that be? One checks ill-will at the thought: So-and-so has done harm to one dear and precious to me; he is doing harm, he will do harm to one dear and precious to me. But how can that be? One checks ill-will at the thought: So-and-so has done good, is doing good, will do good to one not dear and precious to me. But how can that be? Thus one is not groundlessly annoyed.

These are the ten ways of checking ill-will.'

[1] *Sandiṭṭhi-parāmāsā*; *cf. A.* iii, 333; *M.* i, 43, 96, 402.

[2] *Aghāta-*. Five at *A.* iii, 185.

[3] As at *Dhs.* § 1060=*Buddh. Psych. Eth.* 282.

[4] *Kut'ettha labbhā* (=*sakkā*). *Cf. S.* i, 185. Possibly 'it can't be helped.'

Chapter IX.—The Elders.

§ i (81). *Bāhuna.*

Once the Exalted One was staying near Campā[1] on the bank of the Lotus-pond at Gaggarā. Then the venerable Bāhuna came to see the Exalted One, and on coming to him saluted him and sat down at one side. So seated he said this to the Exalted One:

'Pray, sir, from what states free, detached and released does the Wayfarer dwell, with a mind whose barriers are broken down?'[2]

[152] 'Bāhuna, the Wayfarer is free, detached and released from[3] ten states and so dwells with a mind whose barriers are broken down. What are the ten?

The Wayfarer dwells free, detached and released from physical body, feeling, perception, mental factors and (persisting) consciousness . . . from rebirth, decay and death . . . from the passions, Bāhuna, the Wayfarer is free, detached and released, and dwells with a mind whose barriers are broken down.

Just as, Bāhuna, a lotus, blue or red or white, born in water, grown up in water, on reaching the surface rests on the water unsoiled thereby,[4] even so Bāhuna, the Wayfarer, free, detached and released from these ten states, dwells with a mind whose barriers are broken down.'

§ ii (82). *Ānanda.*

Now the venerable Ānanda came to see the Exalted One . . . as he sat at one side the Exalted One said this to him:

'Ānanda, there is no possibility that a monk who is an un-

---

[1] § 94 below; *M.* i, 339; *S.* i, 195. Capital of the Angas, now Bhagulpur. *Cf. MA.* iii, 1. Bāhuna seems unknown.

[2] *Cf. S.* ii, 173; *A.* i, 259, *cetasā vimariyāda-katena*.

[3] The use of the instrumental case throughout here might give the meaning 'by means of.'

[4] *Cf. G.S.* iii, 345 (gāthās).

believer should reach increase, growth and maturity in this dhamma-discipline. There is no possibility that one who is immoral . . . of little learning . . . of foul speech . . . **[153]** having wicked friends . . . indolent . . . muddle-headed . . . discontented . . . of wicked desires . . . there is no possibility that a monk who holds perverse view should reach increase, growth and maturity in this dhamma-discipline. Indeed, Ānanda, there is no possibility that a monk possessed of these ten qualities should do so.

But, Ānanda, there is a possibility that a monk who is a believer, virtuous, deeply learned, minder of what he has heard, that a monk who is fair-spoken, who has a lovely friend, who is ardent in energy, whose mindfulness is sure, **[154]** who is contented, wanting little, who holds right view . . . there is a possibility that such a monk, possessing these ten qualities, should reach increase, growth and maturity in this dhamma-discipline.'

§ iii (83). *Puṇṇiya.*[1]

Now the venerable Puṇṇiya came to see the Exalted One . . . as he sat at one side he asked this:

'Pray, sir, what is the reason, what is the cause why at one time dhamma-teaching occurs to the Wayfarer and at another time does not occur?'

'A monk may be a believer, Puṇṇiya; but if he pays no visit, dhamma-teaching occurs not to the Wayfarer. But if he both be a believer and pay a visit, then dhamma-teaching does occur to the Wayfarer.

But suppose a monk is both a believer and a visitor, but not a constant[2] visitor; or suppose he is all three of these but not a questioner . . . or all these but not one who listens to dhamma with attentive ear; or suppose he does all these but yet on hearing dhamma bears it not in mind . . . or doing all these things, if he does bear dhamma in mind, yet examines not the meaning of the teachings he has borne in mind; or

---

[1] P. seems unknown. He asks the same question at *A.* iv, 337.

[2] *Payirupāsitā,* one who attends constantly or sits beside a teacher.

though he does this [155], yet, by not understanding the meaning and the teaching, fares not onward in accordance with dhamma-teaching; or though he does this, if he be not fair-spoken, possessed of urbane speech, distinctly and clearly enunciated[1] so as to make his meaning clear; or though he does this, yet if he is not one to teach, urge, incite and gladden his fellows in the Brahma-life—under such conditions dhamma-teaching does not occur to the Wayfarer.

But, Puṇṇiya, if he have (all these qualities), then dhamma-teaching does occur to the Wayfarer.'

§ iv (84). *Declaration of gnosis.*

Now the venerable Moggallāna the Great called to the monks, saying: 'Monks, your reverences!'

'Yes, your reverence,' replied those monks to the venerable Moggallāna, who then said:

'In this matter, your reverences, a monk declares gnosis[2] thus: "Destroyed is rebirth, lived is the Brahma-life, done is what should be done. I am assured that there is no more of life in these conditions."

Then the Wayfarer or [156] a Wayfarer's disciple who is a muser, skilled in attaining (musing), skilled in reading others' hearts, skilled in reading the habit of others' hearts, closely examines,[3] questions and talks with him. He, thus closely examined, questioned and talked with by the Wayfarer or a disciple of the Wayfarer, who is a muser . . .—he comes to a desert[4] (so to speak), he comes to a jungle,[5] he comes to an ill pass, to ruin, to an ill pass and ruin alike. For the Wayfarer or Wayfarer's disciple . . . reading his heart with his own thus ponders: How is it that this worthy thus declares gnosis: "Destroyed is rebirth, lived is the Brahma-life, done

---

[1] *Cf. G.S.* ii, 106.

[2] *Aññaŋ vyākaroti.*

[3] *Cf. G.S.* i, 169.

[4] *Iriṇam āpajjati. Iriṇa* (*Skt.*)=barren soil. *Īriṇa*=desert. *Comy.* has *irīṇa*=*tuccha-bhāva* (blank).

[5] *Vijinam āpajjati.* There is a reading *vicinam. Comy.* reads *vipinam* (thicket). It means 'a state of loss of virtue, of one lost in a forest.'

is what should be done; I am assured that there is no more of life in these conditions" ?

Then the Wayfarer or a Wayfarer's disciple . . . reading his heart with his own, comes to know: But this worthy is wrathful, lives generally with heart beset by wrath. Such obsession by wrath means waning in the dhamma-discipline proclaimed by the Wayfarer. This worthy is grudging . . . a detractor of others' virtues . . . spiteful . . . envious . . . stingy . . . **[157]** crafty . . . a trickster . . . of wicked desires . . . of muddled wits . . . this worthy, though there was yet more to be done (to reach perfection), even if the remaining special attainments were but of trifling value, has come to a halt midway of his career;[1] halting midway is waning in the dhamma-discipline proclaimed by the Wayfarer.

Indeed, monks, if he abandon not these ten conditions there is no possibility for a monk to reach increase, growth and maturity in this dhamma-discipline. But if he abandon them he may do so.'

§ v (85). *The boaster.*

Once the venerable Cunda the Great[2] was staying among the Cetī at Sahajātī. On that occasion he addressed the monks, saying: 'Monks, your reverences.'

'Yes, your reverence,' replied those monks to the venerable Cunda the Great, who said:

'In this matter, your reverences, suppose a monk is a boaster[3] and garrulous about his own attainments, thus: I have attained the first musing and can emerge[4] therefrom. **[158]** I can

---

[1] *Antarā-vosāna ; cf. D.* ii, 78; *M.* i, 193; *S.* iii, 168; a term applied to Devadatta at *Itiv.*, p. 85.

[2] At § 24 and *G.S.* iii, 252 (about musing) he speaks to the monks at the same place.

[3] *Katthī* seems not to occur elsewhere. The strengthened form in negative is at *Sn.* 850; *MP.* 414. Here *Comy.* says *kathana-sīlo, vivaṭaŋ katheti.*

[4] 'Emergence' is said to mean the power to return to normal consciousness at a given predetermined moment. *Cf. Path of Purity,* iii, 870.

attain the sphere of nothingness . . . the sphere of neither-perception-nor-not-perception . . . the sphere wherein perception-and-feeling are ended, and can emerge therefrom.

Thereupon the Wayfarer or a disciple of the Wayfarer, who is a muser, one skilled in attaining (musing), skilled in reading others' hearts, skilled in reading the habit of others' hearts, closely examines him, questions and talks with him. He thus closely examined, questioned and talked with by the Wayfarer or Wayfarer's disciple, comes to a desert (so to speak), comes to a jungle, comes to an ill pass, to ruin, both to an ill pass and to ruin; for the Wayfarer or Wayfarer's disciple . . . reading his heart with his own thus ponders: How is it that this worthy is a boaster and garrulous about his own attainments, so as to say: "I have attained the first . . . second . . . third . . . fourth musing and can emerge therefrom . . . the sphere wherein perception and feeling are ended, and can emerge therefrom"?

Then the Wayfarer or Wayfarer's disciple . . . reading his heart with his own, comes to know: For many a day this worthy has been one whose deeds are incongruous, inconsistent, shady and spotted. His deeds, his habits are not consistent with good morals. This worthy is immoral, and immorality like this means waning in the dhamma-discipline proclaimed by the Wayfarer. Moreover this worthy is an unbeliever, and unbelief means waning in the dhamma-discipline proclaimed by the Wayfarer. [159] He is of little learning, and little learning means waning. He is foul-spoken, and foul speech means waning . . . he has wicked friends, and wicked friendship means waning . . . he is slothful, and sloth means waning . . . he is of muddled wits, and muddled wits mean waning . . . he is a fraud, and fraudulence means waning . . . he is not forbearing,[1] and not-forbearance means waning . . . this worthy is weak in wisdom, and weak wisdom means waning in this dhamma-discipline proclaimed by the Wayfarer.

Suppose, your reverences, a friend should say to his friend:

---

[1] *Dubbhara*; *cf. A.* iv, 280.

" When you are in need of money, old man, you will ask me for money and I will give it you." The latter, when need of money arises, says to the former: " I need money, old man. Give me money." The other replies: " Then dig here, old man." He digs there but finds no money, and says to the other: " You told me a lie. You gave me empty words in saying: 'Dig here.'" The other replies: " No! I told you no lie. I gave you not empty words; so dig you here." He does so, but finds no money, and again reproaches his friend with falsehood. Again the friend denies it **[160]**, saying: " I told you no lie. I gave you not empty words, but I was out of my mind; I was distracted."[1]

Just in the same way, your reverences, suppose a monk is a boaster and garrulous about his own attainments . . . (*he repeats the whole of the above*) . . . **[161]** there is no possibility that such a monk, if he abandon not these ten qualities, will make increase, growth and maturity in this dhamma-discipline. But if he abandon them he may do so.'

§ vi (86). *The question of gnosis.*

Once the venerable Kassapa the Great was staying in Bamboo Grove at the Squirrels' Feeding-ground. On that occasion **[162]** he called to the monks, saying: 'Monks, your reverences!'

'Yes, your reverence,' replied those monks to the venerable Kassapa the Great, who said this:

'In this matter, your reverences, a certain monk declares gnosis thus: " Destroyed is rebirth, lived is the Brahma-life, done is what was to be done. I am assured that there is no more of life in these conditions."

Then the Wayfarer or a disciple of the Wayfarer who is a muser, skilled in attaining (musing), skilled in reading others' hearts, skilled in reading the habit of others' hearts, closely examines and questions him, talks with him. He thus closely examined, questioned and talked with, comes to

---

[1] *Cf. S.* i, 126; *G.S.* ii, 90, *ummādaŋ vā pāpuṇeyya citta-vikkhepaŋ vā;* here *cetaso vipariyāyaŋ*. Below, § 8. For *Samma cf. G.S.* i, 211 n.

a desert (so to speak), comes to a jungle, comes to an ill pass, to ruin, to an ill pass and to ruin alike. Then the Wayfarer or Wayfarer's disciple . . . thus ponders: How is it that this worthy declares gnosis thus: Destroyed is rebirth . . .? Then the Wayfarer or Wayfarer's disciple . . . reading his heart with his own, comes to know: This worthy is over-conceited; regarding his own conceit as truth he thinks he has won what he has not won; he thinks he has done what he has not done; he thinks he has attained what he has not attained. From over-conceit he declares gnosis thus: Destroyed is rebirth. . . .

Then the Wayfarer or Wayfarer's disciple who is a muser . . . thus ponders: Dependent on what, I wonder, is this worthy thus conceited, and regarding his own conceit as truth . . . thus declares gnosis?

[163] Then reading his heart with his own he comes to know: But this worthy is of deep learning; he bears in mind what he has heard and treasures it up; those teaching that, lovely in the beginning, lovely midway, lovely at the end (of life), set forth the utterly complete Brahma-life in all its purity—such teachings he has much heard and borne in mind, verbally repeated, mentally examined, penetrated with view. Therefore is this worthy conceited; regarding his over-conceit as truth he thinks he has won what he has not won, he thinks he has done what he has not done . . . attained what he has not attained. It is from over-conceit that he declares gnosis thus: Destroyed is rebirth. . . .

Then the Wayfarer or Wayfarer's disciple . . . comes to know: This worthy is covetous; he lives generally with heart obsessed by coveting. Now obsession by coveting means waning in this dhamma-discipline proclaimed by the Wayfarer. This worthy is malicious. Now malice means waning. . . . This worthy is slothful and torpid. Now sloth-and-torpor means waning. . . . This worthy is unbalanced . . . is a doubter and waverer . . . delights in doing things, delights in deeds, is wholly given over to delight in deeds. **[164]** This worthy delights in gossip, loves gossip, is wholly given over to delight in gossip . . . delights in sleep . . . in society. . . .

Being of muddled wits, this worthy, even if the remaining special attainments were but of trifling value, has come to a halt midway of his career. Halting midway in one's career is waning in the dhamma-discipline proclaimed by the Wayfarer.

Indeed, your reverences, there is no possibility that this monk, without abandoning these ten qualities, should reach increase, growth and maturity in this dhamma-discipline. But should he abandon them there are good grounds for his reaching growth, increase and maturity therein.'

§ vii (87). *Kālaka the monk.*

On that occasion, concerning Kālaka[1] the monk, the Exalted One called to the monks, saying: 'Monks!'

'Yes, sir,' replied those monks to the Exalted One, who said this:

'In this matter, monks, we have a monk who is disputatious,[2] who speaks not in favour of calming disputes. In so far as he is of such a nature, this state of things[3] conduces not to dearness, to respect, to cultivation,[4] to accord and oneness.

[165] Then again a monk is not fond of the training, speaks not in favour of undergoing the training. In so far as he is such, this state of things also conduces not to dearness. . . .

Again a monk is of evil desires, no speaker in favour of restraint of desires. In so far as he is such, this state of things also conduces not to dearness. . . .

Again a monk is wrathful . . . disparaging . . . crafty . . . a deceiver . . . **[166]** is by nature unobservant[5] of teachings,

---

[1] The *uddāna* of text has no title for this and next sutta, but one MS. has what I have given. Neither *Comy.* nor *Ang.* Index notices the name Kālaka, and I have not found it elsewhere. Text gives several variants; perhaps it is due to a confusion with Kokālika of § ix.

[2] *Adhikaraṇika.* Taken by *P.E.D.* as 'judge in a dispute,' but by *Comy.* as 'disputatious.'

[3] *Dhamma.*

[4] *Bhāvanāya,* in the sense of cultivating one's acquaintance. *Cf. sevitabba, bhajitabba, bhāvitabba.*

[5] *Nisāmaka-jātiyo* (? *-jātiko*)=*na upadhāraṇa-sabhāvo, Comy. Cf. G.S.* ii, 106; *A.* iv, 296 (*Comy. sīghaŋ jānituŋ asamattho*).

speaks not in favour of observing teachings. In so far as he is such, this also conduces not to dearness. . . .

Again a monk is not given to seclusion . . . does not kindly welcome his fellows in the Brahma-life, speaks not in favour of welcoming kindly. In so far as he is such, this also conduces not to dearness, to respect, to cultivation, to accord and oneness.

In such a monk, however much this longing arises: O that my fellows in the Brahma-life would honour, respect, appreciate and show deference to me!—yet his fellows in the Brahma-life neither honour, respect, appreciate nor show deference to him. What is the cause of that? Because his discerning fellows in the Brahma-life observe that those bad, unprofitable qualities are not abandoned in him.

Just as if, monks, in an unbroken colt[1] however much this longing should arise: O that men would set me in the place of a trained thoroughbred, feed me with a thoroughbred's food and groom me with the grooming of a thoroughbred!—yet men put him not in the place of a thoroughbred, feed him not with a thoroughbred's food, groom him not with the grooming of a thoroughbred.

[167] Why not? Because discerning men observe that those crafty, roguish tricks, those swervings and crooked ways of his are not abandoned.[2] Even so, monks, however much this longing may arise in such a monk: O that my fellows in the Brahma-life would honour, respect, appreciate and show deference to me!—yet his fellows in the Brahma-life do none of these things. Why not? Because, monks, his discerning fellows in the Brahma-life observe that those qualities are not abandoned in him.

Now, monks, suppose we have a monk who is not disputatious, but who speaks in favour of calming disputes. In so far as he is not disputatious, but speaks in favour of calming disputes, this state of things conduces to dearness, respect, cultivation, to accord and oneness.

---

[1] *Cf. A.* i, 287=*G.S.* i, 266=*A.* iv, 397. *Comy. assakalunkha*=*assa-pota*. Below, XI, x.

[2] At *M.* i, 340 of the young elephant.

Then again he is fond of the training, speaks in favour of undergoing it . . . has small desires, speaks in favour of restraint of desires . . . is not wrathful, speaks in favour of restraining wrath . . . is not disparaging, speaks in favour of restraining disparagement . . . **[168]** is not crafty . . . is no deceiver . . . is by nature observant of teachings, speaks in favour of observing teachings . . . is given to seclusion . . . kindly welcomes his fellows in the Brahma-life and speaks in favour of so doing. In so far as he is such an one, this makes for dearness, respect, cultivation, accord and oneness.

In such a monk, although no such longing arises as: O that my fellows in the Brahma-life would honour, respect, appreciate and show deference to me!—yet his fellows in the Brahma-life do honour, do respect, appreciate, do show deference to him. Why so? Because, monks, his discerning fellows in the Brahma-life observe that in him those wicked, unprofitable qualities are abandoned.

Just as if, monks, such longing as this should arise in a first-rate[1] thoroughbred steed: O that men would put me in the place of a thoroughbred, feed me with a thoroughbred's food, groom me with a thoroughbred's grooming!—yet men do all these things to him. **[169]** Why so? Because discerning men observe that in him those crafty, roguish tricks, those swervings and crooked ways are abandoned.

In the same way, monks, although no such desires arise in a monk of this sort, yet his fellows in the Brahma-life do none the less honour, respect, appreciate and show deference to him. Why so? Because in their discernment they observe that those wicked, unprofitable qualities are abandoned in him.

§ viii (88). *Disaster* (*a*).[2]

'Monks, if any monk abuses and reviles, rails at the Ariyans who are his fellows in the Brahma-life, it is utterly impossible, it is unavoidable, that he should not come to one or other of ten disasters. What ten?

He fails to attain the unattained, from what he has attained

---

[1] *Bhadda.* [2] N° (b) with eleven results is at XI, § 6.

he falls away,[1] true dhamma is not made clear for him;[2] or else he is over-conceited about true dhamma,[3] or he follows the Brahma-life without delight therein, or he commits some foul offence, or falls into some grievous sickness, or goes out of his mind with distraction; he makes an end with mind confused, and when body breaks up, beyond death, he rises up again in the Waste, the Ill-bourn, the Downfall, in purgatory.

Monks, if any monk abuses and reviles . . . it is unavoidable that he should not come to one or other of these ten disasters.'

§ ix (89). *The Kokālikan.*[4]

[170] Now the Kokālikan monk came to see the Exalted One, and on coming to him saluted him and sat down at one side. So seated he said this to the Exalted One:

'Sir, Sāriputta and Moggallāna have wicked desires, they are a prey to wicked desires.'

'Say not so, Kokālikan! Say not so, Kokālikan! Calm your heart towards Sāriputta and Moggallāna. Of dear virtues are Sāriputta and Moggallāna.'

Then for a second time and yet a third time the Kokālikan monk repeated his words, and a second and third time the

---

[1] *Cf. A.* ii, 252; *G.S.* ii, 185.

[2] *Saddhamm'assa na vodāyati. Comy.* has *sāsana-saddhammā assa vodānaŋ na gacchanti.*

[3] *Cf.* § vi. Seven saddhammas frequently named are: *saddhā, hiri-ottappaŋ, bahussutaŋ, saccaŋ, āraddha-viriya, sati, paññā.* These may be regarded as personal convictions or attainments. (I translate at *K.S.* iii, 69, as 'the seven domains of good,' but I doubt whether this is correct.)

[4] This well-known story is brought in to support the teachings of the previous suttas. It occurs at *Sn.* iii, 10=Lord Chalmers's *Trans.*, p. 156 *ff.*; *S.* i, 149=*K.S.* i, 187; *JA.* iv, No. 481, and the gāthās are quoted *Netti* 132 (177). *Comy.*, which is much the same as at *SnA.* ii, 473; *SA.* i, 216, and *AA.*, *ad loc.*, states that he was the younger or Cūla-Kokālika, not Mahā-K. the disciple of Devadatta. He had abused the great disciples in a former birth. *DhpA.* on *Dhp. v.* 363 describes these gāthās as referring to him. He was a native of the town Kokālī.

Exalted One reproved him with the same words. Thereupon the Kokālikan monk rose up from his seat, saluted the Exalted One, keeping his right side towards him, and departed.

Not long after he had departed the whole body of the Kokālikan monk broke out with pustules of the size of mustard-seed. From being of the size of mustard-seed they grew to the size of lentils, then to that of chick-peas,[1] then to that of kola-nut stones, then to the size of a jujube, then to that of myrobalan, then to that of unripe vilva fruit,[2] then to that of billa fruit. Having grown to that size they burst **[171]**, discharging pus and blood. And there he lay on plantain leaves, just like a poisoned fish.[3]

Thereupon Tudu, the individual Brahmā,[4] went to see the Kokālikan monk, and on reaching him stood on a cloud and said this to him:

'Kokālikan, calm your heart towards Sāriputta and Moggallāna! Of dear virtues are Sāriputta and Moggallāna.'

'Who are you, your reverence?'

'I am Tudu, the individual Brahmā.'

'Were you not pronounced a non-returner by the Exalted One? Then how is it that you come here? See how you have erred in this matter.'[5]

Thereupon Tudu the individual Brahmā addressed the Kokālikan monk in these verses:

In sooth to every man that's born
A hatchet grows within his mouth,
Wherewith the fool, whene'er he speaks
And speaks amiss, doth cut himself.

---

[1] *Kaḷāya=caṇaka, Comy.*

[2] At *Sn.* trans. 'a quince.'

[3] *At the porch of Jetavana monastery.* This later addition and the appearance of Tudu is in the *Jātaka C.*, and the previous sutta in the *Saŋyutta* version is from the Commentaries.

[4] *Pacceka Brahmā.* Tudu had been K's guru, and on his death was pronounced a non-returner by the Master.

[5] *Passa yāva te idaŋ aparaddhaŋ—i.e.*, you can't be a non-returner; a mistake has been made. *JA.* has 'You'll become a yakkha on a dung-hill.'

Who praiseth him who should be blamed
Or blameth who should praisèd be,
He by his lips stores up ill-luck,
And by that ill-luck finds no bliss.

Small is the ill-luck of a man
Who gambling loseth all his wealth.
Greater by far th' ill-luck of him
Who, losing all and losing self,
'Gainst the Wellfarers fouls his mind.

Whoso reviles the worthy ones,
In speech and thought designing ill,
For an hundred thousand periods,
For six and thirty, with five more
Such periods, to purgatory's doomed.[1]

[172] But the Kokālikan monk met his end by that same sickness. When he had made an end he rose up again in Paduma[2] Purgatory, for hardening his heart against Sāriputta and Moggallāna.

Then when the night was far spent, the Brahmā Sahampati shedding radiance lit up Jeta Grove from end to end, and came to see the Exalted One, and on coming to him saluted him and stood at one side. Thus standing the Brahmā Sahampati said this to the Exalted One:

'Sir, the Kokālikan monk has met his end, and having met his end has risen up again in Paduma Purgatory, for hardening his heart against Sāriputta and Moggallāna.' Thus spake the Brahmā Sahampati, and so saying saluted the Exalted One, keeping his right side towards him, and vanished there and then.

But the Exalted One, when that night had gone, addressed the monks, saying:

'Monks, last night when night was waning the Brahmā

---

[1] The first verse is from Mrs. Rhys Davids's trans. at *K.S.* i, 188; the rest from mine at *G.S.* ii, 3.

[2] *Comy.* 'not a special purgatory,' but presumably one where periods are reckoned according to the thousand-petalled lotus.

Sahampati shedding radiance lit up Jeta Grove from end to end, and on coming to me saluted me and . . . standing at one side said this to me' (*and he repeated his words*).

At these words a certain monk said to the Exalted One:

'Pray, sir, how long is the measure of life in Paduma Purgatory ?'

'Long indeed, monk, is the measure of life in Paduma Purgatory. It were no easy thing to reckon it thus: **[173]** So many years or so many centuries or so many thousands of years or so many hundreds of thousands of years.'

'But, sir, can a figure be made ?'

'It can, monk.' Then the Exalted One added:

'Suppose, monk, a Kosalan cartload of twenty measures of sesamum seed, and suppose that at the end of every century one took out a single seed. Sooner would that Kosalan cartload of twenty measures of sesamum seed be used up and finished by this method than the period of the Abbuda Purgatory. Just as are twenty such, such is one Nirabbuda Purgatory. Twenty of these make one Ababa . . . twenty of these one Ahaha . . . twenty of these one Aṭaṭa Purgatory. Of these twenty make one Kumuda Purgatory. Of these twenty make one Sogandhika Purgatory. Of these twenty make one Uppalaka Purgatory; twenty of these one Puṇḍarīka Purgatory, and twenty of these make one Paduma Purgatory.[1] Now, monk, it is in the Paduma Purgatory that the Kokālikan monk has risen up again, for hardening his heart against Sāriputta and Moggallāna.'

Thus spake the Exalted One. The Wellfarer having thus spoken, the Teacher added this further:

[174] In sooth to every man that's born
A hatchet grows within his mouth . . . (*as above*).

---

[1] *SnA.* (but not the others) adds that 'some say that the names of the Purgatories are representations of the lamentations (*e.g., ahaha, ababa, aṭaṭa*) or occupations of their inmates. Others that they are cold Purgatories (and presumably these words represent the chattering of teeth, etc.).'

§ x (90). *The powers.*

Now the venerable Sāriputta came to see the Exalted One. As he sat at one side the Exalted One said this to him:

'Pray, Sāriputta, what are the powers of the monk[1] who has destroyed the cankers? Possessed of what powers does such a monk come to know of the destruction of the cankers: Destroyed in me are the cankers'?

'Tenfold, sir, are the powers of the monk who has destroyed the cankers, possessed of which powers he knows: Destroyed in me are the cankers. What are the ten?

In this matter, sir, by the monk who has destroyed the cankers all compounded things are by right insight clearly seen, as they really are, to be of the nature of impermanence. **[175]** In so far as they are thus clearly seen, this is a power of such a monk, by reason of which power he comes to know: Destroyed in me are the cankers.

Then again, sir, by the monk who has destroyed the cankers all compounded things are seen by right insight, as they really are, as being like unto burning charcoal.[2] This is a power of such a monk, by reason of which power he comes to know: Destroyed in me are the cankers.

Again, sir, the thoughts of such a monk flow towards seclusion,[3] slide and tend to seclusion, come to rest in seclusion, take delight in seclusion, come utterly to cease in all conditions that may give rise to cankers. This, sir, is a power of such a monk, by means of which power . . .

Again, sir, by such a monk the four arisings of mindfulness are made to grow, thoroughly made to grow. In so far as this is so . . . this is a power . . .

Again, sir, by such a monk the four best efforts[4] are made to grow, thoroughly made to grow. In so far as this is so . . . this also is a power . . .

Likewise the four bases of psychic power[5] . . . the five faculties . . . the five powers . . . the seven limbs of wisdom

---

[1] Eight of these are at *A*. iv, 224.

[2] One of many similes for *kāmā* at *M*. i, 130.

[3] *Vivekà-*. *Cf. K.S.* v, 223. [4] *Ibid.*, 219. [5] *Ibid.* 225, etc.

. . . the Ariyan eightfold Way is made to grow, thoroughly made to grow. In so far as in a monk the Ariyan eightfold Way is made to grow, thoroughly made to grow, this also, sir, is a power of the monk who has destroyed the cankers, by reason of which power he comes to know: Destroyed in me are the cankers.

These, sir, are the ten powers of the monk who has destroyed the cankers.'

Chapter X.—The Lay-Followers.

§ i (91). *Pleasures of sense.*

[176] Once the Exalted One was staying near Sāvatthī at Jeta Grove in Anāthapiṇḍika's Park. On that occasion the housefather Anāthapiṇḍika came to see the Exalted One . . . as he sat at one side the Exalted One said this to him:

[177] 'Housefather, there are these ten enjoyers of sense-pleasures[1] found existing in the world. What ten?

Herein, housefather, a certain enjoyer of sense-pleasures seeks after wealth unlawfully and arbitrarily; so doing he makes not himself happy and cheerful,[2] he does not share with others, he does no meritorious deeds.

Again a certain enjoyer of sense-pleasures seeks after wealth unlawfully and arbitrarily; but in so doing he does make himself happy and cheerful, but he does not share with others, and he does no meritorious deeds.

Again a certain enjoyer of sense-pleasures seeks after wealth unlawfully and arbitrarily; but in so doing he does make himself happy and cheerful, he does share with others, he does meritorious deeds.

Then again a certain enjoyer of sense-pleasures seeks after wealth both lawfully and unlawfully, both arbitrarily and not so; but in so doing he makes not himself happy and cheerful, nor does he share with others, nor does he do meritorious deeds.

Again a certain enjoyer of sense-pleasures seeks after wealth both lawfully and unlawfully, both arbitrarily and not, and does make himself happy and cheerful, yet shares not with

---

[1] *Kāmā-bhogin*=luxurious. Three sorts are described at *K.S.* iv, 235-41 to the headman Rāsiya, arranged in the same tedious way, but doubtless held suitable for the comprehension of housefathers.

[2] As at *D.* i, 51; *G.S.* ii, 75, etc.

others and does no meritorious deeds. Yet again a certain enjoyer of sense-pleasures, seeking after wealth in this way, does all three of these things.

Now again, housefather, a certain enjoyer . . . seeking after wealth lawfully, not arbitrarily, in so doing neither makes himself happy and cheerful, nor does he share with others, nor does he do meritorious deeds.

Again a certain enjoyer . . . seeking after wealth lawfully, not arbitrarily, [**178**] though he makes himself happy and cheerful, yet shares not with others and does no meritorious deeds.

Yet again a certain enjoyer . . . seeking after wealth lawfully, not arbitrarily, does make himself happy and cheerful, does share with others, does meritorious deeds. But he makes use of his wealth with greed and longing, he is infatuated therewith, heedless of the danger, blind to his own salvation.[1]

On the other hand a certain enjoyer of sense-pleasures, seeking after wealth lawfully, not arbitrarily, and making himself happy and cheerful, both shares with others and does meritorious deeds, but makes use of his wealth without greed and longing, without infatuation; he is not heedless of the danger, he is not blind to his own salvation.

Now, housefather, in the case where this enjoyer of sense-pleasures seeks wealth unlawfully and arbitrarily, and in so doing makes not himself happy and cheerful, shares not with others and does no meritorious deeds, in such a case this enjoyer of sense-pleasures is culpable on three counts: First he seeks wealth unlawfully and arbitrarily; this is the first count. Then he makes not himself happy and cheerful; this is the second count. Thirdly he shares not his wealth with others and does no meritorious deeds; this is the third count on which he is culpable. Thus, housefather, he is culpable on three counts.

Now, housefather, in the case where the enjoyer of sense-

[1] As at *K.S.* iv, 237 *n.*, but there, as here, *ajjhāpanna* (guilty of an offence) should read *ajjhopanna*. See Trenckner-Andersen-Smith, *P. Dict. s.v.*

pleasures seeks wealth unlawfully and arbitrarily, but in so doing makes himself happy and cheerful, yet shares not with others and does no meritorious deeds, in such a case he is culpable on two counts, praiseworthy on one count. For he seeks wealth unlawfully and arbitrarily; this is the first count on which he is culpable. He makes himself happy and cheerful; this is the count on which he is praiseworthy. He shares not with others and does no meritorious deeds; this is the second count on which he is culpable. Thus, housefather, he is culpable on two counts, praiseworthy on one.

[179] Now, housefather, in the case where this enjoyer of sense-pleasures seeks wealth unlawfully and arbitrarily, and in so doing makes himself happy and cheerful, shares with others and does meritorious deeds—in such a case he is culpable on one count, praiseworthy on two. For in seeking wealth unlawfully and arbitrarily he is culpable on one count; in making himself happy and cheerful, sharing with others and doing meritorious deeds, he is praiseworthy on two counts. Thus, housefather, he is culpable on one, praiseworthy on two counts.

Again, housefather, in the case where he seeks wealth both lawfully and unlawfully, both arbitrarily and not, and in so doing neither makes himself happy and cheerful, nor shares with others nor does meritorious deeds—in such a case he is praiseworthy on one count, culpable on three. For in seeking wealth lawfully and not arbitrarily he is praiseworthy on this one count only; in doing so unlawfully and arbitrarily he is culpable on this first count; in not making himself happy and cheerful he is culpable on this second count; in not sharing or doing meritorious deeds he is culpable on this third count. Thus, housefather, on this one count he is praiseworthy, on these three he is culpable.

Again, housefather, in the case where he seeks wealth both lawfully and unlawfully, both arbitrarily and not, but in so doing makes himself happy and cheerful, yet shares not with others and does no meritorious deeds—in such a case he is praiseworthy on two counts, culpable on two. For in seeking wealth lawfully and not arbitrarily he is praiseworthy on this first count; in doing so unlawfully and arbitrarily he is culpable on this first count; in making himself happy and cheerful he is praiseworthy on this second count; in not sharing with others and doing no meritorious deeds he is culpable on this second count. Thus, housefather, **[180]** he is praiseworthy on two counts, culpable on two counts.

Again, housefather, in the case where he seeks wealth both lawfully and unlawfully, both arbitrarily and not, and in so doing makes himself happy and cheerful and shares with others and does meritorious deeds—in such a case he is praiseworthy on three counts, culpable on one. For in seeking wealth lawfully and not arbitrarily he is praiseworthy on this first count; in doing so unlawfully and arbitrarily he is culpable on this one count; in making himself happy and cheerful he is praiseworthy on this second count; in sharing with others and doing meritorious deeds he is praiseworthy on this third count. Thus on these three counts he is praiseworthy, culpable on one count.

Yet again, housefather, in the case where he seeks after wealth lawfully not arbitrarily, but in so doing makes not himself happy and cheerful, nor shares with others and does no meritorious deeds—in such a case he is praiseworthy on one count, culpable on two. For in seeking wealth lawfully not arbitrarily, on this one count he is praiseworthy; in not making himself happy and cheerful he is culpable on this first count; in not sharing and not doing meritorious deeds he is culpable on this second count. Thus on this one count he is praiseworthy, on these two he is culpable.

Again, housefather, in the case where he seeks after wealth lawfully, not arbitrarily, and in doing so makes himself happy and cheerful, yet shares not with others and does no meritorious deeds—in this case he is praiseworthy on two counts, culpable on one count. For in seeking wealth lawfully, not arbitrarily, he is praiseworthy on this first count; in making himself happy and cheerful he is praiseworthy on this second count; in not sharing with others and not doing meritorious deeds he is culpable on this one count. **[181]** Thus, housefather, on these two counts he is praiseworthy, culpable on this one count.

Now, housefather, in the case where he seeks after wealth lawfully, not arbitrarily, and in s doing makes himself happy and cheerful and likewise shares with others and does meritorious deeds, yet makes use of his wealth with greed and longing, is infatuated therewith, heedless of the danger and blind to his own salvation—in such a case this man is praiseworthy on three counts, culpable on one count. For in seeking wealth lawfully, not arbitrarily, he is praiseworthy on this first count; in making himself happy and cheerful he is praiseworthy on this second count; in sharing and doing meritorious deeds he is praiseworthy on this third count; but as he makes use of his wealth with greed and longing . . . he is culpable on this one count. Thus on these three counts he is praiseworthy, on this one count culpable.

But, housefather, in the case where this enjoyer of sense-pleasures seeks after wealth lawfully, not arbitrarily, and in so doing makes himself happy and cheerful, and also shares his wealth with others and does meritorious deeds therewith, and further makes use of it without greed and longing, without infatuation, and is not heedless of the danger or blind to his own salvation—in such a case he is praiseworthy on four counts. For in seeking after wealth lawfully, not arbitrarily, on this first count he is praiseworthy; in making himself happy and cheerful he is praiseworthy on this second count; in sharing his wealth with others and doing meritorious deeds therewith, on this third count also he is praiseworthy; in making use of his wealth without greed and longing, without infatuation, in not being heedless of the danger, in not being blind to his own salvation, on this fourth count he is praiseworthy. Thus on these four counts he is praiseworthy.

Thus, housefather, these ten sorts of enjoyers of sense-pleasures are found existing in the world.

Now, housefather, of these ten enjoyers of sense-pleasures he who seeks after wealth lawfully, not arbitrarily, [**182**] and in so doing makes himself happy and cheerful, also shares his wealth with others, and further does meritorious deeds therewith, and yet makes use of his wealth without greed and longing, without infatuation, heedful of the danger and alive to his own salvation[1]—of these ten this one is best and chief, topmost, highest and supreme. Even as from a cow comes milk, from milk cream, from cream butter, from butter ghee, from ghee the skimmings of ghee, and that is reckoned the best—even so of these ten enjoyers of sense-pleasures . . . this one is reckoned best and chief, topmost, highest and supreme.'

§ ii (92). *Guilty dread.*

Now the housefather Anāthapiṇḍika went to see the Exalted One. . . . As he sat at one side the Exalted One said this to him:

'Housefather, when the fivefold guilty dread[2] is allayed in the Ariyan disciple and he is possessed of the four limbs of stream-winning, and has well seen and well penetrated the Ariyan Method by insight, he may, if he so desire, himself proclaim thus of himself: I am one who has cut off the doom of Purgatory, of rebirth in the womb of an animal, in the realm of ghosts; cut off is the Waste, the Ill-bourn, the Downfall. A Stream-winner am I, one not doomed to the Downfall, assured, bound for enlightenment. Now, housefather, what is the fivefold guilty dread that is allayed in him?

[183] It is that guilty dread, housefather, which he who kills begets in this same visible state, as a result of his killing; it is that guilty dread about the life to come, which he who kills begets; also that mental suffering and dejection which he experiences. By abstaining from killing he begets no guilty dread in this same visible state nor for the life to come; he experiences no mental suffering and dejection. Thus in him who abstains from killing that guilty dread is allayed.

That same guilty dread, housefather, which he who takes what is not given . . . who is a wrongdoer in sexual desires

---

[1] This phrase and the simile following are at *G.S.* ii, 104 (*A.* ii, 95), where the reading is *mokkho* for our *pāmokkho*. *Cf. S.* iii, 264.

[2] Almost the same as at *K.S.* v, 333, but here reckoned a Ten—*i.e.*, freedom from the fivefold guilty dread, possession of the four elements of stream-winning and understanding of the Ariyan Method.

. . . who tells lies . . . who is under the influence of liquor fermented and distilled and so given[1] to negligence—the guilty dread which, as a result of these things, he begets in this same visible state, also about the life to come, also that mental suffering and dejection—these are not begotten by him who abstains from occasions (or places) for taking liquor fermented and distilled. Thus in him who so abstains that guilty dread is allayed.

These are the five guilty dreads that are allayed. And of what four limbs of stream-winning is he possessed?

Herein, housefather, the Ariyan disciple is possessed of unwavering confidence in the Enlightened One thus: That Exalted One is arahant, a perfectly enlightened one, perfect in knowledge and practice, a Wellfarer, world-knower, unsurpassed trainer of men who can be trained, Teacher of devas and mankind, a Buddha is the Exalted One.

He is possessed of unwavering confidence in dhamma, thus: Well proclaimed by the Exalted One is dhamma, to be known in this visible state, not limited to time, but of the sort to come and see, that leads onward, to be understood personally by the discerning ones.

He is possessed of unwavering confidence in the Order, thus: Well faring onward is the Exalted One's order of disciples, straight faring onward, faring onward by the Method, dutifully faring onward; that is, the four pairs of individuals, the eight individual men—that is the Exalted One's order of disciples, one worthy of reverence, worthy of worship, worthy of offerings, worthy of salutations with clasped hands, an unsurpassed field of merit for the world.

He is possessed of the virtues dear to the Ariyans, virtues unbroken, [**184**] whole, unspotted, giving liberty, praised by the discerning ones, virtues untainted, conducing to concentration of mind. Of these four limbs of stream-winning he is possessed.

And what in him is the Ariyan Method that is well seen and well penetrated by insight?

---

[1] *-pamāda-ṭṭhāyī.*

Herein, housefather, the Ariyan disciple thus reflects: This being, that is. By the arising of this, that arises. This not being, that is not. By the ending of this, that comes to cease. That is to say: Because of ignorance, the activities; because of the activities, conscious being; because of conscious being, name-and-shape; because of name-and-shape, the six centres of sense; because of the six centres of sense, contact; because of contact, feeling; because of feeling, craving; because of craving, grasping; because of grasping, becoming; because of becoming, birth; because of birth, decay-and-death, grief, lamentation and woe, dejection and despair come into being. Thus is the arising of this whole mass of Ill.

But with the waning and utter ceasing without remainder of ignorance, the ending of the activities; with the ending of the activities, the ending of conscious being; with the ending of conscious being, the ending of name-and-shape; with the ending of name-and-shape, the ending of the six centres of sense; with the ending of the six centres of sense, the ending of contact; with the ending of contact, the ending of feeling; with the ending of feeling, the ending of craving; with the ending of craving, the ending of grasping; with the ending of grasping, the ending of becoming; with the ending of becoming, the ending of birth; with the ending of birth, decay-and-death, grief, lamentation and woe, dejection and despair cease to become.

Thus is the ending of this whole mass of Ill, and this for him is the Ariyan Method well seen, well penetrated by insight.

Now, housefather, since for the Ariyan disciple these five guilty dreads are allayed, and he is possessed of these four limbs of stream-winning, and for him this Ariyan Method is well seen and well penetrated by insight, he, if he so desires, himself may proclaim of himself: Destroyed is Purgatory for me, destroyed is birth in the womb of an animal, destroyed is the realm of ghosts, destroyed is (rebirth in) the Waste, the Ill-bourn, the Downfall, in Purgatory; a stream-winner am I, one not doomed to the Downfall, one assured, bound for enlightenment.'

§ iii (93). *View.*

[**185**] On a certain occasion the Exalted One was staying near Sāvatthī at Jeta Grove in Anāthapiṇḍika's Park.

Now the housefather Anāthapiṇḍika left Sāvatthī at an early hour to visit the Exalted One. But it occurred to him: It is not time to see the Exalted One, he is in retirement. Nor is it time to see the monks who make the mind to grow;[1] those monks are in retirement. Suppose I were to pay a visit to the Park where dwell the Wanderers who hold other views.

So the housefather Anāthapiṇḍika drew near the Park where dwelt the Wanderers holding other views.

Now on that occasion the Wanderers holding other views, having come together in a great company, were sitting engaged in divers childish talk, all talking loudly, making a great noise and din. But when they saw the housefather Anāthapiṇḍika approaching, while yet he was at some distance, they hushed each other, saying: 'Make little noise, your reverence! Make no noise, your reverence! Here comes the housefather Anāthapiṇḍika, a disciple of Gotama the recluse. This housefather Anāthapiṇḍika is one of those disciples of Gotama the recluse, householders clad in white, who live at Sāvatthī. Now those worthies are fond of little noise, they are schooled to little noise, they speak in praise of little noise. Maybe, if he sees our company making little noise, he will think it worth his while to draw near.' So those Wanderers kept silence.

So the housefather Anāthapiṇḍika drew near to those Wanderers, and on coming to them greeted them courteously, and after courteous greetings and reminiscent talk [**186**] sat down at one side. As he thus sat those Wanderers said this to him:

'Tell us, housefather, what views does Gotama the recluse hold?'

'Indeed, sirs, I know not all the view of the Exalted One.'

[1] *Mano-bhāvanīyā=mano-vaḍḍhanakā, Comy. Cf. K.S.* iii, 1 (where I mistranslate). The whole introductory part is at *M.* ii, 23; *cf. D.* iii, 37.

'You say you know not all the view of Gotama the recluse, housefather. Then tell us what view the monks hold.'

'Indeed, sirs, of the monks also I know not all the view.'

'Well, housefather, since you know not all the view either of Gotama the recluse or of the monks, tell us what sort of view you yourself hold.'

'This, sirs, indeed were no hard task—to tell you of what sort of view I am myself. But first let your reverences expound your own views. Afterward it will be no hard task for me to expound what views I hold myself.'

At these words a certain Wanderer said this to the housefather Anāthapiṇḍika: 'Eternal is the world; this is truth; any other view is infatuation. That is the view I hold, housefather.'

And yet another Wanderer said: 'Not eternal is the world; this is truth; other view is infatuation. That is the view I hold, housefather.'

And yet another . . . and another said: 'Limited is the world . . . unlimited is the world . . . soul[1] is body . . . soul is one thing, body another . . . a wayfarer (man)[2] is beyond death, a wayfarer is not beyond death . . . a wayfarer both is and is not beyond death . . . neither is nor is not beyond death,' adding, 'such is my view, housefather.'

At these words the housefather Anāthapiṇḍika said this to those Wanderers:

'Sirs, when this or that worthy says: "I hold this view, housefather: Eternal is the world" **[187]**—such view arises

---

[1] *Jīva* (the living thing) the later Upanishadic term for 'soul' as distinguished from *ātmā*. *Jīva* is the link (individual soul) joining *ātmā* to *attabhāva* (personality).

[2] *Tathāgata*, as I remarked above, I take this term in this context as applied to any man; the *Tathāgata* (*par excellence*) I have translated *Wayfarer*. This set of views is about the only one put in the mouths of the 'Heretics' by the monks. If they used the word *tathāgata* at all, it would not be in the sense used by the Pāli records. *Comy.* generally interprets as 'just a being.' It is unlikely that the Master called himself *Tathāgata*, certainly not *Buddha*. 'Is' means 'survives.'

either from his own lack of close thinking, or it depends on the words of someone else.[1] A view like this has become, is put together, thought out, has arisen dependent on something. Now whatever has become, is put together, thought out, has arisen dependent on something—that is impermanent. What is impermanent, that is Ill. To what is Ill that worthy clings; to what is Ill that worthy resorts. As to the view, sirs: Not eternal is the world—such view also arises either from his own lack of close thinking . . . that view has become . . . whatever has become . . . that is impermanent. What is impermanent, that is Ill. To what is Ill that worthy clings, to what is Ill that worthy resorts. (And the same is to be said of each of the other views.)'

[**188**] At these words those Wanderers said this to the housefather Anāthapiṇḍika:

'Well, housefather, we have all expressed our several views according as we hold them. Do you now tell us what view you hold yourself.'

'Sirs, whatsoever has become, is put together, is thought out, is dependent on something else, that is impermanent. What is impermanent, that is Ill. What is Ill, that is not of me, I am not that, not for me is that the self. Such is my own view, sirs.'

'Well, housefather, since you hold that whatsoever has become, put together . . . is impermanent, and since you hold that the impermanent is Ill, then, housefather, you cling to Ill, you make Ill your resort.'

'Sirs, since whatsoever has become, whatsoever is put together, thought out, dependent on something else, is impermanent; since what is impermanent is Ill; since what is Ill is not of me, I am not that, not for me is that the self—thus is this matter well seen by me as it really is by right insight; and from that Ill I have come to know to the uttermost the escape, as it really is.'

At these words the Wanderers kept silent, were confounded,

---

[1] *Paraghosa*, to be distinguished from *parato ghosa* (voice from the beyond) of *G.S.* i, 79.

hung the head, looked downward, were disappointed, sat unable to make reply.

So the housefather Anāthapiṇḍika, seeing those Wanderers confounded, unable to make reply, rose up from his seat and went to see the Exalted One, and on coming to him, saluted him and sat down at one side. So seated (he related all the conversation he had had with the Wanderers holding other views). Whereupon the Exalted One said: 'Well done, housefather! Well done, housefather! Even thus righteously are infatuated people from time to time to be confuted and rebuked by you.'

Thereupon the Exalted One instructed, stirred, fired and gladdened the housefather Anāthapiṇḍika with a talk about dhamma. And the housefather Anāthapiṇḍika, thus instructed, stirred, fired and gladdened with a talk about dhamma [**189**], rose up from his seat, saluted the Exalted One by keeping his right side towards him, and so departed.

Not long after the housefather Anāthapiṇḍika had gone, the Exalted One addressed the monks, saying:

'Monks, any monk who had been fully ordained in this dhamma-discipline even for a hundred rain-seasons might reasonably from time to time confute and rebuke the Wanderers holding other views just as they have been confuted by the housefather Anāthapiṇḍika.'

§ iv (94). *Vajjiyamāhita.*[1]

Once the Exalted One was staying at Campā on the bank of the Lotus Pond at Gaggarā.

Now the housefather Vajjiyamāhita left Campā at an early hour to see the Exalted One. But it occurred to him: It is not the time to see the Exalted One . . . (*exactly as in the previous sutta with the different name*). . . . [**190**] So those Wanderers kept silence.

So the housefather Vajjiyamāhita drew near to those Wanderers, and on coming to them greeted them courteously

---

[1] *Cf.* § 81. With a number of other laymen said to have won the deathless at *A.* iii, 451.

. . . and sat down at one side. As he thus sat those Wanderers holding other views said this to him:

'Is it true, housefather, as it is said, that Gotama the recluse blames all ascetic ways, that he downright upbraids and reproaches every ascetic who lives the hard life?'

'No indeed, sirs, the Exalted One blames not all ascetic ways, nor does he downright upbraid and reproach every ascetic who lives the hard life. The Exalted One, sirs, blames the blameworthy, praises the praiseworthy. In so doing the Exalted One is a particularizer;[1] that Exalted One is not one who makes sweeping assertions[1] herein.'

At these words a certain Wanderer said this to the housefather Vajjiyamāhita:

'Stay thou, housefather! That Gotama the recluse, whose praises you utter, is a nihilist,[2] one who defines nothing as certain.'[3]

'Nay, sir, herein I speak with good reason. The Exalted One has thus defined: "This is good; that is bad." By thus defining good and bad the Exalted One is a definer. He is no nihilist, not one who defines nothing as certain.'

[191] At these words those Wanderers were silent, were confounded, hung the head, looked downwards, were disappointed, and sat unable to make reply.

Then the housefather Vajjiyamāhita, seeing that those Wanderers were in such a state, rose up from his seat and went to see the Exalted One. . . . As he sat at one side he told the Exalted One of his conversation with those Wanderers holding other views. Then said the Exalted One to him:

'Well done, housefather! Well done, housefather! Even

---

[1] *Vibhajja-vādo, ekaŋsa-vādo.* See *Gotama the Man*, 73, 106; *Sakya*, 357; *K.S.* ii, 2 *n.*; *M.* ii, 197.

[2] *Venayiko*, a nihilist. *Cf. M.* i, 140, *venayiko samaṇo Gotamo sato sattassa ucchedaŋ vināsaŋ vibhavaŋ paññāpeti* (where *MA.* ii, 117 has *vinayati vināsetī ti, vinayo*). *So yeva venayiko.* Here our *Comy.* has, as alternative, *satta-vināsako*; but puts first *sayaŋ avinīto aññehi vinetabbo.* The words also mean 'versed in Vinaya,' in which sense it is taken by *P.E.D.* in this passage. But at *A.* iv, 175, it is 'disciplinarian.'

[3] *Appaññattiko=apaṇṇattiko, Comy.* Perhaps it means 'a Pyrrhonist' (suspender of judgment).

thus reasonably are infatuated people from time to time to be confuted and rebuked by you. Indeed, housefather, I say not that all ascetic ways are to be pursued. Yet do I not say that all ascetic ways are not to be pursued. I say not that every undertaking, that every effort in training should be undertaken and made. Yet do I not say the opposite. I say not, housefather, that every renunciation should be made, nor yet that it should not be made. I say not that every form of release is to be regarded as such,[1] nor yet that it should not be so regarded.

If, housefather, in one practising austerities unprofitable states wax and profitable states wane, such austerity should not be practised, I declare. If in one practising austerities unprofitable states wane and profitable states wax, such austerities should be practised, I declare. **[192]** If in one undertaking the training . . . making an effort . . . making renunciation, unprofitable states wane and profitable states wax, such undertaking of training, such making of effort, such making of renunciation should not be made, I declare.

If in one who regards himself as released by a certain form of release, unprofitable states wax and profitable states wane, such release should not be regarded as such, I declare. But if in one who regards himself as released by a certain form of release profitable states wax and unprofitable states wane, such form of release should be regarded as release, I declare.'

Then the housefather Vajjiyamāhita, being thus instructed, stirred, fired and gladdened by the Exalted One, rose up from his seat, saluted the Exalted One by keeping his right side towards him and departed.

Not long after he had gone the Exalted One addressed the monks, saying: 'Monks, any monk who had been for a long time stained with but few faults in this dhamma-discipline might reasonably from time to time confute and rebuke the Wanderers holding other views, even as they have been confuted by the housefather Vajjiyamāhita.'

---

[1] For different forms see *G.S.* iii, 15, presumably suitable for some but not others.

§ v (95). *Uttiya.*[1]

[193] The Wanderer Uttiya came to see the Exalted One, and on coming to him greeted him courteously, and after the exchange of greetings and reminiscent talk sat down at one side. So seated the Wanderer Uttiya said this to the Exalted One:

'Pray, Master Gotama, is the world eternal? Is this the truth and other view infatuation?'

'I have not declared that it is so, Uttiya.'

'How then, Master Gotama, is the world not eternal? Is this the truth and other view infatuation?'

'This also, Uttiya, I have not declared.'

'Pray, Master Gotama, is the world limited . . . unlimited . . . is the soul body . . . is the soul one thing, body another thing . . . is a wayfarer (man)[2] beyond death or is he not . . . is he beyond death and yet is not . . . is he neither . . . Can it be said this or that is true, that any other view is infatuation?'

'This also, Uttiya, I have not declared. I have not declared whether he is or is not beyond death, or that this is truth, other view infatuation.'

'Pray, Master Gotama, how is this? To each of my questions you reply, "I have not so declared, Uttiya." **[194]** What then has been declared by the worthy Gotama?'

'With full comprehension, Uttiya, I teach dhamma to disciples for the purification of beings, for the overpassing of sorrow and despair, for the going to an end of grief and dejection, for reaching the Method,[3] for the realizing of nibbāna.'

'If then with full comprehension the worthy Gotama teaches dhamma to disciples for the purification of beings . . . for the realizing of nibbāna, pray, will the whole world escape[4] thereby or only half of it or one third part of it?'

At these words the Exalted One was silent.

---

[1] *Cf.* Andersen, *Pāli Reader*, 89 and notes; *Ud.* 67. At *K.S.* v, 20, 146, Uttiya is a monk; so also at *Brethren*, 34, where *Comy.* states that he was originally a Wanderer. As Mrs. Rhys Davids there remarks, it may be the same person.

[2] *Cf.* above, *n.* on § 93. [3] read *Ñāya.* [4] *Niyyissati*, lit. 'go out.'

Then it occurred to the venerable Ānanda: The Wanderer Uttiya must not be allowed to entertain the harmful view that Gotama the recluse, when asked by him an all-important question,[1] let it drop. Can it be that he cannot answer it? Such a view would be loss and sorrow for a long time to the Wanderer Uttiya. So the venerable Ānanda said this to him:

'See now, Uttiya, your reverence, I will make a figure for you. In a figure sometimes intelligent people understand the meaning of what is said. Suppose a border-town of some rājah, with strong foundations, strong walls and towers, but a single gate; and over that gate is set a warden, shrewd and watchful, who keeps out strangers **[195]** and lets in known people. As he patrols all round that town in due order he might not mark a crevice in the wall or a hole big enough for a cat to slip through, nor would he have the knowledge: So many creatures enter or so many creatures leave this town.[2] But this he would know: Whatsoever creatures of any size[3] enter or leave this town, all of them enter or leave by this gate.

Just in the same way, your reverence (that question of yours, namely): "Will the whole world escape thereby or half of it or one third part of it?" is not a matter of urgent importance to the Wayfarer. What he says is this: "Whosoever have escaped, are escaping or will escape from the world, all of them, by abandoning the five hindrances, those defilements of the heart which cause the weakening of insight—all of them with thoughts well established in the four arisings of mindfulness, by making to grow in very truth the seven limbs of wisdom—all of them have escaped, are escaping or will escape by so doing. So as to that question of yours which

---

[1] *Sabba-sāmukkaŋsikaŋ*. *Comy.* has *mayā sabba-pucchānaŋ uttamaŋ pucchaŋ pucchito*, but does not explain how it came to have this meaning. *DA*. i, 277=*AA*. on *A*. iv, 186, *s.v. dhamma-desana*=*MA*. iii, 92=*UdA*. 283, gives the meaning of 'a self-raised teaching, only intelligible to self.' But here the meaning conveyed is 'essential' (Andersen's *Pāli Glossary*). It does not occur in *Saŋyutta Nikāya* or *Comy.*

[2] This sentence is not at *D*. ii, 83, or *K.S*. v, 139.

[3] *Oḷārikā*.

you put to the Exalted One, you asked it from a different point of view.[1] That is why the Exalted One did not explain the matter to you.'

§ vi (96). *Kokanuda.*

[**196**] Once the venerable Ānanda was staying at Rājagaha in the Tapodā Park.

Now the venerable Ānanda rose up in the night when dawn was at hand and went to Tapodā[2] to bathe his limbs. Having done so and come up again he stood clad in one robe drying his limbs.[3]

Now the Wanderer Kokanuda also had risen in the night when dawn was at hand and went to Tapodā Park to bathe his limbs. And he saw the venerable Ananda approaching while yet at a distance; and at the sight of him he said:

'Who are you, your reverence?'

'I am a monk, your reverence.'

'One of what monks?'

'One of the recluses who are the Sakyan's sons.'

'I would ask your reverence a question on a certain point,[4] if your reverence could give the opportunity for answering my question.'

'Ask on, your reverence. When we hear, we shall know.'

'How is it, friend? Does your worship hold the view: Eternal is the world; this is the truth; other view is infatuation?'

'No indeed, your reverence, I hold not this view: Eternal is the world; this is the truth; other view is infatuation.'

'How then, friend? Does your worship hold the view:

---

[1] *Aññena pariyāyena—i.e.*, not *dhamma-pariyāyena* but *añña-titthiya-pariyāyena.*

[2] *Tapodā* means 'hot waters.' *Cf. K.S.* i, 14; *Vin.* iii, 108 (quoted *UdA.* 72); *VinA.* 512. Here was a hot spring, says *SA.* i, 38, because the Brazen Purgatory was beneath.

[3] *Pubbâpayamāno* as at *M.* i, 161, and *SA.* on *S.* i, 8 (where text has *sukkhâpayamāno*). *Comy.* explains 'make them dry as before (*pubba-sadisāni*).' Trenckner, however, at *M.* i, 453 gives a *Comy. pubba-bhāvaŋ gamayamāno.*

[4] *Kiñci-d-eva desaŋ*; *cf.* § 23 above.

Not eternal is the world . . . limited . . . unlimited is the world . . . what is soul, that is body . . . soul is other than body . . . the wayfarer (man) is beyond death . . . is not beyond death . . . both is and is not beyond death . . . neither is nor is not beyond death; this is the truth; other view is infatuation ?'

[197] 'No indeed, your reverence, I hold not this view.'

'Then your worship knows not, sees not ?'

'No indeed, your reverence, I am not one who knows not, sees not. I know. I see.'

'How is it, friend ?[1] When questioned thus: "Does your worship hold this view ? Eternal is the world, and the rest; this is the truth; other view is infatuation," you reply: "No indeed, your reverence, I hold not this view. . . ." When thus questioned: "Does your worship know not, see not ?" you reply: "No indeed, your reverence, I am not one who knows not, who sees not. I know. I see." Pray how is the meaning of your words to be understood ?'

'Your reverence, to regard the world as eternal, as not eternal, as limited, as unlimited; to regard soul as body, as different; to regard the wayfarer (man) as being[2] beyond death, as not being, as both being and not being, as neither being nor not being beyond death, (and to hold) this is the truth; other view is infatuation **[198]**—all this is going-to-view. As regards going-to-view, your reverence, as regards fixing on view, relying on view, as regards obsession by view, rising up[3] from view and rooting up view[4]—since in all that I am one who knows, who sees, why should I profess that I know not, that I see not ? I know, your reverence, I see.'

'Pray what is the venerable one's name ? And by what name do his fellows in the Brahma-life know the venerable one ?'

---

[1] Here the Wanderer uses the familiar *bho*; Ānanda uses *āvuso*, the term of equals in religious standing, but ends up with *āyasmā*, in addressing him. [2] 'Being'='existing.'

[3] *Samuṭṭhāna*. *Comy.*, however, takes this as a synonym of the word before.

[4] This, according to *Comy.*, constitutes the stream-winner.

'Ānanda is my name, your reverence. By that name my fellows in the Brahma-life know me.'

'What! I have been talking with his worship the great teacher and knew not it was the venerable Ānanda! Had I been aware of its being the venerable Ānanda, I would not have said thus much. So let the venerable Ānanda pardon me.'

§ vii (97). *Worshipful.*

'Monks, possessed of ten[1] qualities a monk is worshipful, worthy of honour, worthy of offerings, worthy of being saluted with clasped hands, a field of merit unsurpassed for the world. What ten qualities?

Herein a monk is virtuous, he dwells restrained with the restraint of the obligation, well equipped in range of practice, seeing grounds for fear in minutest faults, he takes up and trains himself in the training of the precepts.

Then he has heard much, he bears in mind what he has heard, stores up what he has heard. **[199]** Whatsoever teachings, lovely in the beginning, lovely midway, lovely at the end (of life), both in spirit and in letter do stress the Brahma-life in its all-round fulness and utter purity—such teachings are much heard by him, borne in mind, repeated aloud, pondered and well penetrated by vision.

Then he has fellowship with the lovely, fellowship and companionship with the lovely.

He is one who has right view, he is possessed of right seeing.

Also he enjoys divers sorts of more-power:[2] From being one he becomes many; from being many he becomes one; manifest or invisible he goes unhindered through a wall, through a rampart, through a mountain, as if through air: he plunges into the earth and shoots up again as if in water; he walks upon the water without parting it, as if on solid ground; he travels through the air sitting cross-legged, like a bird upon the wing; even this moon and sun, though of such mighty power

---

[1] With four qualities at *G.S.* ii, 177; *cf.* above, §§ 7, 30.

[2] *Cf. G.S.* i, 153, 233.

and majesty, he handles and strokes them with his hand; even as far as the Brahma-world he has power with his body.

With the deva-power of hearing, purified and surpassing that of men, he can hear sound both of devas and of humans, whether far or near.

He comes to know the minds of other beings, of other persons, with his own mind grasping them. Of the mind that is lustful he comes to know that it is lustful. Of the mind that is free from lust he comes to know that it is so. Of the mind that is full of hate . . . free from hate . . . deluded . . . free from delusion . . . cramped . . . diffuse . . . lofty . . . mean . . . inferior . . . superior . . . uncontrolled . . . controlled . . . of the mind in bondage, of the mind that is released, he comes to know that it is so.

He calls to mind his former dwelling in divers ways, thus: **[200]** One birth, two births, three . . . ten . . . fifty . . . even a hundred . . . a thousand, a hundred thousand births. He calls to mind the divers folding up of æons, the divers unfoldings of æons, the divers folding-and-unfoldings of æons, (remembering): At that time I bore such a name, was of such a family, of such complexion, thus and thus supported, thus and thus experiencing weal and woe, of such and such a span of life. I, as that one, thence deceasing rose up again at that time; there too I was of such a name, such a family . . . I, as that one, thence deceasing rose up again here. Thus with all details and characteristics he recalls his manifold dwelling aforetime.

Also with the deva-sight, purified and surpassing that of men, he beholds beings deceasing and rising up again, beings both mean and excellent, fair and foul, gone to a happy bourn, gone to an ill-bourn according to their deeds, (so as to say): "Alas, sirs! these beings, given to the practice of evil deeds, of evil words, of evil thoughts, scoffers at the Ariyans, of perverted view and reaping the fruit of perverted view—these beings, when body broke up, beyond death rose up again in the Waste, the Ill-bourn, the Downfall, in Purgatory": or, "Ah, sirs! these beings, given to the practice of good deeds, words and thoughts, no scoffers at the Ariyans, but of sound view and reaping the fruit of sound view—these beings, when body broke up, beyond death rose up again in the Happy Bourn, in the heaven world. Thus with the deva-sight . . . he beholds beings . . . gone according to their deeds.

Then by the destruction of the cankers, in this same visible state he attains the heart's release, the release by insight that is freed of the cankers, himself thoroughly comprehending it, and realizing it abides therein.

[201] Possessed of these ten qualities a monk is worshipful, worthy of honour, worthy of offerings, of salutations with clasped hands, a field of merit unsurpassed for the world.'

§ viii (98). *The elder monk.*[1]

'Monks, possessed of ten qualities an elder monk, in whatever quarter he may live, lives happily. What are the ten?

An elder monk has seen many a day pass, has long ago gone forth, is virtuous . . . (*as in previous sutta*) . . . has heard much . . . penetrated by vision. Moreover by him both of the obligations in full[2] are thoroughly learned by heart and well analyzed, with full knowledge of the meaning, clearly divided sutta by sutta and in minute detail. He is skilled in the rise and settlement of disputes. He delights in dhamma,[3] is pleasant to converse with, he rejoices exceedingly in further dhamma and further discipline. He is content with whatsoever supply of robe and alms-food, of seat and lodging, of medicines and comforts in sickness he may get. He is charming and perfectly composed in his goings out and his comings in, and when he sits down in the house. He wins at pleasure, without effort, without stint, the four stages of musing which are of the clear consciousness,[4] which are concerned with the happy life in this same visible state. By destroying the cankers in this same visible state, thoroughly comprehending the heart's release, the release by insight, he realizes, attains it and dwells therein.

With these ten qualities an elder monk lives happily wherever he may be.

---

[1] *Thero.*

[2] § 32. Twice a month in full.

[3] § 17.

[4] *Abhicetasika*; *cf. G.S.* ii, 24; above, § 30.

§ ix (99). *Upāli.*

Now the venerable Upāli came to see the Exalted One . . . seated **[202]** at one side he said this to the Exalted One:

'Sir, I desire to frequent woodland haunts in the forest, to be a lodger in solitude.'

'Upāli, to frequent woodland haunts in the forest and to be a lodger in solitude are things hard to compass.[1] A hard thing it is to dwell secluded; it is hard to find delight in living alone; the woods strain the mind,[2] methinks, of a monk who has not won concentration of mind. Whoso, Upāli, should say: "Though I have not won concentration of mind, yet I will frequent woodland haunts in the forest, I will be a lodger in solitude," of him it is to be expected that either he will sink to the bottom or float on the surface.[3]

Suppose, Upāli, a great pool of water. Then comes a bull elephant seven[4] or eight cubits[5] in height. He thinks thus: Suppose I plunge into this pool of water and amuse myself with the sport of squirting water into my ears or over my back. When I have enjoyed this sport and washed and drunk and come out again, suppose I go whithersoever it pleases me. So in he goes and does so, comes out again and goes whithersoever it pleases him. How can he do it? The great bulk of his person, Upāli, finds a footing in deep water.

[203] But suppose a hare or a cat[6] should come and say to itself: What difference is there between myself and a bull elephant? Suppose I plunge into this pool of water and amuse myself with the sport of squirting water into my ears or over my back? When I have enjoyed this sport and washed and drunk and come out again, suppose I go whithersoever it pleases me?

---

[1] *Durabhisambhava; cf. S.* v, 454; *Sn.* 429, 701. *Comy.* 'not attainable by weaklings.'

[2] *Haranti mano. Mano* in accusative is rare, but found in *Sn.*

[3] His lustful thoughts will pull him down and his malicious thoughts will keep him afloat.

[4] This simile is not listed in those of *J.P.T.S.*, 1906-7.

[5] *Ratana; cf. Mil. P.* 282 (of the *nāga* Uposatha).

[6] Cats would hardly do this. For the comparative *ko ca . . . ko ca, cf.* § 75 *n.*

So he springs into that pool of water hastily and without consideration. Then this is to be expected of him: Either he will sink to the bottom or float on the surface. Why so? The smallness of his person, Upāli, finds no footing in deep water.

Just in the same way, Upāli, whoso should say: "Though I have not won concentration of mind, yet I will frequent woodland haunts in the forest, I will be a lodger in solitude" —of him it is to be expected that either he will sink to the bottom or float on the surface.

Again, Upāli, suppose a tender boy-child, feeble and lying on his back and playing with his own excrements. What think you, Upāli? Does not this childish sport come to completion and fulness?'

'It does, sir.'

'Well then, Upāli, that boy-child on another occasion, when he has grown older, following on the ripening of the sense-faculties, plays with whatever may be the playthings of such children, such as a toy-plough,[1] tip-cat,[2] somersaults,[3] windmills, leaf-pannikins, toy-carts and toy-bows. Now what think you, Upāli? Does not this game come to be finer and more valued than the former?'

'It does, sir.'

'Well, Upāli, that child later on, when he has grown older owing to the ripening of his sense-faculties, and has come into possession of the five sense-pleasures and is possessed by them, he becomes a prey to them, to objects cognizable by the eye, objects desirable, agreeable, fascinating, attractive: to sounds cognizable by the ear . . . to odours, tastes **[204]** and touches cognizable by nose, tongue and body, things concerned with sensual desires and passionate. Now what

---

[1] Text *vanka*; *v.l.* and *Comy. vankaka*. *DA.* i, 86; *Mil. Pañh.* 229= *Trans.* ii, 32 and *n.* The list is at *M.* i, 266=*F. Dialog.* i.

[2] *Ghaṭika* (Sinh. *kalli*). A short stick is laid over a stone or other stick, and struck into the air with a long stick, and struck again as it revolves in the air.

[3] *Mokkhacika*, *v.l. mokkhaṭika*; *cf. J.P.T.S.*, 1885, p. 49. *Comy.* as at *DA.* i, 86; *Vin.* i, 275. See refs. in *P.E.D.*

think you, Upāli ? Does not this game come to be finer and more valuable than the former ?'

'It does, sir.'

'Now look you,[1] Upāli. A Wayfarer arises in the world, an arahant, one rightly enlightened, perfect in knowledge and practice, a Wellfarer, world-knower, an unsurpassed trainer of men who can be trained, a teacher of devas and mankind, an awakened one, an Exalted One. He makes known this world, with its Devas, its Māras, its Brahmās, its recluses and brāhmins, its host of devas and mankind, himself realizing it by his own comprehension. He teaches dhamma, lovely in the beginning, lovely midway, lovely at the end (of life), both in its meaning and its letter; he shows forth the Brahma-life utterly fulfilled and purified. Then a housefather or housefather's son or one reborn in some family or other hears that dhamma. On hearing that dhamma he wins faith in the Wayfarer. In possession of that faith which he has won he ponders thus: Oppressive is the home-life, a way of dust ! The way of going forth is of the open air. It is no easy thing for one living the household life to practise the Brahma-life in all its completeness, in utter purity like a polished shell. How if I were to get the hair of my beard shorn and, donning the saffron robe, were to go forth from home to the homeless ? Then he, some time later on, abandoning the whole mass of his wealth whether small or great, abandoning his circle of kinsmen whether small or great, gets the hair of his beard shorn, dons the saffron robes and goes forth from home to the homeless.

He, having thus gone forth, having entered upon the way of life in the training followed by the monks, abandoning the slaying of creatures abstains therefrom. He lives as one who has laid down the rod, who has laid down the knife, who has scruples; he is kind and has compassion for every living thing. Abandoning the taking of what is not given he abstains therefrom. He lives as one who takes only what is given, who waits for what is given; he lives with a self that

---

[1] *Vo*, not *nipāta-mattaŋ*, as *Comy*. What follows is at *G.S.* ii, 221 *ff*.

has become pure, not by stealth. Abandoning the unchaste life he lives chaste, lives a life aloof, abstaining from the sexual act, [205] from dealings with womenfolk. Abandoning falsehood he abstains therefrom; he speaks the truth, joins truth to truth,[1] unswerving, reliable, no deceiver of the world. Abandoning slanderous speech he abstains therefrom. When he hears something at one place he spreads it not abroad elsewhere to cause dissension among these folk. When he hears something at another place he spreads it not abroad elsewhere to cause dissension among those folk.

Thus he reconciles those who are at variance and confirms the friendly. He delights in harmony, finds pleasure therein, rejoices in harmony and utters words that make for harmony. Abandoning bitter speech he abstains therefrom. Whatever speech is blameless, pleasing to the ear, affectionate, speech that goes to the heart, is urbane, delights many folk—such speech does he utter. Abandoning idle babble he abstains therefrom. He is one who speaks in season, speaks of facts, speaks sense, speaks according to dhamma, speaks according to the discipline. He speaks words worth treasuring up, words seasonable, reasonable, discriminating and concerned with profit.

He is one who abstains from injury to seed-life and plant-life; he lives on one meal a day, refrains from food at night and at unseasonable hours; from flowers, scents, unguents, adornments and finery, from shows of nautch-dancing and singing, from beds high and broad, from taking gifts of gold and silver, from gifts of uncooked grain, gifts of uncooked flesh, from gifts of women and girls, female and male slaves, of goats and sheep, fowls and swine, elephants, cattle, horses and mares. He abstains from gifts of fields, cultivated or waste, from buying and selling, sending messengers or going as such, from cheating with scales, [206] copper vessels or measures, from taking bribes to pervert justice, from cheating and crooked ways. He abstains from cutting, flogging, binding, highway robbery, plundering and deeds of violence.

He is content with a robe sufficient to protect the body,

---

[1] *Sacca-sandho.*

with alms-food enough for his belly's need. Wherever he may go he takes these with him. Just as for instance a bird upon the wing, wherever it may fly, flies with the load of its wings, even so a monk is content with a robe . . . with alms-food . . . and takes these with him. Possessed of this Ariyan mass of morals, he experiences in himself the bliss of blamelessness.

Seeing an object with the eye he is not misled by its outer view nor by its lesser details. Since coveting and dejection, evil, unprofitable states, might flow in upon one who lives with the faculty of the eye uncontrolled, he applies himself to such control, sets a guard over the faculty of eye and attains control thereof.

Hearing a sound with the ear or with the nose smelling a scent or with the tongue tasting a savour or with body contacting tangibles, or with mind cognizing mental states, he is not misled by their outer view nor by their lesser details. But since coveting and dejection, evil, unprofitable states, might flow in upon one who lives . . . he sets a guard over the faculty of mind, attains control thereof. Thus possessed of this Ariyan restraint of faculties he experiences in himself unadulterated bliss.

In his goings out and his comings in he acts composedly. In looking in front and looking behind . . . in bending or relaxing . . . in wearing his robe and bearing outer robe and bowl . . . in eating, drinking, chewing and tasting . . . in easing himself, in going, standing, sitting, sleeping, waking, in speaking and keeping silence he acts composedly.

Possessed of this Ariyan mass of morals and this Ariyan restraint of the [**207**] faculties and composure, he resorts to a secluded lodging-place, a forest, the root of a tree, a hill, ravine, grotto or cave, a charnel-field, a jungle-path, an open space, a heap of straw. Thus gone to the forest or root of a tree or a lonely place,[1] he sits down cross-legged, keeping his body erect and fixing attention in front of him. Then abandon-

---

[1] For this passage *G.S.* ii, 224, has, 'After his meal when he has returned from his alms-round.'

ing the hankering after the world, he abides with heart freed therefrom, he cleanses his heart of hankering. Abandoning the taint of ill-will; with heart free from ill-will he abides having regard for the welfare and feeling compassion for every living thing; he cleanses his heart of the taint of ill-will. Abandoning sloth-and-torpor he remains freed therefrom, wide-awake, mindful, composed, and cleanses his heart of sloth-and-torpor. Abandoning distraction-and-flurry he abides undistracted at heart in the inner self, he cleanses his heart of distraction-and-flurry. Abandoning doubt-and-wavering he abides as one who has transcended them; no longer questioning this or that in things profitable, he cleanses his heart of doubt-and-wavering.

Thus abandoning these five hindrances, these taints of the heart which cause the weakening of wisdom, aloof from sense-desires, aloof from unprofitable states, he enters on the first musing, which is accompanied by thought directed and sustained, born of seclusion, zestful and easeful, and so abides.

Now what think you, Upāli ? Is not this way of living[1] more excellent and choice than his former ways ?'

'It is, sir.'

'Now, Upāli, my disciples coming to see this dhamma in the self[2] follow after woodland haunts in the forest and solitary lodging; but not if they have attained their own good do they dwell [there].[3]

Again, Upāli, a monk, by calming down thought directed and sustained[4] . . . attaining the second musing so abides. Now what think you, Upāli ? Is not this way of living more excellent and choice than his former way of living ?'[5]

'It is, sir.'

'Indeed, Upāli, my disciples coming to see this dhamma in

---

[1] *Nanvāyaŋ vihāro* (=*nanu ayaŋ v.*).

[2] *Imam pi kho attani dhammaŋ sampassamānā.*

[3] *No ca kho tāva anuppatta-sadatthā viharanti.* I take this to mean that, as soon as one has won realization, he should return to the outer world to teach and help. Or is it to be translated, 'but, not having realized (*an-uppatta-*), they stay there (in the forest)' ?

[4] *Cf. G.S.* ii, 206 *ff.*

[5] These words are repeated after each item.

the self follow after woodland haunts in the forest and solitary lodging; [**208**] but not if they have attained their own good do they dwell there.

Again, Upāli, a monk, by the fading out of zest, disinterested . . . attains and abides in the third musing. . . .

Again, Upāli, by abandoning both ease and discomfort a monk . . . attains and abides in the fourth musing. . . .

Again, Upāli, passing utterly beyond all sense of object, by the coming to an end of sense-reaction, by paying no attention to the diversity of sense, but realizing: Unlimited is space, a monk attains to the plane of the infinity of space and so abides.

Yet again, Upāli, passing utterly beyond the plane of the infinity of space, realizing: Unlimited is consciousness, a monk attains to the plane of the infinity of consciousness and so abides . . . passing utterly beyond the plane of the infinity of consciousness, realizing: There is nothing at all, he attains the plane of nothingness . . . passing utterly beyond the plane of nothingness, realizing: This is the real,[1] this is the best, [**209**] he attains and abides in the plane of what is neither-consciousness-nor-unconsciousness . . . passing utterly beyond that, he attains the ending of consciousness and feeling, and so abides; and by insight beholding it he knows that in himself the cankers are destroyed.

Now what think you, Upāli? (In each of these stages) is not this way of living more excellent and choice than his former ways?'

'It is, sir.'

'My disciples, Upāli, because they behold this dhamma in the self, follow after woodland haunts in the forest and solitary lodging; but not if they have attained their own good do they dwell there.

Come then, Upāli, do thou dwell in the Order. Dwelling in the Order will be pleasant for thee.'[2]

---

[1] *Santaŋ* (*sat*), gen. trans. 'peace' (?).

[2] Upāli. Our *Comy.* has much the same as that on the Upāli verses at *Thag. v.* 249=*Brethren*, 168, but probably our Upāli was not the barber, so called; for in this passage he wishes to go to the forest (which

§ x (100). *Unfit to grow.*

'Monks, by not abandoning these ten conditions one cannot grow[1] to realize arahantship. What ten ?

Passion, malice, delusion, wrath, grudge, depreciation, spite, jealousy, stinginess. By not abandoning these ten one cannot grow to realize arahantship.

Monks, by abandoning these ten conditions one can grow to realize arahantship. What ten ?

Passion . . . stinginess.'

---

was not the natural inclination of 'Vinaya' Upāli); whereas at *Thag.*, *loc. cit.*, he says, 'Send me *not* away, lord, to dwell in the forest !' The Master replies, 'Bhikkhu, you, dwelling in the forest will develop one subject (*dhura*) only; whereas if you dwell with us you will become proficient both in 'book'-knowledge (*gantha*) and insight.' Nor was he 'one who went forth in faith.' Our *Comy.* conjectures that the Master restrained him for the purpose of afterwards declaring him *etad agga* of Vinaya-reciters ! Hence there is a probable confusion of two or more Upālis. *Cf. Gotama the Man*, 215.

[1] *Abhabbo* (not becomable).

CHAPTER XI.—IDEAS OF A RECLUSE.[1]

§ i (101). *Ideas.*

[210] 'Monks, three ideas of a recluse, if made to grow, made much of, complete seven (other) conditions. What three ?

I am now come to a state of being an outcast. My life is dependent upon others. I must now behave myself differently.

These three ideas of a recluse . . . complete seven conditions. What seven ?

He is one who ever and always makes no pause in action[2] or practice of virtue: he does no harm to any one, he is without self-conceit, he is eager for the training; **[211]** as regards the necessaries of life he thinks: This is[3] my object; he dwells ardent in energy.

Thus, monks, these three ideas of a recluse, if made to grow, if made much of, complete these seven conditions.'

§ ii (102). *Limbs of wisdom.*[4]

'Monks, these seven limbs of wisdom, if made to grow, if made much of, complete the threefold knowledge. What are the seven ?

The limb of wisdom that is mindfulness, that which is investigation of dhamma, energy, zest,[5] tranquillity, concentration, and the limb of wisdom that is equanimity. These seven complete the threefold knowledge.[6] What is that ?

---

[1] *Cf.* § 48. 'Recluse' for *samaṇa* (*çramaṇa*) is not perfectly fitting, for such were not solitaries. 'Austere' is perhaps nearer the meaning. The usual comment is *samita-pāpatta* (calmed as to wickedness).

[2] *Satata-kārī . . . vuttī.*

[3] *Idam atthan ti'ssa=ime paccayā ti.* So also *Comy.* but text has several *v.ll.*

[4] *K.S.* v, 50.

[5] *K.S.* omits.

[6] Bases of psychic power at *K.S.* v, 236.

In this connexion a monk recalls his manifold former dwelling, for instance: One birth . . . two births and so forth. . . . Thus with all details and characteristics he recalls his manifold former dwelling.

With the deva-sight, purified and surpassing that of men . . . he comes to know how beings go according to their deeds.

By destroying the cankers . . . he realizes the heart's release, the release by insight, and abides therein.

So these seven limbs of wisdom, monks, complete this threefold knowledge.'

§ iii (103). *Wrongness.*

'Because of wrongness, monks, there is failure,[1] not making good. How so?

From wrong view proceeds wrong thinking; from that, wrong speech. **[212]** From wrong speech, wrong action. From wrong action, wrong living; from that, wrong effort. From wrong effort proceeds wrong mindfulness; from that, wrong concentration. From wrong concentration proceeds wrong knowledge. From wrong knowledge proceeds wrong release.

Thus, monks, because of wrongness there is failure, not making good.

But because of rightness there is making good, not failure. How so?

From right view proceeds right thinking; from that, right speech. From right speech proceeds right action; from that, right living. From right living proceeds right effort; from that, right mindfulness. From right mindfulness proceeds right concentration; from that, right knowledge. From right knowledge proceeds right release.

Thus, monks, because of rightness there is making good, not failure.'

---

[1] *Virādhanā. Comy. soggato maggato ca virajjhanaŋ; cf. D.* ii, 287, *kathaŋ ārādhanā hoti, kathaŋ hoti virādhanā?* where *Comy.* expl. as *sampādanā* and *asampādanā*.

§ iv (104). *The seed.*

'Monks, for a man, a person, who has wrong view, wrong thinking, speech, action, living, effort, mindfulness, concentration, wrong knowledge and wrong release, whatsoever bodily action is carried to completion and fulfilment according to that view, whatsoever action of speech, of mind, whatsoever intention, aspiration, resolve, whatsoever activities of mind (directed thereto) there may be—all those states conduce to what is unpleasant, not delightful, not charming, not profitable, to what is painful. What is the cause of that? Monks, the view is bad.

Suppose, monks, a nimb-seed[1] or a seed of creeper or bitter gourd be planted in moist soil. [213] Whatever essence it derives from earth or water, all that conduces to its bitterness, its acridity, its unpleasant taste. What is the cause of that? The bad nature of the seed, monks.

Just so in a man, a person of wrong view, of wrong thinking . . . of wrong release, whatsoever bodily action is carried to completion and fulfilment, whatsoever action of speech . . . of mind, whatsoever intention, aspiration, resolve, activities of mind (directed thereto) there be, all those states conduce to what is unpleasant . . . to what is unprofitable, to what is painful. What is the cause of that? Monks, the view is bad.

But, monks, for a man, a person who has right view, right thinking, speech, action, living, effort, mindfulness, concentration, right knowledge and right release, whatsoever intention, aspiration, resolve, whatsoever activities of mind (directed thereto) there may be, all those states conduce to what is pleasant, delightful, charming, profitable, to what is pleasure. What is the cause? Monks, that view of his is auspicious.[2]

Suppose, monks, a seed of sugar-cane or paddy or grape be planted in moist soil. Whatsoever essence it derives from earth and water, all that conduces to its sweetness, pleasant-

---

[1] As at *A.* i, 32=*G.S.* i, 28. [2] *Bhaddikā.*

ness and delicious flavour. What is the cause of that? The happy nature of the seed.

Just so, monks, in a man of right view . . . [**214**] right knowledge and right release, whatsoever intention, aspiration, resolve, activities of mind (directed thereto) there may be, all those states conduce to what is pleasant . . . to what is pleasure. What is the cause of that? Monks, the view is auspicious.'

§ v (105). *By knowledge.*[1]

'Monks, when ignorance leads the way, by the reaching of states unprofitable, shamelessness and recklessness follow in its train. In one who is swayed by ignorance and is void of sense wrong view springs up. Wrong view gives rise to wrong thinking, wrong thinking to wrong speech, wrong speech to wrong action, wrong action to wrong living, wrong living to wrong effort, wrong effort to wrong mindfulness, wrong mindfulness to wrong concentration, that to wrong knowledge, and that to wrong release.[2]

But, monks, when knowledge leads the way, by the attainment of profitable states the sense of shame and self-restraint follow in its train. In one who is swayed by knowledge and has good sense, right view springs up. Right view gives rise to right thinking . . . right concentration gives rise to right knowledge, and that to right release.'

§ vi (106). *Causes of wearing out.*

[**215**] 'Monks, there are these ten bases of wearing out.[3] What ten?

For one who has right view, monks, wrong view is worn out, and those divers evil, unprofitable states which come into being because of wrong view—those also are worn out in him; while those divers good, profitable states, due to right view, reach fulness of culture.[4]

---

[1] *Cf. K.S.* v, i (without the last two items).

[2] Wrong release means that the method is wrong and the result illusory. One is deluded into thinking he has won the essential.

[3] *Nijjara*; *cf. G.S.* ii, 209. [4] *Bhāvanā-pāripūriṃ*, *A.* i, 43.

For one who has right thinking . . . right speech, action, living, effort, mindfulness, concentration [**216**], for one who has right knowledge and right release, wrong release is worn out, and those divers good, profitable states, due to right release, reach fulness of culture.

These, monks, are the ten basic causes of wearing out.'

§ vii (107). *The ablution.*

'Monks, in the southern districts there is an ablution.[1] On that occasion there are food and drink, food soft and hard, syrups and drinks,[2] dancing, singing and music of instruments. But, monks, this is just a wiping, not a wiping out,[3] I declare. For that ablution is low, common, vulgar, unariyan, not bringing profit; it conduces not to revulsion, to fading, to ending, to calming, to comprehension and illumination, it conduces not to nibbāna.

Now, monks, I will teach you the Ariyan ablution, a washing which conduces to downright revulsion, fading, ending, calming, comprehension, illumination, which conduces to nibbāna—an ablution whereby beings whose nature it is to be reborn are released from rebirth; whereby beings whose nature it is to decay are released from decay; whereby beings whose nature it is to die are released from death; whereby beings to whom belong sorrow and lamentation, woe, dejection and despair, are released therefrom. Do ye listen to it attentively and I will speak.'

'We will, sir,' replied those monks to the Exalted One, who said:

'And of what sort, monks, is that Ariyan ablution, that washing which conduces to downright revulsion [**217**], whereby beings are released from rebirth, decay and death, sorrow . . . and despair?

---

[1] *Dhovana. Comy.* 'a bone-washing ceremony. In those parts bodies are not burned but buried. Afterwards the bones are dug up, dried and washed with ceremonies of lamentation.' For Ariyan washing, *cf. S.* v, 389 (*ajjhattaŋ nahānaŋ*).

[2] *Leyya peyya* as at *Mil. P.* 2.

[3] *N'etaŋ n'atthī ti* (non-existence) as at beginning of next sutta. We find *atthitā* and *n'atthitā*. Or should it be *naṭṭhī* (*nassati*), annihilation?

For one who has right view, monks, wrong view is washed away, and those divers evil, unprofitable states which come to be because of wrong view—those also are washed away from him; while those divers good, profitable states due to right view reach fulness of culture.

For one who has right thinking, right speech, action, living, effort, mindfulness, concentration, for one who has right knowledge and release, wrong knowledge and wrong release are washed away from him, and those divers good, profitable states due to right release reach fulness of culture.

This indeed, monks, is the Ariyan ablution, a washing which conduces to downright revulsion, fading, ending, calming, comprehension, illumination, to nibbāna—an ablution whereby beings whose nature it is to be reborn, to decay, to die, to suffer sorrow and lamentation . . . dejection and despair are released therefrom.'

§ viii (108). *Physic.*

[218] 'Monks, physicians administer a purge for checking sickness arising from bile, phlegm, for checking sickness arising from wind.[1] This is a purge, monks, but not a wiping out, I declare. Now, monks, I will teach you the Ariyan purge, a purge which works and fails not; a purge by which beings subject to rebirth are released therefrom, by which beings subject to decay and death, subject to sorrow and lamentation, woe, dejection and despair are released therefrom. Do ye listen to it attentively and I will speak.'

'We will, sir,' replied those monks to the Exalted One, who said this:

'And of what sort, monks, is the Ariyan purge which works and fails not, that purge whereby beings . . . are released from rebirth, decay and death . . . woe, dejection and despair?

For one who has right view . . . right release, wrong view and the rest are purged away, **[219]** and those divers evil, unprofitable states which come to be because of wrong view—

[1] *Cf. K.S.* iv, 155 and notes; refs. to *Mil. P.* 134, etc.

those also are purged away from him; while those divers good, profitable states which come to be because of right view reach fulness of culture. This indeed, monks, is the Ariyan purge which works and fails not, a purge whereby beings . . . are released.'

§ ix (109). *Ejection.*[1]

'Monks, physicians administer an emetic for checking sickness . . . (*the whole as in the previous sutta with* 'vomited' *for* 'purged'). **[220.]**

§ x (110). *To be ejected.*

'Monks, these ten states are to be ejected. What ten ?

In one who has right view wrong view is ejected[2] . . .' **[221]** (*the whole as in the previous two suttas, with* 'ejected' *for* 'purged').

§ xi (111). *Adept* (*a*).

Now a certain monk came to see the Exalted One . . . and said:

'Sir, the words "an adept, an adept,"[3] are used. Pray, sir, how far is a monk an adept ?'

'In this matter, monk, a monk is possessed of the right view of an adept, of an adept's right thinking, speech, action, living, effort, mindfulness, concentration, of an adept's right knowledge and release. Thus far a monk is an adept.'

§ xii (112). *Adept* (*b*).

[222] 'Monks, there are these ten qualities of an adept. What ten ?'

(*The same as before.*)

---

[1] *Niddhamanaŋ* is the *uddāna* (title) of this sutta, for text's *vamaṇa* (vomit).

[2] *Niddhantā=niddhamitā, Comy. Uddāna* has no title.

[3] *Asekho* (not-pupil). At *K.S.* ii, 84 *ff.*, it is possible to be one by insight and to declare gnosis without any super-powers. At *K.S.* v, 154, 265, the adept is such by cultivating the Arisings of Mindfulness; at *K.S.* v, 204, the Five controlling faculties. It is generally applied to defining the arahant, *K.S.* iii, 69. For an adept's virtues see *G.S.* i, 199. Thus the arahant is *asekha*, a master, not a pupil. In theosophical teachings the *asekha* is the next, but much higher stage than that of Arahant, and this is called 'the fifth initiation.'

CHAPTER XII.—THE DESCENT.

§ i (113). *Not-dhamma (a).*

'Monks, not-dhamma and not-aim are to be understood, likewise dhamma and aim. When one knows these two (pairs of) things, one should fare onward according to dhamma and according to aim. And what are not-dhamma and not-aim ?

Wrong view, wrong thinking, speech, action, living, effort, mindfulness, concentration, wrong knowledge and release. These are called "not-dhamma and not-aim."

[223] And what are dhamma and aim ?

Right view and the rest . . . right knowledge and release. These are called "dhamma and aim."

Monks, not-dhamma and not-aim are to be understood . . . when one knows these two things, one should fare onward according to dhamma and aim.'

§ ii (114). *Not-aim (b).*

(*The same, but the opposites are taken together in each case.*)

'Wrong view, monks, is not-dhamma; right view is dhamma; also whatsoever divers evil, unprofitable states come to be because of wrong view, that is not-aim; whereas whatsoever divers good, profitable states due to right view reach fullness of culture, that is the aim.

Wrong thinking is not-dhamma . . . wrong speech and the rest . . . wrong knowledge **[224]** and wrong release are not-dhamma; also whatsoever divers evil, unprofitable states come to be because of . . . wrong release, that is not-aim; whereas whatsoever divers good, profitable states, due to right release, reach fullness of culture, that is profit.

Monks, not-dhamma and not-aim are to be understood. . . . What I have said was said because of this.'

§ iii (115). *Not-dhamma* (*c*).

[225] 'Monks, not-dhamma should be understood and dhamma; not-aim should be understood and aim. Knowing not-dhamma and dhamma, knowing not-aim and aim according to dhamma and aim should one fare onward.'

Thus spake the Exalted One. So saying the Wellfarer rose from his seat and entered the residence.[1]

Now not long after the Exalted One was gone it occurred to those monks: The Exalted One, having given us this pronouncement in brief,[2] without explaining its meaning in detail, has risen from his seat and entered the residence, after saying: 'Monks, not-dhamma should be understood, and so forth.' Now who could expound to us in detail the meaning of this pronouncement made in brief by the Exalted One?

Then it occurred to those monks: There is this venerable Ānanda, one praised by the Master[3] and honoured by his discerning fellows in the Brahma-life. This venerable Ānanda is capable of expounding in detail the meaning of this pronouncement in brief of the Exalted One. Suppose we go to see the venerable Ānanda, suppose on coming to him we ask the venerable Ānanda the meaning of this. According as he shall expound it to us, so will we bear it in mind.

Accordingly those monks went to see the venerable Ānanda and on coming to him greeted him courteously, and, after exchange of greetings and reminiscent talk, sat down at one side. So seated they said this to him:

'Ānanda, your reverence, the Exalted One, after having given us this pronouncement in brief: "Monks, not-dhamma should be understood and dhamma; not-aim should be understood and aim. Knowing not-dhamma and dhamma, knowing not-aim and aim, according to dhamma and aim

---

[1] At *SA.* ii, 388, *Comy.* thinks the Master retired so that Ānanda might have a chance to sing his praises in his absence! *Cf. K.S.* iv, 57, for a similar instance, where a few words are worked up into a discourse, the truth of which is afterwards confirmed by the teacher himself.

[2] *Uddesaŋ*. *Comy. mātikaŋ nikkhipitvā*, 'laying down a summary.'

[3] *Comy.* 'in five matters declared topmost.'

should one fare onward "—but without expounding its meaning in detail he rose from his seat and entered the residence.

Now, your reverence, to us here it occurred not long after the Exalted One was gone: [226] The Exalted One having given us this pronouncement. . . . Now who could expound to us in detail the meaning of this pronouncement in brief? Then it occurred to us: There is this venerable Ānanda, one praised by the Master. . . . Let the venerable Ānanda go into details.'[1]

'Now, your reverences, suppose a man aiming at sound timber,[2] searching for sound timber, ranging about in his quest for sound timber, should neglect the root, the trunk of a great upstanding tree of sound timber, and think he must search for sound timber in the branches and foliage. This is just what has happened to your reverences. For, though you had the Master face to face, you passed by[3] that Exalted One, and think that I am the one to be questioned in this matter. Your reverences, that Exalted One knowing knows and seeing sees; he has become the eye, he has become knowledge, become dhamma, become Brahma; proclaimer and expounder is he; dispenser of weal, giver of the deathless, master of dhamma, the Wayfarer[4] is he. Surely that was the time for you to approach and ask the Exalted One [227] the meaning of this. According as the Exalted One should expound it to you, so should ye bear it in mind.'

'Surely it is true, your reverence, that the Exalted One knowing knows and seeing sees. . . . Moreover that was indeed the time for us to approach and ask the Exalted One the meaning of this. According as the Exalted One should expound it to us, so should we bear it in mind. Still we thought: The venerable Ānanda is praised by the Master and honoured by his discerning fellows in the Brahma-life. The venerable Ānanda is capable of expounding to us in detail the meaning of this pronouncement made in brief by the

---

[1] *Vibhajatu.* [2] Simile at *M.* i, 111; *S.* iv, 94; below, text 256.

[3] *Atisitvā* (*atisarati*), but *Comy. atiyitvā*; *cf. A.* i, 66 and *acceti.*

[4] *Tathāgato.*

Exalted One. So let the venerable Ānanda go into details and not think it a troublesome thing.'[1]

'Well, your reverences, do you listen. Attend carefully and I will speak.'

'We will, your reverence,' replied those monks to the venerable Ānanda, who then said:

'Now as to that pronouncement which the Exalted One made in brief . . . namely, "Monks, not-dhamma should be understood," and so forth—now, your reverences, what is not-dhamma and what is dhamma? What is not-aim and what is aim?

Your reverences, wrong view is not-dhamma, right view is dhamma; and those divers evil, unprofitable states that come to be because of wrong view, that is not-aim; whereas those divers good, profitable states, due to right view, which come to fullness of culture, this is the aim . . . (*as in previous sutta*) . . . **[228]** Right release, your reverences, is dhamma, and those divers good, profitable states, due to right release, which come to fullness of culture, that is the aim.

Thus, your reverences, as to that pronouncement made in brief . . . such do I understand to be the meaning in detail of what was not explained in detail. But if ye wish it ye should approach the Exalted One himself and question him on this matter, and according as the Exalted One explains it to you so do ye bear it in mind.'

'Very good, sir,' replied those monks to the venerable Ānanda, and praised his words, thanked him and rose up and went away to see the Exalted One. On coming to him they saluted him . . . and said:

'Sir, as to that pronouncement made in brief by the Exalted One . . . not long after the Exalted One was gone it occurred to us . . . (*and they repeated their thoughts of a visit to Ānanda*) **[229]** . . . So, sir, we went to see the venerable Ānanda and asked him the meaning of this. Then to us here the meaning

---

[1] *Agaruŋ katvā*; *cf. SA.* ii, 389, 'without making us ask again and again,' the trouble may refer to either party. Elsewhere I have translated, 'and not put us to further trouble.'

of it was well detailed with these reasons, in these words, in these particulars by the venerable Ānanda.'

'Well done, monks! Well done, monks! A sage is Ānanda, of great wisdom is Ānanda, monks. If you had come to me and asked me the meaning of this, I should have explained it even so myself, even as it is explained by Ānanda. This is just the meaning of that thing, and so do ye bear it in mind.'

§ iv (116). *Ajita.*

Now Ajita[1] the Wanderer came to see the Exalted One, and on reaching him greeted him courteously, and after the exchange of greetings and reminiscent talk sat down at one side. So seated [**230**] Ajita the Wanderer said:

'Master Gotama, we have a fellow in the Brahma-life who is reckoned a sage. He has thought out as many as five hundred mental states[2] with which the holders of other views when reproached can know: We are reproached.'

But the Exalted One called to the monks, saying: 'Monks, do ye bear in mind the grounds for (being called) a sage?'

'Now is the time for this, Exalted One! Now is the time for this, O Exalted One! Whatever the Exalted One may say, on hearing it from the Exalted One the monks will bear it in mind.'

'Then listen, monks. Pay careful attention and I will speak.'

'We will, sir,' replied those monks to the Exalted One, who then said:

'In this matter, monks, a certain one counters and crushes speech that is not-dhamma speech[3] with similar speech. Thereby he excites a company that is a not-dhamma company so that it becomes uproarious and noisy, shouting: "A sage indeed! A sage indeed!"

---

[1] Not found elsewhere. There are monks of this name, and the well-known man of the hair garment. *V.l.* of *uddāna* has *Ājina*.

[2] *Citta-ṭṭhānā* (the word does not occur in *Indexes* or *P. Dict.*)= *citt'uppāda, Comy.*

[3] Not *about* dhamma, but according to dhamma.

And the same thing happens when a certain one with not-dhamma speech counters and crushes dhamma-speech.

Again in this matter a certain one with speech that is both dhamma-speech and not-dhamma speech counters and crushes what is not-dhamma speech, with the same results to a company that is a not-dhamma company.

Yet again a certain one with dhamma-speech counters and crushes not-dhamma speech. Thereby he excites a dhamma-company, thereby that dhamma-company becomes uproarious and noisy, shouting: "A sage indeed! A sage indeed!"

[**231**] Monks, what is not-dhamma should be understood, and what is dhamma. What is the aim should be understood and what is not-aim. Knowing both not-dhamma and dhamma, knowing both not-aim and the aim one should fare onward according to dhamma and the aim. And what, monks, is not-dhamma, what is dhamma? What is the aim and what is not-aim?

(*Here he repeats* § iii). . . . It was on this account that these words were said.'

§ v (117). *Sangārava* (*a*).

[**232**] Now the brāhmin Sangārava[1] came to see the Exalted One, and on coming to him greeted him courteously, and, after the exchange of greetings and reminiscent talk, sat down at one side. So seated he said this to the Exalted One:

'Pray, Master Gotama, what is "the hither shore," what is "the further shore"?'

'Wrong view, Sangārava, is the hither shore, right view the further shore. Wrong thinking, speech, action, living, effort, mindfulness, concentration, wrong knowledge and wrong release are the hither shore. Right view and the rest are the further shore.

This, brāhmin, is the hither shore: that is the further shore.

Few are they of mortal men
Who have reached the further shore;
But the crowd of other folk
On this side fare up and down.

[1] *Cf. S.* i, 183; v, 121; *A.* i, 168; iii, 230.

When dhamma rightly is revealed,
Who by dhamma fare along,
They shall reach the shore and pass
The realm of death so hard to cross.

Giving up the state of darkness
Let the wise pursue the light.
Giving up home for the homeless,
In solitude where joys are rare,
Let him long for bliss unbounded.
Leaving lusts and owning naught
Let the wise man cleanse himself
From the passions of the heart.

[**233**] They who in the limbs of wisdom
Rightly make the mind to grow,
Glad to have surrendered clinging,
Glad to be from grasping free,
Canker-cured they, all-resplendent
I' the world are quenchèd utterly.'[1]

§ vi (118). *Hither and further shore* (*a*).

'Monks, I will teach you the hither shore and the further shore. Do ye listen attentively. Apply your minds and I will speak.'

'We will, sir,' replied those monks to the Exalted One, who said:

'And what, monks, is the hither shore and what is the further shore? Wrong view, monks, is the hither shore, right view is the further shore . . . wrong release is the hither shore, right release is the further shore.' (*And he repeated the gāthās of the previous sutta.*)

§ vii (119). *The Ariyan descent* (*a*).

[**234**] Now on that occasion the brāhmin Jāṇussoṇi,[2] the day being the sabbath, having washed his head and put on a

---

[1] *Parinibbuto.* Gāthās at *Dhp. vv.* 85-9; *K.S.* v, 22; again next sutta.

[2] A chapter below is called by his name. *Cf. K.S.* ii, 52 *n.*; v, 2; *A.* i, 36; also Bhāradvāja, the fire-man, *K.S.* i, 207.

fresh pair of linen cloths, holding a handful of wet *kusa* grass, was standing aside not far from the Exalted One.

And the Exalted One saw the brāhmin Jāṇussoṇi . . . so standing, and on seeing him said this:

'How is it, brāhmin, that you on this sabbath day, having washed your head and put on a fresh pair of linen cloths, thus stand aside holding a handful of wet *kusa* grass?'

'Today, Master Gotama, is the (ceremony of) descent of the brāhmin clan.'

'In what manner, brāhmin, is this descent?'

'Herein, Master Gotama, it being the sabbath, brāhmins wash the head, put on a fresh pair of cloths, smear the floor with wet cowdung, strew it with wet *kusa* grass, and make their bed between the boundary[1] and the fire-house.[2]

Rising up thrice in that night, with clasped hands they do homage to fire, saying: "We come down[3] to your worship, we come down to your worship!" Then they feed the fire with oblation of oil of butter and fresh butter. When the night has passed they feed brāhmins with choice food both hard and soft. Thus, Master Gotama, is the descent of the brāhmins.'

'Brāhmin, the descent (ceremony) of the brāhmins is one thing, the descent by the discipline of the Ariyan is quite another thing.'

'Pray, Master Gotama, in what way is the descent by the discipline of the Ariyan done? Well for me if the worthy Gotama would teach me dhamma as to the descent by the discipline of the Ariyan.'

'Then, brāhmin, do you listen. Give heed carefully and I will speak.'

'I will, master,' replied the brāhmin Jāṇussoṇi to the Exalted One, who said:

---

[1] *Velā* (? boundary). *Comy.*, which has nothing to say about all this, simply has 'heap of sand.' I have a reference to *Aśvalāyana Grihya Sūtra* ii, 3 (of the *Śrauta Sūtras*), but I cannot verify it.

[2] *Agyâgāra.*

[3] *Paccorohāma.* The word is used of stepping down from a vehicle or into water. Did they originally step into the fire?

[235] 'In this matter, brāhmin, the Ariyan disciple thus ponders: From wrong view (comes) an evil ripening, both in this same visible state and in the future state. Thus pondering he abandons wrong view, he descends from wrong view. . . . From wrong intent comes an evil ripening . . . from wrong speech . . . wrong action . . . wrong living, wrong effort, mindfulness and concentration . . . from wrong knowledge and wrong release comes an evil ripening, both in this same visible state and in the future state. Thus pondering he abandons wrong release, descends from wrong release. Thus, brāhmin, is the descent by the discipline of the Ariyan.'

'Indeed, Master Gotama, one thing is the descent of the brāhmins, quite another thing is the descent by the discipline of the Ariyan.[1] Why, Master Gotama, compared with the descent by the discipline of the Ariyan that of the brāhmins is not worth one sixteenth part of it.[2]

[236] It is excellent, Master Gotama! It is excellent, Master Gotama![3] It is as if one should raise the fallen, open up the hidden, point out the way to one gone astray, hold up a shining light so that they who have eyes may see objects. Thus has dhamma been expounded in divers ways by the worthy Gotama. I myself, worthy Gotama, do go for resort to the awakened one, to dhamma and to the order of monks. Let the worthy Gotama reckon me as a lay-follower from this day forth, so long as life shall last, as one who has gone to him as resort.'

§ viii (120). *The Ariyan descent* (*b*).

'Monks, I will teach you the Ariyan descent. Do ye listen to it. . . .

And what, monks, is the Ariyan descent?

In this matter, monks, the Ariyan disciple thus ponders: From wrong view comes an evil ripening . . . (*and he repeated that part of the previous sutta down to*) . . . he descends from wrong release.

This, monks, is called "the Ariyan descent."'

---

[1] The brāhmins step into water, the Ariyan disciple steps out of his sin.

[2] See *Appendix*.

[3] *Text* abbreviates this stock paragraph.

§ ix (121). *The harbinger.*

'Just as, monks, the dawn is the forerunner, the harbinger[1] of the sun's arising, even so of profitable states this is the forerunner, the harbinger, namely, right view.

From right view, monks, proceeds right thinking. From right thinking, right speech . . . from right knowledge proceeds right release.'

§ x (122). *Cankers.*

[237] 'Monks, these ten states, if made to grow, if made much of, conduce to the ending of the cankers. What ten?

Right view and the rest . . . right release. These ten states. . . .'

---

[1] *Pubba-nimittaŋ; cf. K.S.* v, 27.

CHAPTER XIII.—PERFECT PURITY.[1]

§ i (123). *States of perfect purity.*

'Monks, these ten states, utterly pure and clear, are not save in the discipline of the Wayfarer. What ten?

Right view, right intent, right speech, right action, right effort, right mindfulness, right concentration, right knowledge and right release.

These are the ten. . . .'

§ ii (124). *States not yet arisen.*

'Monks, these ten states, not yet arisen, arise not save in the discipline of the Wayfarer. What ten?

[238] Right view . . . right release.'

§ iii (125). *States of great fruit.*

'Monks, these ten states, of great fruit, of great advantage, are not save in the discipline of the Wayfarer. What ten?

Right view . . . right release.'

§ iv (126). *Ending in restraint.*

'Monks, these ten states end in restraint of lust, malice and delusion, but only in the discipline of the Wayfarer. What ten?

Right view . . . right release.'

§ v (127). *Conducive.*

'Monks, these ten states conduce to downright revulsion, to fading, ending, calming, comprehension, enlightenment, to nibbāna, but only in the discipline of the Wayfarer. What ten?

Right view . . . right release.'

---

[1] No *uddāna* for this chapter.

§ vi (128). *Made to grow* (*a*).

'Monks, these ten states, if made to grow, if made much of, if not arisen, arise only in the discipline of the Wayfarer. What ten?

Right view . . . right release.'

§ vii (129). *Made to grow* (*b*).

'Monks, these ten states, if made to grow, if made much of, are of great fruit, [**239**] of great profit, but only in the discipline of the Wayfarer. What ten?

Right view . . . right release.'

§ viii (130). *Made to grow* (*c*).

'Monks, these ten states, if made to grow, if made much of, end in the restraint of lust, malice and delusion, but only in the discipline of the Wayfarer. What ten?

Right view . . . right release.'

§ ix (131). *Made to grow* (*d*).

'Monks, these ten states, if made to grow, if made much of, conduce to downright revulsion, fading, calming, comprehension, enlightenment, to nibbāna, but only in the discipline of the Wayfarer. What ten?

Right view . . . right release.'

§ x (132). *Wrong.*

[**240**] 'Monks, there are these ten states of wrongness. What ten?

Wrong view and the rest . . . wrong release. These are the ten. . . .'

§ xi (133). *Right.*

'Monks, there are these ten states of rightness. What ten?

Right view and the rest . . . right release. These are the ten states. . . .'

Chapter XIV.—The Seemly (*a*).[1]

§ i (134). *Right and wrong.*

'Monks, I will teach you the seemly and the unseemly. Do ye listen to it. Pay attention carefully and I will speak.'

'We will, sir,' replied those monks to the Exalted One, who said this:

'And what, monks, is the unseemly?

Wrong view and the rest . . . wrong release. This is called "the unseemly."

And what, monks, is the seemly?

Right view and the rest . . . right release. This is called "the seemly."'

§ ii (135). *Ariyan and unariyan.*

[241] 'Monks, I will teach you the Ariyan and the unariyan dhamma. Do ye listen. . . .

. . . Wrong view . . . is called "unariyan dhamma."

. . . Right view . . . is called "Ariyan dhamma."'

§ iii (136). *Good and bad.*

'. . . Wrong view . . . is called "the bad."

. . . Right view . . . is called "the good."'

§ iv (137). *Aim and not-aim.*

'. . . Wrong view . . . is called "not-aim."

. . . Right view is called "the aim."'

§ v (138). *Dhamma and not-dhamma.*

[242] '. . . Wrong view . . . is called "not-dhamma"; right view . . . is called "dhamma."'

§ vi (139). *With cankers and without.*

'Monks, I will teach you dhamma with cankers and dhamma without cankers. . . .

. . . Wrong view . . . is called "dhamma with cankers."

. . . Right view is called "dhamma without cankers."'

---

[1] *Sādhu*. This chapter has no *uddāna*.

§ vii (140). *Blameworthy and blameless.*

'. . . Wrong view is called " blameworthy dhamma."
. . . Right view . . . is called " blameless dhamma." '

§ viii (141). *Remorse and not-remorse.*

[243] '. . . Wrong view . . . is called "dhamma with remorse."[1]

. . . Right view is called " dhamma without remorse." '

§ ix (142). *Given to heaping up and diminishing.*

'. . . Wrong view is called "dhamma that goes to heaping up" (rebirth).[2]

. . . Right view is called "dhamma that goes to diminishing" (rebirth).'

§ x (143). *Yielding pain and pleasure.*

'. . . Wrong view is called " dhamma that yields[3] pain."
. . . Right view is called " dhamma that yields pleasure." '

§ xi (144). *Pain and pleasure.*

[244] '. . . Wrong view is called "dhamma whose fruit is pain."

. . . Right view is called "dhamma whose fruit is pleasure." '

CHAPTER XV.—THE ARIYAN WAY (*b*).

§ i (145). *Ariyan and unariyan.*

'Monks, I will teach you dhamma that is the Ariyan way, likewise dhamma that is the unariyan way. Do ye listen. . . .

. . . Wrong view is called " the unariyan way."
. . . Right view is called " the Ariyan way." '

§ ii (146). *Bright way and dark way.*

'Monks, I will teach you dhamma that is the bright way, likewise that which is the dark way. . . . Do ye listen. . . .

[245] . . . Wrong view . . . is called " the dark way."
. . . Right view . . . is called " the bright way." '

---

[1] *Tapanīya.* [2] *Ācaya-gāmin.* [3] *Udraya.*

§ iii (147). *True dhamma and false dhamma.*

'. . . Wrong view . . . is called "false dhamma."

. . . Right view . . . is called "true dhamma."'

§ iv (148). *Very-man*[1] *dhamma and its opposite.*

'. . . Wrong view . . . is called "not the dhamma of the very-man."

. . . Right view . . . is called "dhamma of the very-man."'

§ v (149). *To be brought about.*

'. . . Wrong view . . . is called "dhamma not to be brought about."

. . . Right view . . . is called "dhamma to be brought about."

§ vi (150). *To be followed.*

[246] '. . . Wrong view . . . is called "dhamma not to be followed."

. . . Right view . . . is called "dhamma to be followed."'

§ vii (151). *To be made to grow.*

'. . . Wrong view . . . is called "dhamma not to be made to grow."

. . . Right view . . . is called "dhamma to be made to grow."'

§ viii (152). *To be made much of.*

'. . . Wrong view . . . is called "dhamma not to be made much of."

. . . Right view . . . is called "dhamma to be made much of."'

§ ix (153). *To be remembered.*

[247] '. . . Wrong view . . . is called "dhamma not to be remembered."

. . . Right view . . . is called "dhamma to be remembered."'

§ x (154). *To be realized.*

'Monks, I will teach you dhamma to be realized, likewise dhamma not to be realized. Do ye listen. . . .

---

[1] *Sappurisa.*

And what, monks, is dhamma that is not to be realized ?

Wrong view and the rest . . . wrong release. This, monks, is called " dhamma that is not to be realized."

And what, monks, is dhamma that is to be realized ?

Right view and the rest . . . right release. This, monks, is called " dhamma that is to be realized." '

CHAPTER XVI.—PERSONS (*a*).

§ i (155). *Not to be followed.*

' Monks, a person possessed of ten qualities should not be followed. What ten qualities ?

[**248**] A person has wrong view, thinking, speech, action, living, effort, mindfulness, concentration, wrong knowledge and wrong release. Possessed of these ten qualities a person should not be followed.

Possessed of ten qualities a person should be followed. What ten ?

Right view . . . right release. Possessed of these ten a person should be followed.'

§§ ii-x (156-166). *Various persons.*

' Monks, possessed of ten qualities a person should not be associated with . . . should be associated with; should not be cultivated . . . should be cultivated; should not be venerated . . . should be venerated; is not praiseworthy . . . is praiseworthy; is not respected . . . is respected; is not shown deference[1] . . . is shown deference; is not successful . . . is successful; is not purified . . . is purified; conquers not pride . . . conquers pride; [**249**] grows not in insight . . . grows in insight; works much demerit . . . works much merit; what are the ten qualities ?

(In the first term of each pair) He has wrong view . . . wrong release.

(In the second term of each pair) He has right view . . . right release.'

---

[1] Text *appatikkho sappatikkho* (not in *Indexes* or *P. Dict.*). We should read with Burmese MSS. *appatisso sappatisso*.

CHAPTER XVII.—JĀṆUSSOṆI.

§ i (167). *The Ariyan descent* (*c*).[1]

Now at that time the brāhmin Jānussoṇi, the day being the sabbath . . . (*the whole as in last chapter, down to*) . . . 'One thing is the descent of the brāhmins; quite another thing is the descent by the discipline of the Ariyan.'

[**250**] 'Pray, Master Gotama, in what way is the descent by the discipline of the Ariyan? Well for me if the worthy Gotama would teach me dhamma as to this descent.'

'Then, brāhmin, do you listen. Give heed carefully and I will speak.'

'I will, master,' replied the brāhmin Jāṇussoṇi[2] to the Exalted One, who said:

'In this matter, brāhmin, the Ariyan disciple thus ponders: Of the act of taking life the ripening is evil both in this same visible state and in that to come. Thus pondering he abandons taking life, he descends from taking life. . . . Of taking what is not given the ripening is evil. . . . [**251**] Of wrong conduct in things sexual. . . . Of falsehood. . . . Of spiteful speech . . . of bitter speech . . . of idle babble . . . of coveting . . . of harmfulness . . . of wrong view the ripening is evil, both in this same visible state and in the state to come. Thus pondering he abandons wrong view, he descends from wrong view.

Thus, brāhmin, is the descent by the discipline of the Ariyan.'

'Indeed, Master Gotama, the descent of the brāhmin is one thing, quite another thing is the descent by the discipline of the Ariyan. Compared with this latter, the descent of the brāhmin is not worth one sixteenth part of it.[3]

---

[1] There are no more *uddānas* till the Elevens. I have therefore given titles to suit the context.

[2] *Cf.* above, § 119.

[3] See *Appendix*.

It is excellent, Master Gotama! Let the worthy Gotama accept me as a lay-disciple from this day forth so long as life shall last, as one who has so gone to him as resort.'

§ ii (168). *The Ariyan descent* (*d*).

'Monks, I will teach you the Ariyan descent. Do ye listen. . . .'

The Exalted One said:

[**252**] 'Herein, monks, the Ariyan disciple thus ponders: Of the taking of life the ripening is evil . . . (*as in the previous sutta*).

This, monks, is called "the Ariyan descent."'

§ iii (169). *Sangārava* (*b*).[1]

Then Ṣangārava the brahmin came to see the Exalted One, and on coming to him greeted him courteously. . . . Seated at oṇe side, Sangārava the brāhmin said this to the Exalted One:

'Pray, Master Gotama, what is the hither shore and what is the further shore?'

'Taking life, brāhmin, is the hither shore; abstaining therefrom is the further shore. Taking what is not given is the hither shore; abstaining therefrom is the further shore. Wrong conduct in things sexual is the hither shore; abstaining therefrom is the further shore. Falsehood . . . spiteful speech . . . bitter speech . . . idle babble . . . coveting . . . harmfulness . . . wrong view . . . these are the hither shore and abstinence therefrom is the further shore.

This, brāhmin, is (the meaning of) the hither shore and the further shore.

[**253**] Few are they of mortal men
Who have reached the further shore . . .'
(*Gāthās as in* § 117 *and Dhp. vv.* 85-9.)

§ iv (170). *Hither and further shore* (*b*).

'Monks, I will teach you the hither shore and the further shore. Do ye listen. . . .

[1] For (*a*) see § 117.

And what, monks, is the hither shore and what is the further shore?

The taking of life, monks, is the hither shore; abstaining therefrom is the further shore . . . (*as in previous sutta*).

Few are they of mortal men
[254] Who have reached the further shore. . . .'

§ v (171). *Dhamma and not-dhamma* (*d*).

'Monks, not-dhamma and not-aim must be understood, likewise dhamma and the aim. Knowing these two (pairs of) things one should fare onward according to dhamma and the aim. And what is not-dhamma and not-aim?

The taking of life and the rest . . . is called "not-dhamma and not-aim."

And what is dhamma and aim?

Abstaining from these is called "dhamma and the aim." '

§ vi (172). *Dhamma and not-dhamma* (*e*).

[255] 'Monks, not-dhamma and dhamma are to be understood, likewise not-aim and the aim.'

Thus spake the Exalted One. So saying the Welfarer rose up from his seat and entered the residence.

Not long after the Exalted One was gone it occurred to those monks: The Exalted One having given us this pronouncement . . . (*all as in* § 115 *except that they now go to Kacchāna the Great and not Ānanda*) . . . 'Let the venerable Kacchāna the Great go into details.'

[256] 'Now, your reverences, suppose a man aiming at sound timber, searching for sound timber, ranging about in his quest for sound timber, should pass by the root, the trunk of a great upstanding tree of sound timber, and should think he must search for sound timber in the branches and foliage. This is just what has happened to your reverences. For, though you had the Master face to face, you passed by that Exalted One, and think that I am the one to be questioned in this matter.

Your reverences, that Exalted One knowing knows and

seeing sees; he has become the eye, he has become knowledge, become dhamma, become Brahma; proclaimer and expounder is he; dispenser of weal, giver of the deathless; master of dhamma, the Wayfarer is he. Surely that was the time for you to approach and [**257**] ask the Exalted One the meaning of this. According as the Exalted One should expound it to you, so should ye bear it in mind . . . (*as in* § 115 *down to* "as to that pronouncement in brief").

The taking of life is not-dhamma, your reverences; abstaining therefrom is dhamma, and those divers evil, unprofitable states which come to be because of taking life—that is not-aim. Whereas those divers good, profitable states, due to abstinence therefrom, which reach fulness of culture—that is the aim.

Taking what is not given is not-dhamma, your reverences; abstaining therefrom [**258**] is dhamma. Wrong conduct in sexual desires . . . falsehood . . . spiteful speech . . . bitter speech . . . idle babble . . . coveting . . . harmfulness . . . wrong view is not-dhamma; abstaining therefrom is dhamma, and those divers good, profitable states, due to abstaining from wrong view and the rest, which reach fullness of culture—that is the aim . . .' (*as in* § 115 *they go to the Master, who confirms what has been said by Kacchāna*). [**259.**]

§ vii (173). *Dhamma and not-dhamma* (*f*).

[**260**] 'Monks, not-dhamma must be understood and dhamma; likewise not-aim and the aim . . . (*all as in previous sutta*).

[**261**] . . . Herein what was said was said because of this.'

§ viii (174). *Due to lust, malice and delusion.*

'Monks, the taking of life is threefold, I declare. It is due to lust, malice and delusion. Taking what is not given . . . wrong conduct in sexual desires . . . falsehood . . . spiteful speech . . . bitter speech . . . idle babble . . . coveting . . . [**262**] harmfulness . . . wrong view is threefold, I declare. It is due to lust, malice and delusion.

Thus, monks, lust is the coming-to-be of a chain of causal

action;[1] so is malice. Delusion, monks, is the coming-to-be of a chain of causal action. By destroying lust, by destroying malice, by destroying delusion comes the breaking up of the chain of causal action.'

§ ix (175). *All-round approach.*

'Monks, this dhamma is approachable all round, it is not unapproachable.[2] How?

For one who takes life, monks, abstinence therefrom is the way of all-round approach. For one who takes what is not given . . . for one who does wrong in sexual desires . . . who tells lies . . . utters spiteful speech . . . bitter speech . . . idle babble . . . for one who is covetous . . . harmful . . . for one who has wrong view, monks, right view is the way of all-round approach.

Thus, monks, this dhamma is approachable all round, not unapproachable.'

§ x (176). *Cunda the silversmith.*

[**263**] Once the Exalted One was staying at Pāvā in the mango grove of Cunda, the son of the silversmith.

Now Cunda, son of the silversmith,[3] came to see the Exalted One, and on coming to him saluted him and sat down at one side. So seated the Exalted One said this to him:

'Cunda, in whose purifying rites do you find satisfaction?'

'Sir, the brāhmins of the west who carry waterpots and

---

[1] *Kamma-nidāna-sambhava*; *cf. A.* i, 134=*G.S.* i, 117, etc.

[2] *Saparikkamanaŋ* and *aparikkamanaŋ* are explained at *Vin.* iii, 151 (*Sutta-vibhanga*, *Sanghādisesa*, No. vi, and *Pāṭimokkha* (Dickson), *J.R.A.S.*, Oct., 1875, p. 13), and *VinA.* iii, 569, as *sa-upacāraŋ* and *anupacāraŋ*. If a house or vihāra is built for a monk or monks, it must have sufficient space all round it for a bullock-cart to be driven. The only other place where the word seems to occur is at *M.* i, 43, *samo maggo parikkamanāya . . . samaŋ tiṭṭhaŋ parikkamanāya*.

[3] Cunda, the silversmith, apparently, at whose house the Master probably died. *Cf. D.* ii, 126. *Putta* signifies membership of a clan or family, *e.g. devaputta*.

wear lily-garlands, who are purifiers by water, fire-worshippers, enjoin purifying rites.[1] In those I find satisfaction.'

'In what way, Cunda, do those brāhmins who carry waterpots . . . enjoin their purifying rites?'

'Herein, sir, those brāhmins who carry waterpots . . . thus instruct a follower: "Come now, good fellow, rise up in good time from your bed and touch the ground. If you do not touch the ground, touch wet cowdung. If you do not do that, touch green grass; if not that, worship fire; if not that, adore the sun with clasped hands; if not that, descend into water for the third time[2] in the evening." Thus, sir, do the brāhmins who carry waterpots . . . who go down into water, enjoin purifying rites. In them do I find satisfaction.'

'Well, Cunda, the purifying rites enjoined by those brāhmins are quite different from the purification in the discipline of the Ariyan.'[3]

'In what way, sir, [**264**] is there purification in the discipline of the Ariyan? Well for me, sir, if the Exalted One would teach me dhamma about the discipline of the Ariyan.'

'Then, Cunda, do you listen. Pay attention carefully and I will speak.'

'I will, sir,' replied Cunda, the son of the silversmith, to the Exalted One, who said this:

'Threefold, Cunda, is defilement by body; fourfold is defilement by speech; threefold is defilement by thought. And how is defilement by body threefold?

Herein, Cunda, a certain one takes life, he is a hunter, bloody-handed, given up to killing and slaying, void of compassion for all living creatures.[4] A certain one takes what is not given; he takes with thievish intent things not given to him, the property of another person, situated in jungle or in village. In sexual desires he is a wrong-doer; he has intercourse with girls in ward of mother or father, brother,

---

[1] *Cf. S.* iv, 312=*K.S.* iv, 218.

[2] *Sāyā-tatiyaka ; cf. A.* i, 296; ii, 206.

[3] For another comparison *cf. G.S.* i, 146.

[4] As at *M.* i, 286=*Further Dialog.* i, 203. As our *Comy.* has no remarks, consult *MA.* ii, 330 *ff.*

sister or relatives (or clan); with girls lawfully guarded,[1] already pledged to a husband and protected by the rod,[2] even with girls crowned with the flower-garland (of betrothal). Thus, Cunda, threefold is defilement by body.

And how, Cunda, is defilement by speech fourfold ?

Herein again, Cunda, a certain one is a liar. When cited to appear before the council or a company or amid his relatives or guild-men or before the royal family and asked to bear witness with the words: " Come, good fellow ! Say what you know," though he knows not, he says, " I know "; though he knows, he says, " I know not "; though he has not seen, he says he saw; though he saw, he denies it. [265] Thus for his own sake or that of others or to get some carnal profit or other he deliberately utters falsehood.

Also he is a slanderer. Hearing something at one place he proclaims it somewhere else to bring about a quarrel between the parties; what he has heard here he repeats there to bring about a quarrel between the parties. Thus he breaks up harmony, foments strife between those discordant, discord is his delight; exulting in and passionately fond of discord, he utters speech that makes for discord.

Also he is of harsh speech. Whatsoever speech is rough,[3] cutting, bitter about others, abusive of others, provoking wrath and conducive to distraction—such speech does he utter. He is given to idle babble, he speaks out of season, speaks unrealities; he speaks things unprofitable, what is not-dhamma and not-discipline; he utters speech not worth treasuring up, speech unreasonable and not worth listening to, undiscriminating and unconcerned with profit.

Thus, Cunda, defilement by speech is fourfold.

And how is defilement by mind threefold ?

Herein, Cunda, a certain one is covetous, he is one who covets

---

[1] *Dhamma-rakkhitā*. *M.* i, 286 omits this term. *PvA.* 72, in the same context, adds *gottarakkhitā*, and has a list of ten such.

[2] *Sa-paridaṇḍa*, ' ? guarded by a stick,' according to *P. Dict.* and *MA.*, but *daṇḍa* may be taken in the sense of penalty.

[3] *Aṇḍakā* (*v.l. kaṇṭakā*). *MA.* gaṇḍakā (excrescences or warts on a faulty tree).

the property of another, thinking: O that what is another's were mine! He is malevolent of heart, the thoughts of his heart are corrupt, thus: Let these beings be slain, come to destruction,[1] be destroyed, not exist at all. Also he has wrong view, he is perverse in outlook, holding: There is no gift, no offering, no sacrifice; there is no fruit or ripening of deeds well done or ill done; this world is not, the world beyond is not; there is no mother, no father, no beings supernaturally born; there are no recluses and brāhmins in the world who have gone right, who fare rightly, men who by their own comprehension have realized this world and the world beyond and thus declare.

Thus, Cunda, defilement by mind is threefold.

[266], Cunda, there are those ten ways of wrong action. One characterized by those ten ways of wrong action may rise up early and at eventide touch the earth, yet is he still impure. Even if he touch not the earth he is equally impure. Though he handle cowdung he is impure. Even if he does not he is equally impure. He may handle green grasses or not, he is impure just the same. He may worship the fire or not . . . he may clasp his hands and bow to the sun or not . . . he may descend in the evening into water for the third time or not, yet is he still impure. What is the cause of that? Those ten ways of wrong action, Cunda, are impure and cause impurity. Moreover, as a result of being characterized by those ten ways of wrong action, purgatory is declared, birth in the womb of animals is declared, the realm of ghosts is declared, either that or some other form of ill-bourn.

But, Cunda, threefold is cleansing by body, fourfold is cleansing by speech, threefold is cleansing by mind. And how is cleansing by body threefold?

Herein, Cunda, a certain one abandons taking life, abstains therefrom; he has laid aside the rod, has laid aside the knife; he dwells modest, charitable, feeling compassion towards every living creature.

He abandons taking what is not given, abstains therefrom;

---

[1] Text *bajjhantu*; *M.MA. vajjhantu.*

the property of another, situated in jungle or in village, if not given, he takes not with thievish intent.

In sexual desires he abandons wrong action, abstains therefrom. He has no intercourse with girls in ward of mother or father, of brother, sister or relatives (or clan), with girls lawfully guarded, already plighted to a husband and protected by the rod, even with girls crowned with the flower-garlands (of betrothal). Thus, Cunda, **[267]** threefold is cleansing by body.

Abandoning slanderous speech he abstains therefrom. When he hears something at one place he does not proclaim it elsewhere to bring about a quarrel between the parties; what he has heard here he does not report there to bring about a quarrel between the parties; thus he brings together the discordant, restores harmony, harmony is his delight, he exults in, is passionately fond of harmony; he utters speech that makes for harmony. Also he abandons harsh speech, abstains therefrom. Whatsoever speech is blameless, pleasant to the ear, affectionate, going to the heart, urbane, agreeable to many folk, delightful to many folk, of such speech he is a speaker. Also abandoning idle babble he abstains therefrom; he speaks in season, of facts, of the aim, of dhamma, of discipline; he utters speech worth treasuring up, speech seasonable and worth listening to, discriminating and concerned with the aim.

Thus, Cunda, fourfold is cleansing by speech.

And how is cleansing by mind threefold ?

Herein a certain one is not covetous; he covets not the property of another, thinking: O that what is another's were mine ! He is not malevolent of heart, the thoughts of his heart are not corrupt. He wishes: Let these beings carry about the self[1] in peace, free from enmity, free from sorrow and in happiness.

[268] Also he has right view; he is reasonable in outlook, holding that there are such things as gift, offering, oblation, fruit and ripening of deeds done well or ill; that this world is,

---

[1] *Attānaŋ pariharantu : cf. G.S.* ii, 3, 236, 257.

that the world beyond is; that mother, father and beings of supernatural birth (in other worlds) do exist; that there are in the world recluses and brāhmins who have gone rightly, who fare rightly, men who of their own comprehension have realized this world and the world beyond and thus declare it.

Thus, Cunda, threefold is the cleansing by the mind.

So these are the ten ways of right doing. One characterized by those ten ways may rise up early and at evening touch the earth, yet is he pure. If he touch not the earth, yet is he pure. Whether he handle cowdung or not . . . whether he handle green grasses or not . . . whether he worship the fire or not . . . whether he clasp his hands and bow down to the sun or not . . . whether he descend in the evening into water for the third time or not, yet is he pure for all that. And why so?

Because, Cunda, those ten ways of right action are pure and work purity. By being characterized by those ten ways of right action (the state of) devahood is proclaimed, of mankind is proclaimed, or whatsoever other happy bourn there be.'

At these words Cunda, the son of the silversmith, exclaimed to the Exalted One: 'It is excellent, sir![1] Let the Exalted One reckon me a follower of his from this day forth as long as life shall last, as one who has so gone to him as resort.'

§ xi (177). *Jāṇussoṇi.*

[**269**] Now the brāhmin Jāṇussoṇi[2] came to see the Exalted One . . . and sat down at one side. As he thus sat he said this to the Exalted One:

'Master Gotama, let me tell you we brāhmins so-called give charitable gifts: we make the (*shrāddhā*) offerings to the dead,[3] saying: "May this gift to our kinsmen and blood-relations who are dead and gone be of profit.[4] May our kinsmen and blood-relations who are dead and gone enjoy this offering." Pray, Master Gotama, does that gift profit

---

[1] As at § 119.

[2] At *G.S.* i, 150, he asks about sacrifice.

[3] Called *puññāni* in the quotation at *PvA*. 27.

[4] *Cf. Khp.* vii, *ito dinnaŋ petānaŋ upakappati.*

our kinsmen and blood-relations dead and gone? Do they really enjoy that gift?'

'Well, brāhmin, if there be ground for it, it does profit them, but not if there be no ground.'

'Pray, Master Gotama, what is ground, and what is no-ground?'

'Herein, brāhmin, a certain one takes life, takes what is not given, in sexual desires is a wrongdoer, is a slanderer, of bitter speech, an idle babbler, covetous, harmful in thought and wrong in view. When body breaks up, beyond death he rises up again in a purgatory. There he subsists on food proper to dwellers in purgatory. On that he is grounded. This, brāhmin, is the no-ground, standing on which that gift profits him not.

Herein again a certain one takes life . . . and is of wrong view. He, when body breaks up, beyond death rises up again in the womb of an animal. There also he subsists on food proper to creatures so born. On that he is grounded. This also, brāhmin, is no-ground, whereon standing that gift profits him not.

Yet again a certain one abstains from taking life, from taking what is not given, from wrong conduct in sexual desires, from falsehood, from slander [270], from bitter speech, from idle babble; he is not covetous, his thoughts are not harmful and he has right view. When body breaks up, beyond death he rises up again in the company of human beings. There he subsists on food proper to human beings. On that he is grounded. But this also, brāhmin, is no-ground, whereon standing that gift profits him not.

Yet again a certain one abstains from taking life and the rest . . . and has right view. When body breaks up, beyond death he rises up again in the company of the devas. There he subsists on food proper to devas. On that he is grounded. This also, brāhmin, is no-ground, standing on which that gift profits him not.

Herein again, brāhmin, a certain one takes life . . . and has wrong view. When body breaks up, beyond death he rises up again in the region of the departed (*petā*). There he subsists on whatever be the food proper to beings in that region. On that he is grounded. Whatsoever offerings his friends and fellows or kinsmen and blood-relations convey[1] to him, on that he subsists, on that he is grounded. This indeed, brāhmin, is the ground, standing on which that gift is of profit to him.

'But, Master Gotama, suppose that this blood-relation who is dead and gone has not reached that place, who then enjoys that offering ?'

'In that case, brāhmin, other blood-relations dead and gone, who have reached that place, enjoy it.'

'But suppose, Master Gotama, that both that blood-relation and the others who are dead and gone have not reached that place, who then enjoys that offering ?'

'That, brāhmin, is impossible, it cannot come to pass that that place should be empty for so long a time of blood-relations dead and gone. Anyhow, brāhmin, he who offers to the dead[2] and gone is not without reward.'

[271] 'Does the worthy Gotama make any assumption in an impossible case ?'[3]

'I do, brāhmin. In this connexion suppose a certain one takes life, takes what is not given . . . has wrong view; but he has been one who gives to recluses and brāhmins food and drink, cloth and vehicle, flowers, scents and unguents, bed, lodging and light. When body breaks up, beyond death, he rises up again in the company of elephants. There he has gain of food and drink, flowers and various adornments. In so far as he was one who took life and so forth, for that reason he, when body broke up, beyond death arose in the company of elephants. But in so far as he was a giver to recluses and brāhmins of food and drink and the rest, for that reason he has gain of food and drink, flowers and various adornments.

Suppose again, brāhmin, a certain one takes life and so forth . . . and has wrong view. But he was a giver to

---

[1] *Anupavecchanti*, quoted *PvA*. 28. [2] *Dāyako*.
[3] *Aṭṭhāne parikappaŋ vadati.*

recluses and brāhmins of food and drink and the rest. When body breaks up, beyond death he rises up again in the company of horses . . . of cattle . . . of poultry. There too he has gain of food and drink, flowers and various adornments. In so far as he had those vices of taking life and the rest . . . **[272]** that is why he rises up again in the company of horses . . . cattle . . . poultry. But in so far as he was a giver to recluses and brāhmins of food and drink and the rest, that is why he gets these gains of food and drink. . . .

Herein again, brāhmin, a certain one abstains from taking life . . . and has right view. But he has been a giver to recluses and brāhmins of food and drink and the rest. When body breaks up, beyond death he rises up again in the company of human beings. There he has gain of the five sensual delights belonging to human beings. In so far as he abstained from taking life and the rest . . . and had right view, that is why beyond death he rose up again in the company of human beings. As he gave to recluses and brāhmins, in that next life he has gain of the five sensual delights belonging to human beings.'

CHAPTER XVIII.—THE SEEMLY (*b*).

§ i (178). *Right and wrong.*

[**273**] 'Monks, I will teach you the seemly, also the unseemly. Do ye listen to it. Attend carefully and I will speak.'

'We will, sir,' replied those monks to the Exalted One, who then said:

[**274**] 'And what, monks, is the unseemly?

Taking life, taking what is not given, wrong conduct in sexual desires, falsehood, slander, bitter speech, idle babble, coveting, harmfulness and wrong view. This, monks, is called "the unseemly."

And what is the seemly?

Abstaining from taking life and the rest . . . and right view. This is called "the seemly."'

(*As above in chap. xiv., the next ten suttas have the same titles, but substitute* 'taking life . . . [**275**] wrong view' *and* 'abstaining . . . right view' *for* 'wrong view . . . wrong release' *and* 'right view . . . right release.')

§§ ii-xi (179-188).

[**275-277**] *Titles: Ariyan and unariyan. Good and bad. The aim and not-aim. Dhamma and not-dhamma. With cankers and without. Blameworthy and blameless. Remorse and no-remorse. Going to heaping up and diminishing. Yielding pain and pleasure. Whose fruit is pain and pleasure.*

CHAPTER XIX.—THE ARIYAN WAY (*b*).

[**278**] (*The same remarks as the above apply to this chapter also.*)

§§ i-x (189-198).

Titles: Ariyan and unariyan. Bright way and dark way. True dhamma and false dhamma. Very-man dhamma and its opposite. [**279**] *To be brought about. To be followed. To be made to grow.* [**280**] *To be made much of. To be remembered. To be realized.*

Chapter XX.—Persons (199) (*b*).

[**281-282**] (*The same remarks as regards chap.* xvi *with the same substituted words.*)

Titles: Not to be followed, etc.

Chapter XXI.—The Body Born of Deeds.[1]

§ i (200). *Purgatory and heaven* (*a*).

[**283**] 'Monks, characterized by ten qualities one is cast into purgatory according[2] to his deserts. What ten?

Herein a certain one takes life; he is a hunter, bloody-handed, given up to killing and slaying, void of compassion for all tiny creatures. He takes what is not given . . . (*all as above*, § 176) . . . he has wrong view . . . he says that [**284**] there are no recluses and brāhmins . . . who have realized this world . . . and thus declare it. Characterized by these ten qualities one is cast into purgatory according to his deserts.

Characterized by ten qualities, monks, one is put into heaven according to his deserts. What ten?

Herein a certain one abandons taking life, abstains therefrom, he has laid aside the rod. . . .' [**285**] (*The opposite of the above qualities.*)

§ ii (201). *Purgatory and heaven* (*b*).

'Monks, characterized by ten qualities one is cast into purgatory according to his deserts. What ten?

(*The same with:*) He has wrong view, he is perverse in outlook, holding: There is no gift, no offering, no sacrifice; there is no fruit and ripening of deeds well or ill done; this world is not, the world beyond is not; there is no mother, no father, no beings of supernatural birth; there are no recluses or brāhmins in the world who have gone right, who fare rightly,

---

[1] *Karaja-kāya*, explained in § 208.

[2] *Yathābhataṃ nikkhitto*; *cf. G.S.* i, 6, 83, 90, 248, 270; ii, 19 *n.* (as I noted there, it may refer to the casting of a true die; see below, § 206, *apaṇṇako maṇi*).

men who of their own comprehension have realized this world and the world beyond and so declare it. [**286.**]

Characterized by these ten qualities one is thrown into purgatory according to his deserts.

Characterized by ten qualities one is put into heaven according to his deserts. What ten?' (*The opposite of the above.*)

§ iii (202). *Womenfolk.*

'Monks, characterized by ten qualities womenfolk are cast into purgatory according to their deserts. What ten?

[**287**] A woman takes life and the rest . . . and has wrong view.

Characterized by these ten . . .

Characterized by ten qualities womenfolk are put into heaven according to their deserts. What ten?' (*The opposite of the above.*)

§ iv (203). *Woman lay-follower.*

'Monks, characterized by ten qualities a woman lay-follower is cast into purgatory according to her deserts. What ten?' (*The same as before, with the reverse for the heaven-world.*)

§ v (204). *Diffident and confident.*

[**288**] 'Monks, characterized by ten qualities a woman lay-follower dwells at home with diffidence.[1] What ten?

She takes life and the rest . . . has wrong view.

Characterized by ten qualities a woman lay-follower dwells at home with confidence. What ten?' (*The same as above.*)

§ vi (205). *Dhamma-teaching on crookedness.*

'Monks, I will teach you dhamma-teaching, dhamma-teaching on crookedness.[2] Do ye listen to it. Pay attention carefully and I will speak.'

---

[1] *Visāradā.*

[2] *Saṃsappaniya*, 'slinking along' (of a reptile). *Ṭīkā*, 'the irresolution of a child.' *Cf. Path of Purity* iii, 546 (slinking along); *Expositor* i, 175 (the function of resolution is opposition to 'slinking along'). At *A.* iii, 354, *Comy.* has *paripphandati*. Probably it refers to the from-side-to-side action of a snake as is shown by the word *jimha* used below; but in the list of animals the idea is that of stealth.

"We will, sir," replied those monks to the Exalted One, who said this:

'And what, monks, is dhamma-teaching which teaches about crookedness?

Monks, beings are responsible for their deeds,[1] heirs to their deeds, they are the womb of their deeds, kinsmen of their deeds, to them their deeds come home again.[2] Whatsoever deed they do, be it lovely or ugly, of that thing they are the heirs.

[**289**] In this connexion, monks, a certain one takes life, he is a hunter, bloody-handed, given over to killing and slaying, void of compassion to all living creatures. He goes crookedly[3] in body, crookedly in speech, crookedly in mind. His action with body is crooked, so is that with speech and mind; crooked is his bourn and crooked his rising up again in birth. Moreover, monks, for one whose bourn is crooked, whose rebirth is crooked, for him there is one of two bourns, either downright woe in purgatory or to be born in the womb of an animal, one that creeps crookedly along.

And of what sort, monks, is that birth in the womb of an animal, one that creeps crookedly along? A snake, a scorpion, a centipede, a mongoose, a cat, a mouse, an owl or whatsoever other animal goes stealthily on seeing human beings.

Herein again a certain one takes what is not given . . . is a wrong-doer in sensual desires, is a liar, a slanderer, of bitter speech, of idle babble, covetous, of harmful thoughts, of wrong view, of perverse view, holding: There is no gift . . . that this world is not . . . that there are no recluses or brāhmins in the world who . . . have realized this world and the world beyond and so declare it. He goes crookedly in body, speech and mind. His action with body is crooked . . . [**290**] his bourn is crooked . . . for one whose bourn is crooked . . . for him I declare there is one of two bourns, either downright woe in purgatory or to be born in the womb of an animal . . .

---

[1] *Kamma-ssaka.* See *Buddh. Psych. Ethics*, p. 356 *n.* Above, § 48. *Mil. Pañh.* 65 adds *kammaŋ satte vibhajati* (differentiates).

[2] *Kamma-paṭisaraṇa* (resort). [3] *Saŋsappati*, see *n.* above.

a cat, an owl, or whatsoever other animal goes stealthily on seeing human beings.

Monks, beings are responsible for their deeds, heirs to their deeds, the womb of their deeds, the kinsmen of their deeds, to them their deeds come home again. Whatsoever deed they do, be it lovely or ugly, of that they are the heirs.

Herein again, monks, a certain one abandons taking life, abstains therefrom: he lays aside the rod, he lays aside the knife; he dwells modest, charitable, feeling compassion for all living creatures. He goes not crookedly in body, speech and mind. His action with body, speech and mind is straight; straightforward is his bourn and straight his rebirth. Now, monks, for one whose bourn and rebirth are straight I declare one of two bourns, either those heaven-worlds that are utter bliss or (rebirth in) whatsoever families are exalted, such as the families of nobles or brāhmins, or housefathers of a great household, wealthy, of great resources, of great property, with great store of gold and silver, with great store of possessions, with great store of wealth and grain. Thus become, monks, is the rebirth of one who has come to be. What he does, by that he is reborn; when reborn (appropriate) contacts contact such an one. Thus I declare that beings are the heirs of their deeds.

Herein again, monks, a certain one abandons taking what is not given, he abstains therefrom . . . he abandons wrong action in sensual desires . . . [**291**] he abandons falsehood, slander, bitter speech, coveting; he is of harmless thoughts, he has right view, he holds the reasonable view that there is gift, that there is offering, sacrifice; that there is fruit and ripening of deeds done well or ill; that this world is, that the world beyond is; that there are mother and father and beings supernaturally born (in other worlds); that in this world there are recluses and brāhmins who go right, who fare rightly, who by their own comprehension have realized both this world and the world beyond and so declare it. Such an one goes not crookedly in body, speech and mind. His action of body, speech and mind is straight; straightforward is his bourn and straight his rebirth.

Now, monks, for one whose bourn is straight I declare one of two bourns, either those heavens that are utter bliss or (rebirth in) whatsoever families are exalted . . . (*as above*) . . . with great store of wealth and grain. Thus become, monks, is the rebirth of one who has come to be. What he does, by that he is reborn; when reborn (appropriate) contacts contact such an one. Thus do I declare that beings are the heirs of their deeds.

Indeed, monks, beings are responsible for their deeds,[1] heirs of their deeds, the womb of their deeds, the kinsmen of their deeds, to them their deeds come home again. Whatsoever deed they do, be it lovely or ugly, of that they are the heirs.

Such, monks, is the dhamma-teaching, the teaching about crookedness.'

§ vii (206). *Ruin and prosperity* (*a*).

[**292**] 'I declare, monks, that of intentional[2] deeds done and accumulated there can be no wiping out without experiencing the result thereof, and that too whenever arising, either in this same visible state or in some other state hereafter. I declare, monks, that there is no ending of Ill as regards intentional deeds done and accumulated without experiencing the results thereof.

Herein threefold is the fault and guilt of bodily action done with deliberate intent, causing pain and resulting in pain. Fourfold is the fault and guilt of action by speech, done with deliberate intent, causing pain and resulting in pain. Threefold is the fault and guilt of mental action, done with deliberate intent . . . and resulting in pain.

Now herein, monks, a certain one takes life, he is a hunter . . . (*above*) . . . he takes what is not given, he takes with thievish intent things not given to him, the property of another person, situated in village or in jungle. In sensual desires he is a wrong-doer; he has intercourse with girls in ward of

---

[1] *Kammasaka.*

[2] *Sañcetanika ; cf. M.* iii, 207; *Vin.* iii, 112; *Points of Controv.* 266, 313.

mother or father, brother, sister or relatives (or clan); with girls lawfully guarded, already plighted to a husband and protected by the rod, even with girls crowned with the flower-garlands (of betrothal).

Thus threefold is the fault and guilt of bodily action done with deliberate intent, causing pain and resulting in pain. And how, monks, is the fault and guilt of action by speech . . . resulting in pain, of a fourfold nature ?

[**293**] Herein a certain one is a liar. When cited to appear before the council or a company or amid his relatives or guild-men or the royal family, and asked to bear witness, with the words: "Come, good fellow ! Say what you know"; though he knows not, he says "I know"; though he knows, he says "I know not"; though he saw not, he says he saw; though he saw, he denies it. Thus for his own sake or that of others or to get some carnal profit or other he deliberately utters falsehood.

Also he is a slanderer. Hearing something at one place he proclaims it at another place to bring about a quarrel between the parties. What he has heard here he repeats there to bring about a quarrel between the parties. Thus he breaks up harmony and foments strife between those discordant; discord is his delight; exulting in discord, passionately fond of discord he utters speech that makes for discord.

Also he is harsh of speech. Whatsoever speech is rough, cutting, bitter about others, abusive of others, provoking wrath and conducive to distraction—such speech does he utter.

He is given to idle babble, he speaks out of season, speaks unrealities, he speaks unprofitable things, speaks what is not-dhamma, what is not-discipline. He utters words not worth treasuring up, words unseasonable and not worth listening to, undiscriminating and not concerned with the aim.

Thus, monks, fourfold is the fault and guilt of action by speech, done with deliberate intent, causing pain and resulting in pain. And how is the fault and guilt of action by mind . . . of a threefold nature ?

Herein a certain one is covetous, he is one who covets

the property of another, thinking: O that what is another's were mine! He is malevolent of heart, the thoughts of his heart are corrupt, thus: Let these beings be slain, come to destruction, be destroyed, let them not exist at all. Likewise he has wrong view, he is perverse in outlook, holding: There is no gift, no offering, no sacrifice; there is no fruit or ripening of deeds ill done or well done; this world is not; the world beyond is not; there is no mother or father or beings born by supernatural birth (in another state); **[294]** there are no recluses and brāhmins in the world who have gone right, who fare aright, men who by their own comprehension have realized this world and the world beyond and so declare it. Thus, monks, threefold is the fault and guilt of action by mind causing pain and resulting in pain.

Monks, it is because of this threefold fault and guilt of bodily action done with deliberate intent of wrong that beings, when body breaks up, beyond death arise again in the Waste, the Ill-bourn, the Downfall, in Purgatory. It is because of this fourfold fault and guilt of action by speech . . . of action by mind that beings . . . arise again . . . in Purgatory.

Just as, monks, a true die[1] when cast upwards alights sure wherever it alights (when it falls), even so it is because of this threefold fault and guilt of bodily action deliberately done with wrong intent that beings . . . arise again . . . in Purgatory. It is because of this fourfold fault and guilt of action by speech . . . of mental action . . . that beings so arise again.

Monks, I declare that of intentional deeds done and accumulated there can be no wiping out without experiencing the result thereof, and that too wherever arising, either in this same visible state or in some other state hereafter. I declare, monks, that there is no ending of Ill as regards intentional

---

[1] *Apaṇṇako maṇi=samantato caturasso pāsako, Comy.* As I have noted at *G.S.* i, 248, the phrase *yathâbhataŋ nikkhitto* may refer to this throwing of a true die. The word *apaṇṇaka* (derivation unknown) is also an epithet for *nibbāna*. See *Trenckner-Andersen, P. Dict. s.v.*

deeds done and accumulated without experiencing the result thereof.

Herein, monks, threefold is the prosperity of bodily action done with deliberate good intent, causing happiness and resulting in happiness. Fourfold is that of action by speech . . . threefold that of mental action. . . .

[**295**] And how is the prosperity of bodily action done with deliberate good intent . . . threefold ?

Herein a certain one abandoning the taking of life . . . (*as in* § 205) abandoning falsehood . . . has right view . . . holds the reasonable outlook . . . and so declares it.

It is because of this threefold prosperity of bodily action . . . action by speech . . . [**296**] mental action . . . that beings, when body breaks up, beyond death rise up again in the happy bourn, in the heaven world.

Just as a true die when cast upwards alights sure wherever it falls, [**297**] even so it is because of this threefold prosperity . . . that beings so arise.

Monks, I declare that of intentional deeds done and accumulated there can be no wiping out without experiencing the result thereof.'

§ viii (207). *Ruin and prosperity* (*b*).

[**298-9**] (*There seems no reason for this sutta, for it is exactly the same as the previous one.*)

§ ix (208). *The Brahma-moods.*[1]

[**300**] 'Monks, I declare that of intentional deeds done and accumulated there can be no wiping out without experiencing the result thereof, and that too whenever arising, either in this same visible state or in some other state hereafter.

I declare, monks, that there is no ending of Ill as regards intentional deeds done and accumulated without experiencing the results thereof.

---

[1] *Brahma-vihārā ; cf. K.S.* v, 98 *n.*

Monks, that Ariyan disciple[1] thus freed from coveting, freed from malevolence, not bewildered but self-possessed and concentrated, with a heart possessed of amity, abides irradiating one quarter of the world, likewise the second, third and fourth quarters of the world, likewise above, below, across, everywhere, for all sorts and conditions—he abides irradiating the whole world with a heart possessed of amity that is wide-spreading, grown great and boundless, free from enmity and untroubled.

He comes to know thus: Formerly this heart of mine was confined,[2] it was not made to grow; but now my heart is boundless, well made to grow. Moreover whatsoever deed belongs to a limited range, now it stays not in that range, it stands not still in that range.[3]

[**301**] Now what think ye, monks? If from his youth up[4] this young man should make the heart's release by amity to grow, pray would he do any wicked deed?'

'Surely not, sir.'

'Pray, can any ill contact one who does no wicked deed?'

'Surely not, sir. How shall ill contact such an one?'

'Indeed, monks, this heart's release by amity must be made to grow whether by a woman or by a man. A woman

---

[1] As at *S.* iv, 322=*K.S.* iv, 227; *G.S.* ii, 132. Apparently all this is borrowed from some other sutta, for it is introduced without apparent reason thus suddenly. Below we have 'that young man.'

[2] *Paritta; cf. D.* i, 251=*Dialog.* i, 318; *K.S.* iv, 227.

[3] *Yaŋ pamāṇa-kataŋ kammaŋ* is taken by *Comy.* as equal to *kāmâvacara* (sphere of sense-activities), while *appamāṇa-kataŋ kammaŋ* is of *rūpâvacara* (the realm of finer matter). This passage in the Brahmavihāras has hitherto been taken (by Rhys Davids at *D.* i, *loc. cit.*, and by myself at *K.S.* iv) to refer to the all-embracing range of amity, 'whatsoever finite *thing* there be, naught is passed over or left aside'—*i.e.*, he leaves out no finite object from his heart; but re-reading *Text* and *Comy.* I think this trans. will not stand for *kammaŋ* and *na tatrâvasissati*, for another idea seems thus introduced. *Comy.*, which repeats a part of *SA.* iii on *S.* iv, 322, seems to think it means, 'by shutting out the result of this or that act, of himself he is carried onwards to the Company of the Brahma-world.'

[4] *Dahara-t-agge.*

or a man cannot take this body and go away.[1] This mortal being, monks, is but a between-thoughts.[2] He comes to know thus: Whatever wicked deed has been done by me here with this body born of action,[3] all of that must be felt here; then it will not follow me and come to be hereafter.[4]

Thus made to grow, monks, the heart's release by amity conduces to not-returning for the monk of insight won in this life,[5] but who has not yet penetrated the release beyond that.

Then again he irradiates one quarter of the world with a heart possessed of compassion . . . possessed of sympathy . . . possessed of equanimity; so also as regards the second, third and fourth quarters of the world; likewise above, below, across, everywhere, for all sorts and conditions; he abides irradiating the whole world with a heart possessed of equanimity that is widespreading, grown great and boundless, free from enmity and untroubled. Thus he comes to know: Formerly this heart of mine was confined, it was not made to grow; but now my heart is boundless, well made to grow. Moreover whatever deed done belongs to a limited range, now it stays not in that range, it stands not still in that range.

Now what think ye, monks? If from his youth up this

---

[1] Lit., 'there is not a going away of body, taking it along, for a man or woman.'

[2] *Citt'antaro ayaŋ macco.* I have not found the word *c.a.* in *P. Dicts. Comy.* says it is *citta-kārano* or *citten'eva antariko—i.e.*, at one thought-moment one is in this world, at the next in the deva-world or purgatory, etc. Editor of *Text* misprints *anatthiko* (?) at p. 364 (in *Appendix*).

[3] *Karaja-kāya* (this gives the name to this chapter), translated 'sentient body' at *Expositor* ii, 485, where note has: 'It is also explained as the "constituted body" (*sasambhāra-kāya*) or "body born of becoming." . . . *Comy.* on *Dīg.* ii takes it to mean "the body derived from the four great essentials." . . . The rendering by "frail body" in *Buddhist Psychological Ethics*, p. 213, is wrong.'

[4] *Na taŋ anugaŋ bhavissati.* So Text, but *Comy. anubhavissati* (=*na anugataŋ bhavissati*), referring to one on the Fourfold Path.

[5] *Idha-paññassa bhikkhuno. Comy. imasmiŋ sāsane paññā idha-paññā nāma sāsana-caritāya ariya-paññāya yuttassa ariya-sāvakassa.* Text has *idha paññ'assa* (?), as if it were *paññāssa* (would be wisdom). The release 'beyond' is arahantship.

young man should make the heart's release by compassion . . . by sympathy . . . by equanimity to grow, would he do any wicked deed ?'

'Surely not, sir.'

'Pray, can any ill contact one who does no wicked deed ?'

'Surely not, sir. How can ill contact such an one ?'

'Indeed, monks, this heart's release . . . by equanimity must be made to grow, whether by a woman or by a man. A woman or a man, monks, cannot take this body and go away. This mortal being, monks, is but a between-thoughts. He comes to know thus: Whatsoever wicked deed has been done by me here with the body born of action, all that must be felt here, then it will not follow me and come to be hereafter.

Thus made to grow, monks, the heart's release by equanimity conduces to not returning for a monk of insight won in this life, but who has not yet penetrated the release beyond that.'

§ x (209). *After death* (*a*).

Now a certain brāhmin came to see the Exalted One, and on coming to him greeted him courteously, and after the exchange of greetings and reminiscent talk sat down at one side. So seated he said this to the Exalted One:

'Pray, Master Gotama, what is the reason, what is the cause why certain beings of this world, when body breaks up, beyond death rise up again in the Waste, the Ill-bourn, the Downfall, in Purgatory ?'

'Brāhmin, the reason and cause for this are conduct that is not-dhamma and crooked ways of life. That is why beings are so born.'

[**302**] 'But pray, Master Gotama, what is the reason, what is the cause why certain beings . . . rise up again in the Happy Bourn, the heaven-world ?'

'Brāhmin, the reason and cause are conduct that is dhamma and straight ways. That is the reason why they are so reborn.'

'For my part I don't understand in full the meaning of this pronouncement in brief made by the worthy Gotama. Well for me if the worthy Gotama would teach me dhamma in such a way that I could understand in full the meaning of this brief utterance of the worthy Gotama.'

'Then listen, brāhmin. Pay attention carefully and I will speak.'

'I will, master,' replied that brāhmin to the Exalted One, who said this:

'Threefold, brāhmin, is conduct by body that is not-dhamma and crooked ways of life. Fourfold is the same by speech and threefold that by mind. And how is bodily conduct that is not-dhamma and crooked ways of life threefold? (*Here text abbreviates. He repeats the previous teachings on the subject, with their opposites.*)

[**303**] 'Excellent, Master Gotama! . . . let the worthy Gotama reckon me as a follower from this day forth, so long as life shall last, as one who has gone to him as resort.'

CHAPTER XXII.—CHARACTERISTICS.[1]

§ i (210). *Ten qualities.*

'Monks, possessing ten qualities one is cast into purgatory according to his deserts. He takes life, steals, acts wrongly in sensual desires, is a liar, a slanderer, of bitter speech, an idle babbler, covetous, of harmful thoughts, and has wrong view. These are the ten qualities. . . .

[**304**] Possessing ten qualities one is put into heaven according to his deserts. What ten?

He abstains from taking life and the rest . . . and has right view.

Possessing these ten qualities one is put into heaven according to his deserts.'

§ ii (211). *Twenty qualities.*

'Monks, possessing twenty qualities one is cast into purgatory according to his deserts. What are the twenty?

He himself takes life and encourages another to do so . . . he has wrong view himself and encourages another in wrong view. . . .

Possessing twenty qualities one is put into heaven according to his deserts. What twenty?

He abstains from taking life and the rest and encourages another to abstain therefrom . . . he has right view himself and encourages another in right view. These are the twenty qualities. . . .'

§ iii (212). *Thirty qualities.*

[**305**] 'Monks, possessing thirty qualities one is cast into Purgatory according to his deserts. What thirty?

He takes life himself, encourages another to do so and

---

[1] Text has no title to this chapter, nor are the suttas named.

approves[1] of so doing . . . he has wrong view, encourages another in wrong view and approves of wrong view.' (*The opposite for the abstentions.*)

§ iv (213). *Forty qualities.*

[**306–7**] 'Monks, possessing forty qualities one is cast into purgatory according to his deserts. What forty?

He takes life himself, encourages another to do so, approves of taking life and speaks in praise thereof . . . he has wrong view, encourages another in wrong view, approves of wrong view and speaks in praise thereof.' (*The opposite for the abstentions.*)

§ v (214). *Uprooted.*

[**308**] 'Monks, possessing ten qualities . . . twenty . . . thirty . . . forty qualities, one carries about with him a lifeless, uprooted self.[2]

Possessing ten . . . twenty . . . thirty . . . forty qualities one carries about with him a self not lifeless, not uprooted.' (*Abbreviation of the previous sutta.*)

§ vi (215). *After death* (*b*).

'Monks, possessing ten . . . twenty . . . thirty . . . forty qualities a certain one here when body breaks up, beyond death [**309**] rises up again in the Waste, the Ill-bourn, the Downfall, in Purgatory.' (*As before, with the opposite qualities for the heaven-world.*)

§ vii (216). *Fool and wise.*

'Monks, possessing ten . . . twenty . . . thirty . . . forty qualities one should be understood to be a fool. . . .

Possessing the opposite qualities one should be understood to be a wise man.'

---

[1] *Samanuñño* (*samanujānāti*); *cf. A.* ii, 253; iii, 359.

[2] *Khataŋ attānaŋ pariharati,* as at *G.S.* ii, 3, etc., where the title is thus.

§ viii (217). *Lust (a).*

'Monks, for the thorough comprehension of lust ten qualities should be made to grow. What ten?

The idea of the foul, of death, of the repulsiveness in food, of non-delight in all the world, of impermanence, of ill, of the not-self, of abandoning, of fading interest and the idea of ending.

These are the ten qualities to be made to grow for the thorough comprehension of lust.

[**310**] Ten (other) qualities should be made to grow for the thorough comprehension of lust. What ten?

The idea of impermanence, of the not-self, of the repulsiveness in food, of non-delight in all the world, of the bony (skeleton),[1] of the worm-eaten corpse, of the discoloured corpse, of the fissured corpse, and the idea of the inflated corpse. These are the ten qualities. . . .'

§ ix (218). *Lust (b).*

'Monks, for the thorough comprehension of lust ten qualities should be made to grow. What ten?

Right view, right thinking, right speech, right action, right living, right effort, right mindfulness, right concentration, right knowledge and right release. These are the ten. . . .'

§ x (219). *Lust, malice and the rest.*[2]

'Monks, for the perfect understanding, utter destruction, abandoning, wearing out, passing away, of lust, for the fading of interest in lust, for the ending, calming down, giving up, casting away of lust these ten qualities should be made to grow. What ten? (*The same as above.*)

For the perfect understanding . . . casting away of malice,

---

[1] *Cf. G.S.* ii, 16.

[2] As at *G.S.* i, 276 (where three conditions are to be made to grow).

delusion, wrath, enmity, depreciation,[1] illusion, treachery, stubbornness, impetuosity, pride, overbearing arrogance, intoxication of mind and negligence, these (same) ten qualities must be made to grow.'

HERE ENDS THE BOOK OF THE TENS.

---

[1] As I pointed out before, *makkha* (generally translated 'hypocrisy') means, according to *Comy.*, 'smearing over another's virtues.' In Skt. it has the two meanings of hypocrisy and wrath.

THE BOOK OF THE ELEVENS

CHAPTER I.—DEPENDENCE.[1]

§ i (1). *What is the use?*

[**311**] Now the venerable Ānanda came to see the Exalted One, and on coming to him saluted him and sat down at one side. So seated he said this to the Exalted One:

'Pray, sir, what is the object, what is the profit of good conduct?'

(*This sutta is exactly the same as No.* 1 *of this volume, except that one of the ten qualities,* 'nibbidā-virāga,' *is here divided so as to make eleven.*)

§ ii (2). *Thinking with intention.*

[**312**] (*The same remarks apply to this sutta.*)

§ iii (3). *Lacking basis* (*a*) (*by the Teacher*).

§ iv (4). *Lacking basis* (*b*) (*by Sāriputta*).

§ v (5). *Lacking basis* (*c*) (*by Ānanda*).

[**313-7**] (*The same remarks apply to these three suttas also, but the title in the* uddāna *of the Tens is* 'basis' *only.*)

§ vi (6). *Disaster* (*b*).[2]

'Monks, if any monk abuses and reviles, rails at the Ariyans who are his fellows in the Brahma-life, it is utterly impossible, it is unavoidable that he should not come to one or other of eleven disasters. What eleven?

---

[1] *Nissāya* is the name given to this chapter, from the frequent occurrence of the word in § 9. Text wrongly prints *nissaya* (pupillage), the name of a sutta of the Tens, No. 34.

[2] At § 88 this sutta occurs with ten results.

He fails to attain the unattained; from what he has attained he falls away; true dhamma is not made clear for him; or else he is conceited about true dhammas, or he follows the Brahma-life without delight therein, or commits some foul offence [**318**], or gives up the training and falls back to the low life;[1] or he falls into some grievous sickness, or goes out of his mind with distraction; he makes an end with mind confused and when body breaks up, beyond death, rises up again in the Waste, the Ill-bourn, the Downfall, in Purgatory.

Monks, if any monk abuses . . . it is unavoidable that he should not come to one or other of these eleven disasters.'

§ vii (7). *Conscious work-of-mind.*[2]

Now the venerable Ānanda came to see the Exalted One. . . . Seated at one side he asked:

'Pray, sir, may it be that a monk's winning of concentration is of such a sort that in earth he is unaware of earth, in water unaware of water, in fire unaware of fire, in air unaware of it, in the realm of unbounded space unaware of it, in the realm of infinite intellection, in the realm of nothingness, in the realm of neither-perception-nor-not-perception unaware of it; that in this world he is unaware of this world, in the world beyond unaware of the world beyond; that whatsoever is seen, heard, sensed, cognized, attained, sought after, thought over by mind[3]—of all that he is unaware, and yet is conscious?'

'It may be so, Ānanda. A monk's winning of concentration may be of such a sort that in earth he is unaware of earth . . . [**319**] of all that he may be unaware, and yet be conscious.'

'But, sir, in what way may a monk's winning of concentration be of such a sort . . . that of all that he is unaware and yet may be conscious?'

---

[1] This item is inserted to make eleven.

[2] *Saññā-manasikāra* (in *uddāna*). This almost similar sutta is called *samādhi* at X, § 6.

[3] *Cf. K.S.* iii, 165; *Buddh. Psych. Ethics* on § 961 of *Dhammasangaṇi*.

'Herein, Ānanda, a monk is conscious thus: This is the real,[1] this is the best, namely, the calming of all activities, the rejection of every substrate, the ending of craving, the fading of interest, stopping and nibbāna In such a way, Ānanda, a monk's winning of concentration may be of such a sort that in earth he is unaware of earth and the rest; that in whatsoever is seen, heard, sensed, cognized, attained, sought after, thought out by mind—of all that he is unaware, and yet at the same time he is conscious.'

§ viii (8). *Conscious work of mind* (*b*).[2]

Then the venerable Ānanda, having thanked the Exalted One for what he had said, rose up from his seat, saluted him by keeping his right side towards him, and went to see the venerable Sāriputta, whom he greeted courteously, and, after the exchange of greetings and reminiscent talk, sat down at one side. So seated he said this to the venerable Sāriputta:

[320] 'Pray, your reverence, may it be that a monk's winning of concentration may be of such a sort that in earth he is unaware of earth . . . (*and he repeats his questions of the previous sutta, and gets exactly the same replies*).

'It is wonderful, your reverence! It is marvellous, your reverence, how the explanation both of Master and disciple will agree, will harmonize, meaning with meaning, letter with letter; how they will not be inconsistent—that is, in any word about the highest. **[321]** Just now, your reverence, I went to the Exalted One and asked him the meaning of this, and he explained the meaning to me in these very same words and syllables as the venerable Sāriputta! It is indeed a wonder, a marvel, your reverence, how the explanation both of Master and disciple will agree . . . that is, in any word about the highest!'[3]

---

[1] *Santaŋ*.

[2] Apparently *Comy.* regards this sutta as part of the previous one.

[3] *Cf. S.* iv, 379=*K.S.* iv, 269, where see *Appendix*, p. 298, for readings. *Agga-padasmiŋ=nibbāne, Comy.*

§ ix (9). *Conscious work of mind* (*c*).

Now the venerable Ānanda went to see the Exalted One . . . and said:

'Pray, sir, may it be that a monk's winning of concentration may be of such a sort that, though he pay no heed to eye or object seen, or to ear or sound, to nose or scent, to tongue or savour, to body or tangibles; though he heed not earth, water, fire, air, the realm of unbounded space, the realm of consciousness, that of nothingness, that of neither-perception-nor-not-perception, though he heed not this world nor the world beyond; though whatever is seen, heard, sensed, cognized, attained, sought after, thought out by mind—to all that he pays no mental heed, and yet does so?'

'It may be so, Ānanda. . . .'

[322] 'Pray, sir, in what way is a monk's winning of concentration of such a sort that . . . though he pays no mental heed to all that, yet he does?'

'Herein, Ānanda, a monk's work-of-mind is thus: This is the real, this is the best, namely: the calming of all activities, the rejection of every substrate, the ending of craving, the fading of interest, stopping and nibbāna. In such a way, Ānanda, a monk's winning of concentration is of such a sort that, though he pays no mental heed to eye or object seen, to ear or sound . . . to whatever is seen . . . thought out by mind—though he pays no mental heed to all that, yet he does so.'[1]

§ x (10). *Sandha.*[2]

[323] Once the Exalted One was staying at Nātika[3] in the Brick Hall. Then the venerable Sandha came to see the Exalted One. As he sat at one side the Exalted One said this to him:

---

[1] *Comy. paccāvekkhanā* (contemplation) is spoken of here.

[2] I have not found this name elsewhere. Text has *v.l. saddha*, and uddāna has *sekho*. In § 15 below is a monk named Saddho, but it is doubtful whether this is a name or an epithet. *Cf.* S. ii, 153: *infr.* 216 n.

[3] At *Dial.* ii, 97, Nādika (of the Nādikas); *cf. K.S.* ii, 51; iv, 55, 282; v, 311 *n.* [*SA., ad loc.*, Ñātika=the village of two kinsmen, Cūḷapitā and Mahāpitā, uncle and grandfather]; *G.S.* iii, 217, 278 has Nādika.

'Sandha, do you muse with the musing of the trained thoroughbred. Muse not with the musing of the unbroken colt.[1] And what is the musing of the unbroken colt?

The unbroken colt, Sandha, when tied up by the feeding-trough muses: Fodder! Fodder! Why is that? When thus tied up by the feeding-trough it never occurs to him:[2] I wonder what task the trainer will set me today? What can I do for him in return? But tied up there by the feeding-trough he just muses of fodder.

In the same way, Sandha, a certain one here, an untrained man-colt, who has gone to the forest or the root of a tree or a lonely dwelling-place, lives with a heart obsessed by desire and lust, overwhelmed by desire and lust, and he has not come to know the way out of desire and lust when they arise. Keeping desire and lust within him[3] he muses, he is bemused, he is im-mused, he is de-mused.[4]

[324] He muses dependent on earth, he muses dependent on water . . . fire . . . air . . . the realm of unbounded space . . . of consciousness . . . of nothingness . . . of neither-consciousness-nor-unconsciousness, he muses dependent on this world, dependent on the world beyond; whatever is seen, heard, sensed, cognized, attained, sought after, thought out by mind—on that also dependent he muses.[5] Of such a nature, Sandha, is the musing of the unbroken man-colt.

And what, Sandha, is the musing of the thoroughbred?

The goodly, trained thoroughbred, when tied up near the feeding-trough, muses not thus: Fodder! Fodder! Why not?

---

[1] Def. at *A.* iv, 397; *cf. G.S.* i, 223, 266.

[2] For this idea *cf. G.S.* ii, 118.

[3] *Antaraŋ katvā=abbhantare karitvā, Comy.*

[4] *Jhāyati, pajjhāyati, nijjhāyati, avajjhāyati*; *cf. G.S.* ii, 229, where I quoted Lord Chalmers' translation at *M.* i, 334 ('they trance, and en-trance, and un-trance, and de-trance'), said in scorn of the 'shaveling monks.' The prefixes seem to disparage the quality of his musing. *Comy. MA.* seems to miss the point of all this, saying 'the words are just strengthened by prefixes.' Our *Comy.* here is more explicit: *jhāyati*= he ponders; *sañjhāyati* = he muses diversely hither and thither; *nijjhāyati*=he muses definitely without break.

[5] This passage quoted at *Netti*, pp. 38, 39, differs slightly there.

When the goodly, trained thoroughbred, Sandha, is tied up near the feeding-trough it occurs thus to him: I wonder what task the trainer will set me today? What return can I make to him? He muses not on fodder always when tied up near the feeding-trough. The goodly, trained thoroughbred, Sandha, looks (with dread) upon the application of the goad as one would look upon a debt, imprisonment, loss, a piece of ill-luck.[1]

In the same way, Sandha, the goodly thoroughbred man who has gone to the forest, to the root of a tree, to a lonely dwelling-place, lives not with his heart obsessed by desire and lust, not overwhelmed by desire and lust, but he comes to know the way out of desire and lust, as it really is. He dwells not with his heart obsessed by malice . . . sloth-and-torpor . . . worry-and-flurry . . . by doubt-and-wavering . . . with heart not overwhelmed by doubt-and-wavering, but he comes to know the way out of doubt-and-wavering when it arises.

He muses not dependent[2] on earth, water, fire, air, and the rest . . . whatever is seen, heard, sensed, cognized, attained, sought after, thought out by mind—dependent on all that he muses not, and yet he does muse. **[325]** Moreover, Sandha, to him thus musing the devas, with their lord,[3] and the Brahmās with their consorts even from afar bow down, saying:

We worship thee, thou thoroughbred of men,
We worship thee, most excellent of men;
For what it is whereon depending thou
Art musing—that we cannot comprehend.'[4]

At these words the venerable Sandha said this to the Exalted One:

---

[1] *Cf. G.S.* ii, 119.

[2] *Nā nissāya*=' owing to absence of restraint (check or hindrance), *niyantiyā abhāvena*. He makes nibbāna with the fruits of attainment his object of musing,' *Comy.*

[3] *Sa-inda*=*Sakka.*

[4] *Cf. Sn. v.* 544; *S.* iii, 91=*K.S.* iii, 76 *n.*; *SA.* ii, 297; *D.* iii, 198=*DA.* iii, 791. Here and at *S.* iii text should read *yassa te nâbhijānāma* for *tenâbhijānāma.*

'But pray, sir, how musing does the goodly thoroughbred man muse? For he muses not dependent on earth, water, fire, air and the rest . . . and yet he does muse.

To him how musing, sir, do the devas with their lord and the Brahmās with their consorts even from afar bow down saying:

We worship thee, thou thoroughbred of men . . .?'

'Herein, Sandha, for the goodly thoroughbred man in earth the consciousness of earth is made clear;[1] in water the consciousness of water is made clear; in fire . . . air and the rest **[326]** . . . in this world . . . in the world beyond . . . in whatsoever is seen . . . therein consciousness is made clear. Musing thus the goodly thoroughbred man muses not dependent on earth and the rest . . . and yet he does muse.[2] Thus musing the devas . . . bow down saying:

We worship thee, thou thoroughbred of men . . .'

§ xi (11). *At Peacocks' Feeding-ground.*[3]

Once the Exalted One was staying near Rājagaha at Peacocks' Feeding-ground in the Wanderers' Park. On that occasion the Exalted One called to the monks, saying: 'Monks!'

'Yes, sir,' replied those monks to the Exalted One, who said this:

'Monks, if he be gifted with three qualities a monk is fully proficient, has fully reached release from bondage, has fully lived the Brahma-life, has fully reached the goal, is best of devas and mankind. What three qualities?

The aggregate of virtues, of concentration, and of insight belonging to an adept.

[327] Gifted with these three qualities a monk . . . is best of devas and mankind.

---

[1] *Vibhūtā=pākatā, Comy.*

[2] Not explained, but see note above.

[3] *Mora-nivāpa* as at *G.S.* i, 270 *n.* (for three sets of threes *cf. K.S.* iii, 14).

If he be gifted with three other qualities . . . he is best of devas and mankind. What three other qualities?

The marvel of more-power, the marvel of mind-reading, the marvel of exhorting others. Gifted with these three . . . he is best of devas and mankind.

If he be gifted with three further qualities a monk . . . is best of devas and mankind. What three further qualities?

Right view, right understanding and right release. . . .

If he be gifted with yet two other qualities a monk . . . is best of devas and mankind. What two other qualities?

Knowledge and practice.

Gifted with these two other qualities a monk is fully proficient, has fully reached release from bondage, fully lived the Brahma-life, fully reached the goal, is best of devas and mankind.

Monks, these verses were uttered by the Brahmā, the Eternal Youth:[1]

> The noble is the best among the folk
> Who put their trust in lineage.
> But one in wisdom and in virtue clothed
> Is best of devas and mankind.

Now, monks, these verses were well sung, not ill sung, by the Brahmā, the Eternal Youth, well spoken not ill spoken, [**328**], they are fraught with meaning, not void of meaning, and they are approved by me too.[2] I, too, say, monks:

> The noble is the best among the folk
> Who put their trust in lineage.
> But one in wisdom and in virtue clothed
> Is best of devas and mankind.'

---

[1] *Brahmā Sanankumāra* (or 'Five-Crest'), *D.* i, 99; *cf. K.S.* i, 192 *n.*; ii, 194; also *D.* iii, *Aggañña-Suttanta.*

[2] As at *D.* i, 99; *M.* i, 358. *Anumatā* (from *anumaññati*)=*anuññāṭā*, *Comy.*

Chapter II.—Recollection.[1]

§ i (12). *Mahānāma (a).*

On a certain occasion the Exalted One was staying among the Sakyans at Kapilavatthu in Banyan Park. Now on that occasion a number of monks were busy making robes for the Exalted One: 'For,' said they, 'when the rains are over the Exalted One will go forth on his rounds.'

Now Mahānāma the Sakyan[2] heard it said that a number of monks were busy making robes for the Exalted One . . . so he went to see the Exalted One, and on coming to him saluted the Exalted One and sat down at one side. So seated he said this to the Exalted One:

'I have heard it said, sir, that a number of monks are busy making robes for the Exalted One, and that when the rains are over the Exalted One will set forth on his rounds. Pray, sir, among those who live in various ways, in whose way of living should we live?'[3]

[**329**] 'Well asked, Mahānāma! Well asked, Mahānāma! It is a fit thing for you clansmen to come to see the Wayfarer and ask such a question.

He who means business,[4] Mahānāma, is a believer, not an unbeliever. He who means business is of ardent energy, no sluggard. He who means business has mindfulness fixed, not distracted. He who means business is composed, not discomposed. He who means business is strong in insight, not weak in insight. When you have established yourself in these five qualities, Mahānāma, you should further make six qualities to grow.

In this matter, Mahānāma, you should recollect the Wayfarer thus:

---

[1] *Anussati*; *cf. G.S.* ii, 39, 65, etc.; iii, 204 *n.*

[2] He was reckoned *etad agga* in giving choice alms-food. *Cf. K.S.* v, 290, 320, 323, 338; *G.S.* i, 23, 198, 254; iii, 204, etc.

[3] *Cf.* Mrs. Rhys Davids' *Sakya*, 337. This same introduction is at *K.S.* v, 349, but there he asks about comforting the sick.

[4] *Ārādhako.*

The Exalted One is an arahant, fully enlightened, perfect in knowledge and practice, a Welfarer, a world-knower, an unsurpassed trainer of men to be trained, teacher of devas and mankind, an awakened one, Exalted One is he. At such time, Mahānāma, as the Ariyan disciple thus calls to mind the Wayfarer, at that time his heart is not obsessed by lust, not obsessed by malice, not obsessed by delusion; at such time his heart is firmly fixed on the Wayfarer; with upright heart the Ariyan disciple wins the joyful thrill of the weal,[1] wins the joyful thrill of dhamma, wins the joyful thrill of joy that goes with dhamma; in one so joyous is born zest; in one of zestful mind the body is calmed; he whose body is calmed experiences happiness; the mind of the happy man is concentrated. This one, Mahānāma, is thus spoken of: "The Ariyan disciple dwells evenly[2] 'mid folk who are at strife; void of malice he dwells 'mid folk who are malevolent; blest with the ear of dhamma he makes recollection of the Awakened One to grow."

Then again, Mahānāma, you should recollect dhamma thus:

Well declared by the Exalted One is dhamma that is of this visible life, unhindered by time, that bids one come to see it, that leads onward, to be understood by the discerning, each for himself. At such time, Mahānāma, as the Ariyan disciple recollects dhamma, at that time his heart is not obsessed **[330]** by lust, malice, delusion. At such time his upright heart is fixed on dhamma; upright in heart the Ariyan disciple wins the joyful thrill of the weal, wins the joyful thrill of dhamma, wins the joyful thrill of the joy that goes with dhamma. In one joyous is born zest; in one of zestful mind the body is calmed; he whose body is calmed experiences happiness; the mind of the happy man is concentrated. This one, Mahānāma, is thus spoken of: "The Ariyan disciple dwells evenly . . . he makes recollection of dhamma to grow."

---

[1] *Attha-veda*, as at *M.* i, 37, and below, § 18. *Veda=somanassa*, *MA*. (*P. Dict.* translates, 'joy caused by the comprehension of the truth.') *Cf. G.S.* iii, 205 *n*.

[2] *Visama* and *sama* ('he keeps the even tenor of his way').

Then again, Mahānāma, you should recollect the Order thus: Well-faring on the way is the Order of disciples of the Exalted One, straightforward-faring on the way is the Order of disciples of the Exalted One, faring on in the Method is the Order of disciples of the Exalted One, dutifully faring onward is the Order of disciples of the Exalted One, namely: The four pairs of men, the eight persons who are males.[1] Such is the Exalted One's Order of disciples. Worthy of honour, worthy of reverence, worthy of offerings, worthy of salutations with clasped hands are they, a field of merit unsurpassed for the world.

At such time, Mahānāma, as the Ariyan disciple recollects the Order, at that time his heart is not obsessed by lust, malice and delusion. His heart is upright, is firmly fixed on the Order; with heart thus upright the Ariyan disciple wins the joyful thrill of the weal, wins the joyful thrill of dhamma, of the joy that goes with dhamma . . . he makes recollection of the Order to grow.

Then again, Mahānāma, you should recollect your own virtues as being unbroken, whole, unspotted, untarnished, giving freedom, as praised by the discerning ones, virtues untainted, which lead to concentration of the mind. At such time, Mahānāma, as the Ariyan disciple recollects his virtues, at that time his heart is not obsessed by lust, malice and delusion. At such a time his heart is upright, firmly fixed on virtue. With heart thus upright the Ariyan disciple wins the joyful thrill of the weal, of dhamma, of the joy that goes with dhamma . . . he makes recollection of virtue to grow.

[**331**] Then again, Mahānāma, you should recollect your own liberality, thus: A gain, indeed, it is to me, well gained it is by me that, amid folk o'ergrown with the blight of stinginess, I live at home with heart cleansed of the blight of stinginess, open-handed, pure-handed, delighting in self-surrender, one to ask a favour of, one who rejoices in dispensing charitable

---

[1] Those on the eight stages of the Arahant path. Elsewhere I have translated *purisa-puggala* as 'male-man'—*e.g.*, at § 75, where there is a contrast between an ignorant woman disciple and the expert male.

gifts.[1] At such time, Mahānāma, as the Ariyan disciple recollects liberality, at that time his heart is not obsessed by lust, malice and delusion. . . . This one, Mahānāma, is thus spoken of: "The Ariyan disciple dwells evenly 'mid folk who are at strife, void of malice he dwells 'mid folk who are malevolent, blest with the ear of dhamma[2] he makes recollection of liberality to grow."

Again, Mahānāma, you should recollect the devas, thus: There are the devas of the Four Great Kings,[3] those of the suite of the Thirty-three, the devas of Yama, the devas of delight, the devas who delight in creation, those who have power over the creations of others, the devas of the body of Brahmā, the devas beyond that. In me too is seen that sort of faith blest with which those devas deceased hence and rose up again there. **[332]** In me too is seen that sort of virtue, that sort of learning,[4] that sort of liberality, that sort of insight, blest with which those devas deceased here and rose up again there. At such time, Mahānāma, as the Ariyan disciple recollects the faith, virtue, learning, liberality and insight both of himself and of those devas, at that time his heart is not obsessed by lust, malice and delusion. At that time his heart is upright, fixed upon the devas. With upright heart the Ariyan disciple wins the joyful thrill of the weal, of dhamma, of the joy that goes with dhamma. In one joyous is born zest; in one of zestful mind the body is calmed; he whose body is calmed experiences happiness; the mind of the happy man is concentrated. This one, Mahānāma, is thus spoken of: The Ariyan disciple dwells evenly 'mid folk who are at strife; void of malice he dwells 'mid folk who are malevolent; blest with the ear of dhamma[2] he makes recollection of the devas to grow.'

---

[1] The same advice is given to Mahānāma at *K.S.* v, 339 (*S.* v, 395).

[2] So at *G.S.* iii, 206, but *ibid.* 248, 'stream of dhamma.' See above, § 75 *n.* I take 'ear of dhamma' to mean the 'still small voice' (of conscience) or the higher clairaudience.

[3] Again at *K.S.* v, 350; *cf. Path of Purity* ii, 339.

[4] *Sutaŋ.*

§ ii (13). *Mahānāma (b).*

On a certain occasion the Exalted One was staying among the Sakyans at Kapilavatthu in Banyan Park. Now on that occasion Mahānāma the Sakyan had risen from the bed of sickness, had not long arisen from sickness. At that time a number of monks were busy making robes for the Exalted One . . . (*as in previous sutta*).

[333] Now Mahānāma the Sakyan heard it said that a number of monks were busy making robes for the Exalted One . . . so he went to the Exalted One and told him what he had heard, and asked:

'Pray, sir, among those who live in various ways, in whose way of living should we live ?'

'Well asked, well asked, Mahānāma ! . . . he who means business is strong in insight, not weak in insight. When you have established yourself in these five qualities, Mahānāma, you should further make six qualities to grow.

Herein, Mahānāma, you should recollect the Wayfarer thus: That Exalted One is arahant. . . . At such time as the Ariyan disciple thus calls to mind the Wayfarer . . . at such time his heart is firmly fixed on the Wayfarer . . . the mind of the happy man is concentrated. This recollection of the awakened one, Mahānāma, you should make to grow as you go along, as you stand, as you sit, as you lie, as you apply yourself to business; you should make it to grow as you dwell at home in your lodging crowded with children.

[334] Again, Mahānāma, you should recollect dhamma . . . the Order . . . your own virtues . . . your own liberality (*all as in previous sutta*) . . . also the devas . . . the mind of the happy man is concentrated.

This recollection of the devas, Mahānāma, you should make to grow as you go along . . . as you dwell at home in your lodging crowded with children.'

§ iii (14). *Nandiya.*[1]

On a certain occasion the Exalted One was staying among the Sakyans at Kapilavatthu in Banyan Park. Now on that

[1] **Similar advice is given to Nandiya at *K.S.* v, 340.**

occasion the Exalted One was desirous of taking up residence during the rainy season at Sāvatthī. And Nandiya the Sakyan heard it said that the Exalted One so desired.

[**335**] Then it occurred to him: Suppose I also were to take up residence at Sāvatthī during the rainy season. Then I could both apply myself[1] to my business and at the same time get a chance of seeing the Exalted One from time to time.

So the Exalted One took up residence at Sāvatthī during the rainy season and Nandiya the Sakyan did the same. There he applied himself to his business and from time to time got a chance of seeing the Exalted One.

Now at that time a number of monks were busy making robes for the Exalted One. . . . And Nandiya the Sakyan heard it said . . . and went to the Exalted One . . . and asked him:

'Pray, sir, among those who live in various ways, in whose way of living should we live ?'

And the Exalted One replied: 'Well asked, well asked, Nandiya ! It is a fitting thing for you clansmen to come to the Wayfarer and ask such a question. He who means business, Nandiya, is a believer, not an unbeliever. He who means business is virtuous, not immoral.[2] He who means business is of ardent energy, no sluggard. He who means business has mindfulness fixed, not distracted. He who means business is composed, not discomposed. He who means business is strong in insight, not weak in insight. When you have established yourself in these six qualities, Nandiya, you should set up mindfulness in the inner self in five[3] qualities.

Herein, Nandiya, you should recollect the Wayfarer thus: [**336**] That Exalted One is an arahant. . . . Thus, Nandiya, firmly fixed on the Wayfarer you should set up mindfulness in the inner self.

Again, Nandiya, you should recollect dhamma thus: Well

---

[1] Text should read *adhiṭṭhahissāmi* for *adiṭṭha-*.

[2] This item is added to the five of the previous sutta.

[3] *Six* in previous sutta.

declared by the Exalted One is dhamma that is of this visible life, unlimited by time . . . to be understood by the discerning, each for himself. Thus, Nandiya, firmly fixed on dhamma you should set up mindfulness in the inner self.

Again, Nandiya, you should recollect lovely friends thus: A gain to me it is indeed! Well gotten indeed by me it is, that I have lovely friends, compassionate, desirous of my welfare, who encourage and exhort me. Thus, Nandiya, firmly fixed on lovely friends you should set up mindfulness in the inner self.

Again, Nandiya, you should recollect your own liberality thus: A gain it is to me indeed! Well gotten indeed it is by me, that amid folk overgrown with the blight of stinginess I live at home cleansed of the blight of stinginess, open-handed, pure-handed, delighting in self-surrender, one to ask a favour of, rejoicing in dispensing charitable gifts. Thus, Nandiya, firmly fixed on liberality you should set up mindfulness in the inner self.

Once more, Nandiya, you should recollect the devas thus: Whatsoever devas, passing beyond the company of those devas who subsist on food material,[1] do rise up again in a certain mind-made body—such devas observe in the self nothing more to do, no need for repeating what is done.[2]

Just as, Nandiya, a monk who is definitely released[3] observes in the self no more to do, observes no need for repeating

---

[1] *Kabalinkāra-bhakkhā*=' of the *kāmâvacarā*, *Comy*. *Cf*. *G.S.* iii, 141-2 and *n*., where Sāriputta says: ' It is possible for a monk who has achieved virtue, concentration and insight both to attain the ending of consciousness of feeling and to arise from that state; and, if in this visible world he has established gnosis, he may pass beyond the company of devas supported by (more or less) material sustenance, and, rising up in a certain mind-made body, he may attain the same state and arise therefrom.'

[2] *Cf*. *A*. iii, 378 (*katassa paṭicayo n'atthi, karaṇīyaŋ na vijjati*); iv, 355 (*n'atthi kiñci uttariŋ karaṇīyaŋ, n'atthi katassa paṭicayo*); and *Ud*. 35, where *Comy*. has *na hi bhāvita-maggo puna bhāvīyati*.

[3] *Asamaya-vimutto*; *cf*. *samaya-vimutto* (temporarily released). *Comy*. has *abhisamaya-vimuttiyā vimutto, khīnâsava* (evidently wrong, for *abhisameti* means to comprehend). *Cf*. *SA*. i, 182-3; *A*. iii, 173.

what is done, even so, Nandiya, whatsoever devas, passing beyond the company of those devas who subsist on food material, do rise up again in a certain mind-made body, **[337]** such devas observe in the self nothing more to do, no need for repeating what is done. Thus, Nandiya, fixed upon the devas you should cause mindfulness to arise in the inner self.

So, Nandiya, possessing these eleven qualities the Ariyan disciple just abandons evil, unprofitable states, he clings not to them. Just as, Nandiya, a pot upset pours out its water and cannot take it in again;[1] or just as fire let loose in a dry grass-jungle goes blazing on and turns not back to what is burnt out, even so, Nandiya, the Ariyan disciple possessed of these eleven qualities just abandons evil, unprofitable states and clings not to them.'

§ iv (15). *Subhūti.*

Now the venerable Subhūti[2] came along with a believing monk to see the Exalted One, and on coming to him saluted the Exalted One and sat down at one side. As he sat at one side the Exalted One said this to the venerable Subhūti:

'Pray who is this monk, Subhūti ?'

'He is a believer, sir. He is the son of a believing disciple and went forth from a believer's home to the homeless.'

'But, Subhūti, does this believing monk, the son of a believing disciple who went forth from a believer's home to the homeless—does he conform to the traditional marks of the believer ?'

'Now is the time for this, O Exalted One ! Now is the time for this, O Welfarer, for the Exalted One to tell the traditional marks of belief in a believer. Now I shall understand whether this monk does conform[3] to the traditional marks or not.'

---

[1] *Cf. S.* v, 48, where the reading is better.

[2] S. was younger brother of Anāthapiṇḍika; *cf. Brethren,* p. 4. *Comy.* thinks this monk was his nephew. *Saddho* may, however, be his name. *Cf. Sandha* above, p. 204 *n.*: *S.* ii, 153 *Āyasmā Saddho.*

[3] *Sandissati saddhâpadānesu,* lit. 'does he harmonize with the believer's characteristics ?' *Comy.* takes the word (which also means 'legend') to be equal to *lakkhaṇa,* as at *A.* i, 102, *kamma-lakkhaṇo paṇḍito ; apadāne sobhati paññā.*

'Then, Subhūti, do you listen. Pay attention carefully and I will speak.'

'I will, sir,' replied the venerable Subhūti to the Exalted One, who said:

[**338**] 'In this connexion, Subhūti, a monk is virtuous,[1] he lives restrained with the restraint of the Obligation, well equipped with range of practice, seeing danger in minutest faults, and undertaking the practice of the precepts of the training applies himself thereto. In so far as a monk is such, Subhūti, this is a traditional mark of belief in a believer.

Again, a monk has heard much; he bears in mind what he has heard, stores up what he has heard. Whatsoever teachings, lovely in the beginning, lovely midway, lovely at the end (of life), both in spirit and in letter do stress the Brahma-life in its all-round fullness and utter purity—such teachings are much heard by him, borne in mind, repeated aloud, pondered and well penetrated by vision. In so far as a monk has heard much, Subhūti, this is a traditional mark of belief in a believer.

Again, Subhūti, a monk has friendship with the lovely, fellowship with the lovely, companionship with the lovely. In so far as a monk is such an one, Subhūti, this also is a traditional mark of belief in a believer.

Again, a monk is pleasant to speak to, blest with qualities that make him easy to speak to; he is patient and clever at grasping instruction given. In so far as a monk is such, this also is a traditional mark. . . .

Again, in all the undertakings of his fellows in the Brahma-life, be they matters weighty or trivial, he is shrewd and energetic, possessing ability to give proper consideration thereto, as to what is the fit thing to do and how to manage it. In so far as a monk is such, this also is a traditional mark. . . .

[**339**] Again, a monk delights in dhamma, is pleasant to converse with, he rejoices exceedingly in further dhamma, in further discipline. In so far as a monk is such, Subhūti, this also is a mark. . . .

---

[1] As at § 17.

Again, a monk dwells resolute in energy for the abandoning of bad qualities, stout and strong to acquire good qualities, not shirking the burden in good qualities. In so far as a monk is such, this also is a traditional mark.

Again, Subhūti, a monk wins at pleasure, without pain and without stint,[1] the four musings which are of the clear consciousness, which are concerned with the happy life in this visible world. In so far as a monk is such, this also, Subhūti, is a traditional mark. . . .[2]

Then again, a monk can recall his manifold dwelling aforetime, to wit: one birth, two, three . . . ten, up to a hundred births, a hundred thousand births; also the divers foldings up of æons, the divers unfoldings of æons, the divers folding-and-unfoldings of æons (remembering): At that time I was of such a name, of such a family, of such complexion, so supported, thus and thus experiencing weal and woe, of such and such a span of life: I, as that one, thence deceasing, rose up again at that time; there too I was of such a name, of such a family, of such complexion . . . I, as that one, thence deceasing, rose up again here. Thus with all details and characteristics he can recall his **[340]** manifold dwelling aforetime. In so far as a monk can do this, this also is a traditional mark of belief in a believer.

Again, Subhūti, a monk with the deva-sight, purified and surpassing that of men, beholds beings deceasing and rising up again (*as in* § 30 *of the Tens*). . . . In so far as a monk can do this, Subhūti, this also is a traditional mark. . . .

Yet again, Subhūti, by the destruction of the cankers, a monk in this same visible life attains the heart's release, the release by insight, acquiring it by his own comprehension, and realizing it so abides. In so far as a monk is such an one, Subhūti, this also is a traditional mark of belief in a believer.'

At these words the venerable Subhūti said this to the Exalted One:

---

[1] As in § 30 of the Tens.

[2] Most of these qualities are ascribed to the Master himself by the rājah Pasenadi at 30 of the Tens.

'Sir, all these traditional marks of belief in a believer, spoken of by the Exalted One, are seen to exist in this monk, and he conforms to them.' [**341**] (*And he repeated them all as before.*)

'It is well, Subhūti! It is well, Subhūti! Therefore do you live along with this believing monk, and when you wish to do so, Subhūti, you should come along with this believing monk to see the Wayfarer.'

§ v (16). *Advantages.*[1]

[**342**] 'Monks, eleven advantages are to be looked for from the release of heart by the practice of amity, by making amity to grow, by making much of it, by making amity a vehicle and basis, by persisting in it, by becoming familiar with it, by well establishing it. What are the eleven?

One sleeps happy and wakes happy; he sees no evil dream; he is dear to human beings and non-human beings alike;[2] the devas guard him; fire, poison or sword affect him not; quickly he concentrates his mind; his complexion is serene; he makes an end without bewilderment; and if he has penetrated no further (to Arahantship) he reaches (at death) the Brahma-world.

These eleven advantages are to be looked for from the release of the heart by the practice of amity . . . by well establishing amity.'

§ vi (17). *Dasama, the housefather.*[3]

On a certain occasion the venerable Ānanda was staying near Vesālī at Beluva hamlet.[4] Now on that occasion the

---

[1] This favourite sutta, quoted *JA.* No. 169; *Mil. Pañh.* 198 (trans. i, 279); *Path of Purity*, ii, 352 (which passage *Comy.* quotes).

[2] *Comy.* and *V.M.* 312, 'like the elder Visākha.' *Cf. G.S.* ii, 59.

[3] This sutta, here called Dasama by *uddāna*, is at *M.* i, 350 (*Aṭṭhakanagarasutta*)=*F. Dialog.* i, 257. Our *Comy.*=*MA.* iii, 12 *ff.*

[4] Beluva (*vilva*-tree) was, according to *Comy.*, on the slope at the foot of a hill to the south of Vesālī. *Cf. K.S.* v, 130; *DA.* ii, 546. Pāṭaliputta, capital of Magadha, is some distance to the south-west of Vesālī, on the Ganges.

housefather Dasama[1] of Aṭṭhaka town had come to Pāṭaliputta on some business or other.

Now the housefather Dasama came up to a certain monk in Cock's Pleasaunce,[2] and on reaching him said this to that monk:

'Pray, sir, where is the venerable Ānanda now staying? We are anxious to see the venerable Ānanda, sir.'

'Housefather, the venerable Ānanda is staying here near Vesālī, at Beluva hamlet.'

So the housefather Dasama of Aṭṭhaka town, having settled his business at Pāṭaliputta, went to Beluva hamlet near Vesālī, to see the venerable Ānanda, and on coming to him saluted him and sat down at one side. So seated he said this to the venerable Ānanda:

[**343**] 'Pray, Ānanda, sir, is there any one condition enunciated by that Exalted One who knows, who sees, that arahant who is a perfectly enlightened one—a condition whereby a monk who lives in earnest, ardent, with the self established,[3] can get release for his heart yet unreleased; or whereby the cankers not yet destroyed will come to an end—a condition whereby he wins the unsurpassed peace from bondage[4] not yet won?'

'There is such a condition, housefather, enunciated by that Exalted One . . . whereby a monk . . . wins the unsurpassed peace from bondage not yet won.'

'And pray, sir, what is that one condition?'

'Herein, housefather, a monk aloof from sense-desires, aloof from unprofitable states, enters upon the first musing, which is accompanied by thought directed and sustained, born of seclusion, zestful and easeful, and abides therein. He thus ponders: This first musing is just a higher product,

---

[1] 'The tenth.' He was so reckoned in his family relationship according to *Comy*.

[2] *Kukkuṭārāma*. I have so called it at *K.S.* v, 14. *Comy.*, however, says it was made by Kukkuṭa, the rich man. *Cf. G.S.* iii, 48 *n*.

[3] *Pahitatta*. See *Minor Anthologies* xiii (Mrs. Rhys Davids) on the commentarial explanation as *pesitatta* ('who has the self *sent away*').

[4] *Yoga-kkhema*.

it is produced by higher thought. Then he comes to know: Now even that which is a higher product, produced by higher thought, is impermanent, of a nature to end. Fixed on that he wins destruction of the cankers; and, if not that, yet by his passion for dhamma,[1] by his delight in dhamma, by utterly making an end of the five fetters belonging to this world, he is reborn spontaneously,[2] and in that state passes utterly away, never to return (hither) from that world.

This one condition, housefather, has been clearly enunciated by that Exalted One . . . whereby a monk . . . wins the unsurpassed peace from bondage not yet won.

[**344**] Then again, housefather, a monk, by the calming down of thought directed and sustained, enters upon the second musing, that calming of the inner self, that one-pointedness of mind apart from thought directed and sustained, that is born of mental balance, zestful and easeful, and having attained it abides therein. Likewise he attains the third musing . . . the fourth musing. . . .[3] He thus ponders: This fourth musing is just a higher product, it is produced by higher thought. Then he comes to know: Now even that which is a higher product . . . is impermanent, of a nature to end. Fixed on that he wins destruction of the cankers (*as in the previous section*) . . . by delight in dhamma . . . he passes utterly away, not to return (hither) from that world.

This one condition, housefather, has been clearly enunciated by that Exalted One . . . whereby a monk . . . wins the unsurpassed peace from bondage not yet won.

Then again, housefather, with a heart possessed by amity . . . by compassion . . . by sympathy . . . possessed by equanimity (*as in* § 207), he irradiates one quarter of the world; so also as regards the second, third and fourth quarters of the world; likewise above, below, across, everywhere, for all sorts and conditions; he abides irradiating the

---

[1] *Dhamma-rāgena*, according to *Comy.* 'passionate desire for calm and insight.' (If he can master this passion he becomes arahant; if not, he is a non-returner.)

[2] *Opapātiko.*

[3] So abbreviated in text. For full version *cf. G.S.* ii, 130.

whole world with a heart possessed by equanimity that is widespreading, grown great and boundless, free from enmity and untroubled.

[**345**] Then he thus ponders: This heart's release by amity . . . by compassion . . . by sympathy . . . by equanimity is just a higher product; it is produced by higher thought. Then he comes to know: Now even that which is a higher product . . . is impermanent, of a nature to end. Fixed on that idea he wins destruction of the cankers; or if not that, yet by his passion for dhamma, by his delight in dhamma, by utterly making an end of the five fetters belonging to this world, he is reborn spontaneously, and in that state passes utterly away, never to return (hither) from that world.

This one condition, housefather, has been clearly enunciated by that Exalted One . . . whereby a monk . . . wins the unsurpassed peace from bondage not yet won.

Then again, housefather, a monk, by passing utterly beyond all perception of objective form, by coming to an end of reaction to sense, by paying no heed to the variety of perceptions, with the idea: Infinite is space, attains and abides in the realm of infinity of space.

Then he thus ponders: This attainment also of the realm of the infinity of space is just a higher product, it is produced by higher thought. Then he comes to know: Whatsoever is even a higher product . . . that is impermanent, of a nature to end. Fixed on that idea he wins destruction of the cankers, [**346**] and if not that yet by his passion for dhamma . . . he is reborn spontaneously, and in that state passes utterly away, never to return (hither) from that world. This one condition, housefather, has been clearly enunciated by that Exalted One . . . whereby a monk . . . wins the unsurpassed peace from bondage not yet won.

Yet again, housefather, a monk, by passing utterly beyond the realm of the infinity of space, with the idea: Infinite is consciousness, attains and abides in the realm of infinity of consciousness . . . or, passing utterly beyond that, with the idea: Nothing at all exists, attains and abides in the realm of nothingness. Then he thus ponders: This attainment also of the realm of nothingness is just a higher product, it is produced by higher thought.

Then he comes to know: Whatsoever is even a higher product, produced by higher thought, even that is impermanent, of a nature to end. Fixed on that idea he wins destruction of the cankers; and if not that, yet by his passion for dhamma, by his delight in dhamma, by utterly making an end of the five fetters belonging to this world, he is reborn spontaneously and in that state passes utterly away, never to return (hither) from that world.

This one condition, housefather, has been clearly enunciated by that Exalted One who knows, who sees, that arahant who is a perfectly enlightened one—a condition whereby a monk who lives earnest, ardent, with the self established, can get release for his heart yet unreleased; or whereby the cankers not yet destroyed will come to an end—a condition whereby he wins the unsurpassed peace from the bondage not yet won.'

At these words Dasama, the housefather of Aṭṭhaka town, said this to the venerable Ānanda:

'Just as if, Ānanda, your reverence, a man searching for the entrance to a single hidden treasure[1] should at one and the same time come upon the entrance to eleven such treasures; even so I, your reverence, in my search for a single door to the deathless, at one and the same time have come to win eleven such doors whereby to enter in.[2]

[347] Just as if, your reverence, a man should own a house with eleven doors. If that house were ablaze, he could win safety for himself by any one door; even so, your reverence, shall I be able to make the self safe by any one of those eleven doors to the deathless.

Now, your reverence, those who hold other views will search for a fee for the teacher.[3] Why then should not I do worship to the venerable Ānanda?'

---

[1] *Nidhi-mukhaŋ*. *Comy*. has simply 'a treasure.' *P. Dict*. 'an excellent treasure.' But the parallel of *dvāra* in the simile points to the meaning 'opening,' or 'mouth' (of a cave or hole).

[2] Text *sevanāya*; but *M. savanāya* (for the hearing of).

[3] *Comy*. 'if such pupils have no gift, they will ask their relatives. Failing here, they go a-begging till they get it.'

So Dasama, the housefather of Aṭṭhaka town, assembled the Order of monks at Vesālī and Pāṭaliputta, and with his own hands served them with choice food both hard and soft till they had eaten their fill, and clothed each one with a separate set of cloth for robes; but the venerable Ānanda he clothed with three robes complete, and in addition caused a lodging[1] that cost five hundred pieces to be built.'

§ vii (18). *The cowherd* (*a*).[2]

'Possessing eleven qualities, monks, a cowherd cannot become[3] the man to lead a herd about and make it prosperous. What eleven qualities?

[**348**] Herein, monks, a cowherd knows not bodily forms[4] and is unskilled in distinguishing the marks; he does not remove flies' eggs or dress wounds; he makes no fumigation;[5] he knows not the ford, the watering-place or the road; he is unskilled in pastures; he milks dry; pays no special respect to the bulls, the sires and leaders of the herd. Possessing these eleven qualities a cowherd cannot become the man to lead about a herd and make it prosperous.

In the same way a monk possessing eleven qualities cannot become the man to reach growth, increase and maturity in this dhamma-discipline. What eleven?

Herein a monk knows not objects, is unskilled in the marks, removes no flies' eggs, dresses not a wound, makes no fumigation, knows not the ford, knows not the watering-place, knows not the road, is unskilled in pastures, pays no special respect to those elder monks who have gone forth many a day, who are sires of the Order, leaders of the Order.

And how is a monk one who knows not bodily forms?

Herein a monk comes not to know of any object whatsoever that it is the four great essentials or derived therefrom. That is how . . .

And how is a monk unskilled in distinguishing the marks?

---

[1] *Vihāraŋ*=' a leaf-hut,' *Comy.*

[2] At *M.* i, 220 (*Mahāgopālaka-sutta*). [3] *Abhabbo.*

[4] *Comy.* 'cannot recognize them by counting or by colour.'

[5] *Dhūmaŋ.* *Comy.* 'against mosquitoes, etc.'

Herein a monk comes not to know that a fool is marked by his deed, that a sage is marked by his deed. That is how . . .

And how is a monk one who removes not flies' eggs?

Herein a monk cleaves to sensual thinking when it arises, abandons it not, restrains it not, makes not an end thereof, causes it not to go to non-existence; he cleaves to malicious thinking . . . to harmful thinking when arisen . . . to evil, unprofitable states whensoever arisen he cleaves, abandons them not, restrains them not, makes not an end thereof, causes them not to go to non-existence. That is how . . .

And how does a monk not dress wounds?

Herein a monk, seeing an object with the eye,[1] is entranced by its general features and by its details. Although coveting and dejection, those evil, unprofitable states, might flow in upon one who dwells with the eye-faculty uncontrolled, yet he applies not himself to such control, he sets no guard over the faculty of eye, wins no restraint thereof. Hearing a sound with the ear or with the nose **[349]** smelling an odour, with tongue tasting a savour, with body contacting tangibles, or with mind cognizing mental states, he is entranced by their general features and by their details. Though coveting and dejection, those evil, unprofitable states, might flow in upon one who dwells with this mental faculty uncontrolled, yet he applies not himself to such control, he sets no guard over the mental faculty, wins no restraint thereof. That is how a monk is one who does not dress wounds.

And how is a monk one who makes no fumigation?

Herein a monk expounds not to others in detail dhamma as he himself has heard it and borne it in mind. That is how . . .

And how is a monk one who knows not the ford?

Herein a monk frequents not from time to time the company of monks of wide knowledge,[2] who are versed in the sayings, who know the outlines thoroughly, who know the discipline and summaries by heart. He inquires not of them nor questions them thus: 'How is this, your reverence? What

[1] *Cf. D.* i, 70; *A.* ii, 16; *K.S.* iv, 63.

[2] *Cf. G.S.* i, 101.

is the meaning of this?' To him those worthies open not up what was sealed, make not clear what was obscure, and on divers doubtful points of doctrine resolve not his doubts. That is how a monk is one who knows not the ford.

And how is a monk one who knows not the watering-place?

Herein a monk, when dhamma proclaimed by the Wayfarer is preached, gets no thrill of the meaning, no thrill of dhamma, he gets no thrill of the joy[1] that goes along with dhamma. Thus he knows not the watering-place. Thus a monk . . .

And how is a monk one who knows not the road?

Herein a monk comes not to know the Ariyan eightfold way as it really is. That is how . . .

And how is a monk one not skilled in pastures?

[**350**] Herein a monk comes not to know, as they really are, the four arisings of mindfulness. That is how . . .

And how is a monk one who milks dry?

Herein a monk, when believing householders supply a monk to the full[2] with offerings of robe and almsfood, lodging and seat, medicines and comforts in sickness, knows no moderation in accepting such. That is how . . .

And how is a monk one who pays no special respect to the bulls, the sires and leaders of the herd?

Herein a monk treats not with kindly action of body, speech and mind, either openly or in secret, those elder monks who have gone forth many a day, who are sires of the Order, leaders of the Order. That is how . . .

Thus, monks, possessing these eleven qualities a monk cannot become one to lead about a herd or make it prosperous.

Now a cowherd who possesses eleven qualities can become the man to lead about a herd and make it prosperous. What eleven? . . .

---

[1] *Attha-veda* and *dhamma-veda* (=*somanassa*) seem explained by the following sentences. *Comy.* at *MA.* i, 173 explains 'unwavering confidence in.' *Vedo ti gantho pi ñāṇam pi somanassam pi.* *Cf.* above, § 12 of the Elevens.

[2] *Abhihaṭṭhuŋ* (*Comy.*=*abhihāritvā*) *pavārenti.* The two *abhihārā* are of speech and necessaries. Also infin. of *abhihaŋsati*, 'to serve till satisfied.'

In like manner a monk possessing these eleven qualities can become the man to reach growth, increase and maturity in this dhamma-discipline.'

[351-3] (*Here the opposite qualities are repeated for both.*)

§ viii (19). *Concentration* (*c*).

(*This is the same as* § 6 *of the Tens, except that Ānanda is there the questioner. It is repeated in the next sutta. The eleventh item here is* :)

[354] '. . . And in whatsoever is seen, heard, sensed, cognized, attained, searched into, pondered over by mind.'

§ ix (20). *Concentration* (*d*).

Thereupon the Exalted One addressed the monks, saying: 'Monks!'

'Yes, sir,' replied those monks to the Exalted One, who said this:

'May it be, monks, that a monk's winning of concentration is of such a sort that **[355]** in earth he is unaware of earth, in water unaware thereof, in fire . . . in air is unaware of them; that in the realm of unbounded space . . . of infinite intellection . . . of nothingness . . . of neither-perception-nor-not-perception he is unaware of them; that in this world he is unaware of this world, that in the world beyond he is unaware of it; that in whatsoever is seen, heard, sensed, cognized, attained, searched into, pondered over by the mind, there too he is unaware of it, and yet at the same time he may be aware ?'

'Sir, for us things are rooted in the Exalted One; they have the Exalted One for guide, the Exalted One for resort. Well for us, sir, if the meaning of this saying were to occur to the Exalted One. Hearing it from the Exalted One the monks will bear it in mind.'

'Then, monks, do ye listen. Pay attention carefully and I will speak.'

'We will, sir,' replied those monks to the Exalted One who said this:

'It may be the case, monks, that a monk's winning of concentration is of such a sort that in earth . . . and the rest . . . he is unaware of them, and yet at the same time is aware.

Herein, monks, a monk is conscious thus: This is the real, this is the best—namely, the calming of all activities, the rejection of all substrate, the ending of craving, the fading of interest, stopping, nibbāna. In such a way a monk's winning of concentration may be of such a sort that neither in earth . . . nor in the rest . . . is he aware of them, yet at the same time he is aware.'

§ x (21). *Concentration* (*e*).

[356] Now a number of monks went to see the venerable Sāriputta, and on coming to him greeted him courteously . . . (*and asked the same question as in* § 7 *of the Tens, which is the same as the previous sutta*).

§ xi (22). *Concentration* (*f*).

[357] Now the venerable Sāriputta addressed the monks, saying: 'Monks, may it be that a monk's winning of concentration . . . ?' (*as in the previous suttas*).

'We would come a long way, your reverence, to learn the meaning of this saying from the venerable Sāriputta. Well for us, sir, if the meaning of this saying were to occur to the venerable Sāriputta. Hearing it from the venerable Sāriputta the monks would bear it in mind . . .' (*as in* § ix *above*). **[358.]**

Chapter III.—Recapitulation.[1]

§ i (23). *The cowherd* (*b*).

[359] 'Monks, possessing eleven qualities a cowherd cannot become the man to lead about a herd and make it prosperous. What eleven ?

(*As in* § vii *of last chapter.*)

[1] There is no title to this chapter.

. . . A monk who has these eleven qualities cannot become the man to live seeing impermanence in eye . . . ear . . . to live seeing Ill . . . the not-self . . . dissolution . . . decay . . . fading . . . stopping . . . seeing giving-up in the eye. He cannot become the man to live seeing (all these things as inherent) in the ear . . . nose . . . tongue . . . body . . . mind . . . in objects . . . sounds . . . scents . . . savours . . . tangibles . . . mental states . . . in eye-consciousness . . . in ear-, nose- (and the rest) contacts . . . in feeling that is born of eye-contacts, in ear- (and the rest) contacts . . . in awareness of objects, sounds, scents, savours, tangibles [**360**] and mind-states . . . in perception of objects, sounds and the rest . . . in craving for objects, sounds (and the rest) . . . in discursive thought about objects, sounds (and the rest) . . . in sustained thought about objects, sounds (and the rest).

Monks, possessing eleven qualities a cowherd can become the man to lead about a herd and make it prosperous (*the opposite qualities*).

In the same way a monk can become the man to live seeing impermanence . . .' (*as before*).

§ ii (24). *Lust* (*a*).

'Monks, for the full comprehension of lust, eleven qualities must be made to grow. What eleven ?

The first, second, third and fourth musings; the heart's release by amity, by compassion, sympathy and equanimity; the realization of the realm of infinite space, of infinite consciousness, of no-thing. These are the eleven.'

§ iii (25). *Lust* (*b*).

'Monks, for the full comprehension, understanding, utter destruction, abandoning, ending, decay, fading, stopping, giving up and renouncing of lust these (same) eleven qualities must be made to grow.

[**361**] (*The same for*) Malice, delusion, wrath, ill-will, depreciation, spite, jealousy, stinginess, illusion, treachery, stubborn-

ness, impetuosity, pride, overbearing pride and intoxication of mind, these same eleven qualities should be made to grow.'

Thus spake the Exalted One. And the monks, delighted therewith, thanked the Exalted One for what he had said.

THE BOOK OF THE ELEVENS IS ENDED.

THE GRADUAL SAYINGS ARE ENDED.

INDEXES

I.—GENERAL

II.—SOME PĀLI WORDS IN THE NOTES

III.—APPENDIX ON SOḶASĪ

The phrase *kaḷaŋ n'agghati soḷasiŋ*, 'is not worth one sixteenth part of,' at p. 171, occurs fairly often in the Pāli Tipiṭakas—*e.g.*, at *S.* iii, 156; v, 44, 343; *Dhp.*, 70; *It.* 19; *A.* iv, 252 and elsewhere. Why was this particular fraction used to express a minute value? It is common in Skt. works (*shoḍacī*), early and late [the late *Jātakamāla*, xli, has 'the 16 parts (phases) of the moon], and it became a conventional number, perhaps owing to the Sānkhyan system of subdividing. I have found a number of passages which I give here, (*a*) to show a similar use, and (*b*) the ideas from which this use probably arose.

(*a*) *Mahābh. Moksh. Dh.*, § 276, 6. 'Happiness here and in heaven equals not even one sixteenth of the happiness of the utter vanishing of desire.'

Ib., *Sabha P.* 41. 'Worship, gifts, study, all equal not in merit one sixteenth part of that won by having a son.'

Ib., *Vana P.* 91. 'In battle Karna equals not even one sixteenth of Prītha's son.'

Ib., *V.P.* 189. 'Then the life of men will be reckoned as of sixteen years.'

(*b*) The Vedanta reckoning of the psychic organs is sixteenfold. *Cf.*, *Shatap. Br.* x, 4, 11, 17.

Bṛ. Aran. Up. Brāh. i, 14. 'That Prajāpati in his likeness to the year is of sixteen parts (*kaḷā*). His nights fifteen parts; his fixed part is the sixteenth. Entering with this sixteenth part all that is endowed with life, he is next day born in the morning.'

Ib., *ch.* iii, *Brāh.* ii. 'There are eight fetters and eight auxiliaries. (The sense-organs and their functions.)

Svet. Up. i, 4. 'Him we consider as a wheel (*see* below), with one circumference of sixteen parts.' (The eleven organs and the five gross elements.)

Ib., v, 14. 'He who is the cause of the origin of the sixteen parts.'

Chhandog. Up. vi, vii. 'Man, my child, is sixteen-fold . . . of thy sixteen parts only one now remains . . . when the last remnant of thy sixteen parts is invigorated by food, thou canst understand the Vedas.'

Praśna Up. 6. 'Let man know the spirit who ought to be known, in whom the (sixteen) parts abide, as the spokes in the nave (of the wheel).'

Mahābh. Mokshadh. P., § 184, 35. 'These (attributes) are the sixteen different kinds of form which constitute the property of light or vision.' *Ib.*, § 199. 'The sixteen attributes' (the five breaths, the ten senses and mind).

Ib., 232, 12. 'The same total (of those limbs), invested with form and having sixteen constituent parts, becomes what is called body.'

Ib., 241, 17. 'He takes rebirth with a body of eleven elements . . . with subtle form making a total of sixteen.'

Ib., 305, 8. 'That body of sixteen parts called the unmanifest.'

Ib., 311, 15. 'Those knowing *adhyâtma* regard mind as the sixteenth.'

Ib., 321, 108. 'The sixteenth principle is *avidyā*.'

Ib., *Aśvamedha P.* (*Anugītā* 36, 34). 'By action a creature is born with a body and made up of the sixteen.'

Cf. also *Manu* ix, 124. 'Fifteen cows and a bull.'

It seems then that of these sixteen parts one is chief, the others negligible.

TRANSLATIONS OF THE FOUR NIKĀYAS

(Now completed)

1. Dīgha-Nikāya: Dialogues of the Buddha, I. By T. W. Rhys Davids in Sacred Books of the Buddhists, II.
2. Dīgha-Nikāya: Dialogues of the Buddha, II. By T. W. and C. A. F. Rhys Davids in Sacred Books of the Buddhists, III.
3. Dīgha-Nikāya: Dialogues of the Buddha, III. By the Same. Sacred Books of the Buddhists, IV.
4. Majjhima-Nikāya: Further Dialogues of the Buddha, I. By Lord Chalmers. Sacred Books of the Buddhists, V.
5. Majjhima-Nikāya: Further Dialogues of the Buddha, II. By the Same. Sacred Books of the Buddhists, VI.
6. Saŋyutta-Nikāya: Book of the Kindred Sayings, I. By C. A. F. Rhys Davids. Pali Text Society.
7. Saŋyutta-Nikāya: Book of the Kindred Sayings, II. By the Same. Pali Text Society.
8. Saŋyutta-Nikāya: Book of the Kindred Sayings, III. By F. L. Woodward. Pali Text Society.
9. Saŋyutta-Nikāya: Book of the Kindred Sayings, IV. By the Same. Pali Text Society.
10. Saŋyutta-Nikāya: Book of the Kindred Sayings, V. By the Same. Pali Text Society.
11. Anguttara-Nikāya, I.: Book of the Gradual Sayings, I. By the Same. Pali Text Society.
12. Anguttara-Nikāya, II.: Book of the Gradual Sayings, II. By the Same. Pali Text Society.
13. Anguttara-Nikāya, III.: Book of the Gradual Sayings, III. By E. M. Hare. Pali Text Society.
14. Anguttara-Nikāya, IV.: Book of the Gradual Sayings, IV. By the Same. Pali Text Society.
15. Anguttara-Nikāya, V.: Book of the Gradual Sayings, V. By the Same. Pali Text Society.

TRANSLATIONS OF THE KHUDDAKA- (OR FIFTH) NIKĀYA

1. Dhammapada, Khuddakapātha. By C. A. F. Rhys Davids. Minor Anthologies, I. Sacred Books of the Buddhists, VII.
2. Udāna, Iti-Vuttaka. By F. L. Woodward. Minor Anthologies, II. Sacred Books of the Buddhists, VIII.
3. Theragāthā and Therīgāthā: Psalms of the Early Buddhists, I. and II. By C. A. F. Rhys Davids. Pali Text Society.